"This generous and appealing book offers constructed solution-focused questions, engaging training exercises, and creative therapeutic strategies that therapists at all levels of experience and expertise are sure to find useful."

—YVONNE DOLAN, MA,
Director of the Institute for Solution-focused Brief Therapy,
Past President of the Solution-focused Brief Therapy Association

"As always, Fredrike Bannink writes with clarity, calling on her wide knowledge of the field as a trainer and a practitioner. Having worked in other cultures gives her an unusual ability to express complex ideas in clean, simple language. The concept of 1001 questions is original and has a lot to recommend it as a tool for both beginners and experienced practitioners. The book also addresses the relation between solution-focused therapy and cognitive behavioral therapy. It provides advice on dealing with impasse and failure, both from the perspective of the therapist and of the client."

—DR. ALASDAIR MACDONALD,
psychiatrist and international trainer

"Bannink is an effective and practical communicator. She listens very carefully and attentively, and when she makes a move she is fast and asks questions that direct the minds involved to focus on what is useful for what is wanted. Easy to say, hard to do! This book is full of practical wisdom that she cultivated over the years of solution building experiences with people."

—AOKI YASUTERU, PRESIDENT,
Solution Focus Consulting Inc., Japan

"This extremely useful book highlights key aspects of the solution-focused approach while providing fresh ideas for enhancing therapists' creativity and effectiveness."

—TERRY TREPPER, PhD,
Professor of Psychology, Purdue University Calumet

1001

Solution-Focused Questions

1001

Solution-Focused Questions

• • • • • • • •

Handbook for
Solution-Focused Interviewing

Fredrike Bannink

REVISED SECOND EDITION

W. W. NORTON & COMPANY

New York • London

Translated by Inge De Taeye

Copyright © 2006 Pearson Assessment and Information
B.V., Amsterdam, the Netherlands
Translation copyright © 2010 by W. W. Norton & Company, Inc.

Originally published in Dutch as OPLOSSINGSGERICHTE VRAGEN: Handboek oplossingsgerichte gespreksvoering

For information about permission to reproduce selections from this book, write to Permissions, W. W. Norton & Company, Inc., 500 Fifth Avenue, New York, NY 10110

For information about special discounts for bulk purchases, please contact W. W. Norton Special Sales at specialsales@wwnorton.com or 800-233-4830

Manufacturing by LSC Harrisonburg
Book design by Gilda Hannah
Production manager: Leeann Graham

Library of Congress Cataloging-in-Publication Data

Bannink, Fredrike.
    [Oplossingsgerichte vragen. English]
    1001 solution-focused questions : handbook for solution-focused interviewing /
        Fredrike Bannink. — Rev. 2nd ed.
        p. cm. — (A Norton professional book)
    Includes bibliographical references and index.
    ISBN 978-0-393-70634-5 (pbk.)
1. Behavioral assessment. 2. Psychology—Methodology. 3. Interviews. I. Title. II.
Title: One thousand and one solution-focused questions. III. Title: One thousand one
solution-focused questions. IV. Title: Solution-focused questions.
    BF176.5.B36 2010
    158'.39—dc22
                                                                    2010013104

ISBN: 978-0-393-70634-5 (pbk.)

W. W. Norton & Company, Inc., 500 Fifth Avenue, New York, N.Y. 10110
www.wwnorton.com
W. W. Norton & Company Ltd., 15 Carlisle Street, London W1D 3BS

12 13 14 15 16 17 18 19 20

Nothing is constant in the whole world.
Everything is in a state of flux, and comes into being
as a transient appearance.
Time itself flows on with constant motion,
just like a river: for no more than a river
can the fleeting hour stand still. As wave is driven on by wave,
and, itself pursued, pursues the one before,
so the moments of time at once flee and follow,
and are ever new. What was before is left behind,
that which was not comes to be,
and every minute gives place to another.
—Ovid, *The Metamorphoses*

Contents

Acknowledgments

· · · · · · · · · · · · · · · · ·

An author never writes a book alone. It is always a product of many people who work together and ultimately ensure that the name of the author appears on the cover.

I thank my husband, Hidde, and my daughters, Eva and Eline, for giving me the opportunity and encouragement to write my books. I thank my friends, colleagues, students, and clients at home and abroad who have helped me discover, apply, and improve solution-focused interviewing over the years. I also thank my publishers, my translator, and everyone else who has contributed to the realization of this book. *Grazie* also to my Italian cats for keeping me company during many pleasant hours of thinking and writing.

I am very grateful that Insoo Kim Berg wrote the foreword, sadly, just a few months before she passed away. As one of the founders of solution-focused brief therapy, she remains a constant source of inspiration to me. I admired her for the tenaciousness with which she pursued her clients' goals, as well as for her gift for normalizing her clients' problems and for molding conversations about problems into conversations about possibilities.

I also thank my colleague Arnoud Huibers for his contribution to the writing of the foreword: Through him, Insoo had the opportunity to acquaint herself with the contents of this book, which was originally written in Dutch.

Foreword

· · · · · · · · · · · · · · · · ·

Solution-focused interviewing is based on the respectful assumption that clients have the inner resources to construct highly individualized and uniquely effective solutions to their problems. It is a great pleasure to welcome this valuable addition to the growing collection of writings worldwide about the use of the solution-focused approach.

With this clear and well-written book, Fredrike Bannink makes the solution-building approach accessible to many readers. It is a handbook that is meant for both students and advanced practitioners who are interested in sharpening their solution-focused skills.

The format of the book has something of a workshop-like quality. Exercises are offered throughout the book to give the reader the opportunity to integrate the solution-building approach through action learning. A wide variety of solution-focused techniques are introduced that allow the practitioner to reach out to clients to mobilize their resources. The 1001 solution-focused questions presented in this book will give the reader a very good idea of the importance of the precise use of language as a tool in solution-focused interviewing. Questions are included with which to negotiate the goal in the beginning of the therapy, questions for measuring progress, and questions for finding out what successful steps clients have taken to achieve their goals.

Readers of *1001 Solution-Focused Questions: Handbook for Solution-Focused Interviewing* are invited to open themselves to a "new light" on interviewing clients.

Insoo Kim Berg (1934–2007)

Preface

·················

You are hungry and decide to go eat at a restaurant. After you have waited awhile, you are invited to take a seat. The maître d' introduces himself and starts asking you questions about your hunger: How severe is your hunger; how did you come by it; how long have you had it; have you been hungry before; what role has your hunger played in your family or in your relationship with other relatives; what disadvantages and, perhaps, advantages does it have for you? When you ask to eat after this, hungrier still, the maître d' first wants you to fill out a few questionnaires about hunger (and probably about other matters that the maître d' feels are important as well). After all this, you are served a meal that you did not choose yourself, but rather one that the maître d' claims is good for you and has helped hungry people in the past. What do you suppose the chances are that you will leave the restaurant satisfied?

As an alternative to the problem focused vein, it has been possible since the 1980s to conduct solution-focused conversations in mental health care, education, coaching, and mediation. Such conversations are not concerned with the exploration and analysis of a problem, the assertion of a diagnosis, and the prescription of a treatment by an expert to bring about symptom reduction (diagnosis + treatment prescription = symptom reduction). Solution-focused interviewing is concerned with mapping a situation in the future that the client desires and with finding ways to help the client reach that goal (goal formulation + solutions designed by the client = desired outcome). In solution-focused interviewing, one speaks of "clients" instead of "patients," as use of the term "patient" needlessly pathologizes.

De Shazer (1994) viewed solution-focused interviewing as a "tap on the shoulder." The solution-focused professional does not need to push or pull; rather, he or she is always one step behind the client and looking in the same direction. A tap on the shoulder directs the client's attention and helps him or her look at something from a different angle. This stance is also called the stance of *leading from one step behind*. Solution-focused questions are that tap on the shoulder.

I would like to pass along the solution-focused questions that I have gathered over the years, with the help of my students, to others who currently practice or want to practice solution-focused interviewing. The idea for this book arose when I was writing the book *Oplossingsgerichte Mediation* (Bannink, 2006). I initially wanted to append the questions to the book as an addendum. However, because solution-focused questions may be of interest to a broader readership than just professionals who work with people with conflicts, I decided to collect the questions in the book now before you. In addition to a description of the way in which solution-focused interviewing can be applied, you will find 1,001 solution-focused questions in this book. While I do not pretend to have mapped *all* solution-focused questions—you will surely be able to think of others—and you would probably classify some questions under a different heading than I have done, many students tell me that practicing with these questions again and again helps them hold on to and continue the solution-focused thread in sessions with clients.

This book is not intended for professionals who are satisfied with the current concepts and models of interviewing. This book is meant for professionals who reflect seriously enough on their profession and its possibilities to be dissatisfied with the current state of affairs. And it is meant for professionals who are interested in examining where the concept and model of solution-focused interviewing may lead.

This book aims to inspire and invite professionals in the fields of therapy, education, coaching, and mediation to expand their existing skills and to optimally deploy their creative powers to help their clients.

Each chapter contains a section about the theory and a section about the practice of solution-focused interviewing. Throughout the book are twenty-four exercises, which are an invitation to engage in self-reflection and experimentation with the solution-focused model. You may of course think up other exercises as well.

Chapter 1 provides an overview of the history, principles, theory, research, and practice of solution-focused interviewing. Chapter 2 discusses the cooperative relationship of the therapist with the client and raises the important topic of motivation for behavior change. Chapter 3 elaborates on the first session in solution-focused interviewing. Chapter 4 describes the subsequent session and the solution-focused professional's options of addressing client responses to the question "What is better?"

Chapter 5 offers suggestions for homework that the professional may assign to the client. Chapter 6 discusses possibilities for concluding the sessions. In Chapter 7 other solution-focused skills are addressed, including externalizing the problem, projecting into the future, and using the interactional matrix. Chapter 8 examines points of consideration for a productive collaboration with other (usually problem-focused) professionals, such as colleagues and referrers, groups, and organizations. Chapter 9 explains how one can prevent or counteract impasse and failure. Chapter 10 incorporates the 1,001 questions, categorized as questions for general use and questions for use in specific situations or with specific clients. Chapter 11 considers how solution-focused professionals can reflect upon the session and their role in it—they may ask themselves a number of solution-focused questions, too. Chapter 12 describes solution-focused interviewing from start to finish. Finally, Chapter 13 expounds on the view that solution-focused brief therapy can be considered a form of cognitive behavioral therapy.

I hope that you enjoy this book, and I invite you to share your comments and this book and suggestions for the next 999 questions. You may contact me via e-mail at solutions@fredrikebannink.com or through my Web site at www.fredrikebannink.com.

1001

Solution-Focused Questions

·················

CHAPTER 1

Solution-Focused Interviewing

> The pessimist sees difficulty in every opportunity.
> The optimist sees the opportunity in every difficulty.
> —Winston Churchill

FINDING SOLUTIONS OR SOLVING PROBLEMS?

According to the cause-effect model (also called the medical model or the problem-focused *model*), one must find out exactly what is the matter in order to assert a correct diagnosis before a remedy can be provided. In Western thinking, the cause-effect model is the preeminent model that allows us to make the world understandable. The model is useful if one is dealing with relatively straightforward problems that can be reduced to simple and unambiguous causes, as is the case with medical and mechanical problems. The medical model is based on the equation diagnosis + prescribed treatment = symptom reduction. As far as interviewing is concerned, however, this model has a major disadvantage: It is heavily problem-focused. When the problem and its possible causes are studied in depth, a vicious circle of ever-growing problems may develop. The atmosphere becomes laden with problems, which poses the risk that the solution recedes ever further from view and also that the hope of improvement dwindles. A colleague of mine sometimes refers to problem-focused therapy as "problem-seeking" therapy.

Exploring or analyzing the factors that cause or perpetuate a problem does not automatically result in an improvement or alleviation of the problem. Positing a diagnosis is usually considered unimportant in solution-focused interviewing. One adopts, rather, a model of stepped diagnosis analogous to the model of stepped care (Bakker & Bannink, 2008). Hence, solution-focused brief therapy is a diagnosis-transcending treatment method.

There is growing dissatisfaction among clients and professionals with the use of problem-focused models of interviewing. Studying problems in depth often leads to the premature discontinuation of sessions, because nothing changes and the client loses hope for improvement. The solution-focused model changes all that. Problems are viewed as *challenges*. Clients and professionals regain hope as clients are aided in designing the future they wish to achieve and the means of achieving their goals. You can find out more about the importance of hope and hope theory and how offering hope may lead to success in Chapters 2 and 3.

BRIEF HISTORY

Solution-focused interviewing was developed in the 1980s by de Shazer, Berg, and their colleagues at the Brief Family Therapy Center in Milwaukee. They built on the findings of Bateson (1979) and Watzlawick, Weakland, and Fisch (1974), who believed that the attempted solution often perpetuated the problem and did not solve it, and that insight into the origin of the problem was not always necessary.

De Shazer (1985) developed a number of principles concerning solution-focused interviewing, to which I have added a few remarks:

- *The class of problems is distinct from the class of solutions.* To reach a solution, it is not necessary to analyze problems, but it is necessary to analyze client solutions (e.g., "What have you already attempted in order to solve the problem, and which of those things have helped?").
- *The client is the expert.* In the solution-focused model, one talks about the "client" and sometimes about the "customer"—not about the "patient," as one does in the medical model. It is the client who determines his or her goal as well as the path to reach it. De Shazer has submitted that problems are like subway tickets. They help the client get through the turnstile, but they do not determine what train the client will take or where he or she will get off. In other words, where someone wants to go is not determined by the point of departure.
- *If it works, don't fix it.* The professional is not judgmental of what the client experiences as positive.

- *If something works (better), do more of it.* Even if it is something unexpected.
- *Look for "differences that make a difference."* Usually, differences are not automatically effective: They need to be recognized by the client and significant to him or her in order to make a difference. The solution-focused model is aimed at describing exceptions to the rule of the problem, which the client often overlooks. Problems persist if only because the client thinks or says that the problems "always" occur. Times when the problem is absent or less of a problem lie at the surface, but they are dismissed by the client as insignificant or are not even noticed and hence remain hidden. They are simply not yet viewed by the client as differences that make a difference. The solution-focused professional keeps an eye out for the exceptions, however; the interventions are aimed at helping the client shift attention to precisely those times when things are different, through which solutions may reveal themselves. In this way, the client is encouraged to do more of what works (better). Moreover, the following applies: If you are not part of the solution, you are part of the problem.
- *If something does not work, do something else.* More of the same leads to nothing. According to a Japanese legend, a coastal village was threatened by a tsunami. A farmer at work in the rice paddies above the village saw the tidal wave approach from afar. Because there was no time to run back to the village and he was too far away to be heard by others, he stopped screaming and immediately set the fields on fire. The villagers came running at once to save their crops. That is how they were saved from drowning.

The staff at the Brief Family Therapy Center discovered that three specific types of therapist behavior made clients 4 times as likely to talk about solutions, change, and resources:

- *Asking eliciting questions:* "What would you like to see instead of the problem?" or "What is better?" (to be asked at the start of subsequent sessions).
- *Asking questions about details:* "How exactly did you do that? What exactly did you do differently that made it go better?"
- *Giving verbal rewards by paying compliments and asking compe-*

tence questions: "How did you manage that? How did you come up with that fine idea?"

In 1985 de Shazer published his book *Keys to Solution in Brief Therapy*. That same year a book by de Bono was released, titled *Conflicts: A Better Way to Resolve Them*, which showed marked similarities with de Shazer's book. I asked them whether they had ever met; they had not. In his book, de Bono identified "designing a desired outcome" as the best way to resolve conflicts. He also described the use of dream solutions, "what if" questions (hypothetical questions), and the importance of making a small difference. For a comprehensive description of his ideas about conflict resolution and designing a desired outcome, I refer you to de Bono (1985) and Bannink (2006a, 2006b, 2008c,d,e,f).

Erickson (1980) also contributed to the development of solution-focused intervention. He gave students the task of reading the last page of a book and speculating about what had preceded it. Solution-focused interviewing similarly departs from the ultimate goal. Erickson, a psychiatrist, emphasized the competence of the client and argued that the point was not to adapt the treatment to the diagnostic classification but to find out what possibilities for taking a (different) course of action the client him- or herself reveals. Erickson also used the hypnotic technique of pseudo-orientation in time. During hypnosis, he had his clients imagine running into him in 6 months and telling him that their problem had been solved and how they had achieved that. He ended the hypnosis by offering a few suggestions for the client to "forget" what had happened during the hypnosis. And even though they did not always apply the same solutions that they had put forward under hypnosis, it turned out that many of these patients reported doing better 6 months later. Covey wrote in *The Seven Habits of Highly Effective People*:

> Begin with the end in mind. . . . To begin with the end in mind means to start with a clear understanding of your destination. It means to know where you're going so that you better understand where you are now and so that the steps you take are always in the right direction. (1989, p. 98)

Among other things, Chapter 7 describes his technique of projection into the future, whereby one attends one's own funeral.

Viktor Frankl is often cited in solution-focused literature as providing an example of the way in which future-oriented thinking can make a difference.

Look around and notice at least five objects that are beige. Before you tell me what they are, I want you to quickly name the blue objects that you see. You will probably not be able to name any or will only be able to name a few and you will have to take another look in order to find something blue.

This exercise makes clear how clients view their situation when they come to the first session. They will describe it as only beige. They do not want beige; they may even hate beige. By asking clients to give a description of what they do want (e.g., blue), of the times when there is already an element of blue in their lives, of things that might be signs that point to the possibility of more blue, the professional directs attention toward the possibility of blue as an alternative to beige.

You can do this exercise with your client if he or she says that the problems are always there. It is also a nice exercise to use during a lecture if you want to explain to your listeners in a quick and simple fashion how problem-focused interviewing differs from solution-focused interviewing.

In his book he described his stay in a German concentration camp: "The prisoner who had lost faith in the future—his future—was doomed. With his loss of belief in the future, he also lost his spiritual hold" (Frankl, 2006, p. 74). He described his experience limping from the camp to the work site, in the cold and without food. He found himself thinking of something else. Suddenly he saw himself standing at the podium of a large lecture hall, where he was giving a lecture about the psychology of the concentration camp. "By this method I succeeded somehow in rising above the situation, above the sufferings of the moment, and I observed them as if they were already of the past" (p. 73). At that moment, his focus on this image of the future saved his life.

Seligman (2002) is the founder of positive psychology. In the 1970s he became known for his books about learned helplessness (the firm conviction that one cannot solve one's own problems). Now he researches learned optimism. Positive psychology begins with the strengths of the client and the assumption that happiness is not the consequence of just the right genes or coincidence, but that it can be found through the identification and use of the strengths that the client already possesses, such as kindness, originality, humor, optimism, and generosity (Bannink, 2009c). Positive psychology, in which optimism, hope, and self-efficacy take center stage, and solution-focused brief therapy have much in common. The following chapters revisit

Examine which three strengths have brought you to where you currently are in your profession. You may discuss this with a colleague and ask him or her which three strengths of yours he or she would name. You can also do the same with your colleague, discussing his or her strengths.

the import of offering hope. A time when the emancipation of the client is growing and he or she is no longer viewed as someone who fails and who doesn't know, but rather as an expert who sometimes does not *yet* know, calls for a modest attitude on the part of the professional. The latter coaches the client in finding his or her own way in reaching the future that he or she hopes for, and in relying on his or her own abilities as much as possible in the process. Solution-focused interviewing is consistent with this societal development (Bannink, 2007a, 2007b).

TEN PRINCIPLES OF SOLUTION-FOCUSED INTERVIEWING

Selekman (1993) formulated 10 assumptions for solution-focused interviewing. The assumptions are pragmatic and provide the professional with a new lens through which to view the client. I have added a few notes to the assumptions.

Resistance Is Not a Useful Concept
The concept of resistance implies that the client does not want to change and that the professional is at a remove from the client. It is better to approach the client from a position of cooperation than from a position of resistance, power, and control. Chapter 2 revisits this issue.

Cooperation Is Inevitable
The solution-focused professional must adapt to the client's manner of cooperating. Together they dance a "solution-focused tango," as it were, whereby one always complements the other. The client leads; the professional follows. If the client and the professional lose one another on the dance floor, it is incumbent upon the professional to ask the client what he or she needs to do differently in order to retrieve the connection. In a problem-focused tango, the reverse applies: The professional leads, the client follows, and it is up to the client to find the professional if they lose one another on the dance floor. If this does not occur, terms like "resistance" are invoked. The solution-

focused professional draws upon the client's strengths and resources and his or her words and opinions and elicits compliments by asking competence questions. Humor and normalization are useful in this respect. Compliments constitute a form of positive reinforcement of desired behavior. They can take various forms:

- The professional provides a positive new label, also called positive character interpretation—for example, worry can be seen as a sign of commitment ("You must be a committed person to . . . Would you like to tell me more?").
- The professional pays the client direct compliments on what he or she does or says.
- The best solution-focused compliments are indirect compliments that the client can pay him- or herself by answering competence questions: "How did you do that? How did you accomplish that? How did you come up with that fine idea? How did you know that that would help?"
- Asking about exceptions, about the times when the client has not had the problem or when it has been less of a problem, can be considered complimentary as well. After all, at those moments the client did something that worked, and by paying heed to this, the professional can direct the client's attention to his or her solutions rather than limitations.

Change Is Inevitable

Change is a continuous process; stability is an illusion. The question is not *whether* but *when* change will occur. As Ovid puts it in his *Metamorphoses*, "Nothing is constant in the whole world. Everything is in a state of flux, and comes into being as a transient appearance" (trans. 1955). The client can be encouraged to create positive self-fulfilling prophecies. There appears to be a direct correlation between talking about change and the outcome of the therapy. Talking about successes in the past, present, and future is helpful. Gathering information about present and past failures, on the other hand, leads to negative outcomes. Observing for oneself that one is doing well improves one's performance.

Only a Small Change Is Needed

As soon as clients are encouraged to notice and value small changes (exceptions), they begin to expect further changes and believe in the snowball effect of small changes. Unbeknownst to them, clients usually already carry the rudiments of solutions within themselves. These are the exceptions to the problem (hidden successes). Inquiring about exceptions offers indications of what positive steps one could take again or could take more often. Asking about hypothetical solutions, about how things should be different, also yields indications about the directions in which solutions can be sought. Because the client is the expert and comes up with solutions him- or herself, they are a natural fit for the client and his or her situation, they are found more quickly, and they are permanent (Cladder, 1999).

Most Clients Already Possess the Resources They Need in Order to Change

Most people solve their own problems without the help of doctors, psychotherapists, mediators, or self-help groups. Solution-focused professionals maintain a non-pathological view of human beings. People always have one difficulty or more in their lives. Those difficulties may or may not be chronic, depending on how the client and his or her environment (including those who extended professional help) have responded to them. But the client also has resources and strengths that can be harnessed. That is how hope, self-efficacy, and self-esteem can be rebuilt.

Walter and Peller shared three solution-focused questions with which they invite clients to tell their success stories: "How did you do that?" "How did you decide to do that?" and "How did you manage to do that?" (2000, p. 111).

The first question presupposes that the client has done something and therefore assumes action, competence, and responsibility. The second question assumes that the client has made a conscious decision, thus inviting him or her to write a new life story in which he or she has influence over his or her own future. The third question invites the client to relate his or her successes.

Lamarre and Gregoire (1999) described how they invite clients to talk about other areas of competence in their lives, such as sports or a hobby or a special talent. They then ask clients to bring those abilities to bear in order to reach their goals. For instance, they describe how a client prone to panic attacks learned to relax by applying his knowledge of deep-sea diving whenever he experienced anxiety.

Problems Are Unsuccessful Attempts to Resolve Difficulties

Watzlawick et al. (1974) listed three ways in which the client may mishandle his or her problems:

- The client needs to take action but does nothing (denying the problem).
- The client takes action when there is no or little need for it (e.g., the client goes on a diet so restrictive he or she cannot maintain it when he or she does not need to lose weight).
- The client takes action with inaccurate logic (e.g. the "be spontaneous" paradox).

What follows is an example of the "be spontaneous" paradox. A woman notices that the man next door brings his wife a bouquet of flowers every Friday when he comes home from work. She draws her husband's attention to this and says she would like that too. When her husband comes home the following Friday with a bouquet and hands it to her, the woman is upset: "That's not how I want to get flowers from you. I only want them if you think to get them yourself!"

Bateson (1979) provided a description of logical levels. Lifting a conversation to a higher logical level (e.g., from talking about behavior to talking about motivation, or even about outlook and objective) increases the chance of a successful outcome. Therefore, if people have differences in outlook, it is useful to lift the conversation to a hierarchically higher plane, for example, one of goal formulation.

In addition, it is important that the solution-focused professional not do the same as his or her predecessors if that didn't help. "What was agreeable or annoying in your previous experiences with other professionals, what was useful, and what has helped?"

One Does Not Need to Know Much About the Problem in Order to Solve It

The point of departure here is that a problem does not always manifest itself to the same degree. The professional can examine what the client is doing differently or what is different at those moments when the problem is absent or is less of a problem, or when it ceases to be a problem for a short period of time. This concerns both what he or she *does* differently and how he or she *thinks* differently. Over two thirds of clients in psychotherapy have already taken positive action in the time between when they phone to make an appointment and the intake session (see the discussion of the solution-focused decision tree later in this chapter). In addition, the professional may assign the following task by phone: "Between now and our first session, pay attention to positive things that happen and that you want to continue to happen." The result is that some clients call to cancel the appointment, because they notice that things aren't so bad after all. Solution-focused interviewing looks to the past not to explore or analyze earlier problems or failures but rather to bring to light the client's previous successes. The professional may accomplish this by asking questions about exceptions: periods or moments in the client's life during which he or she was doing well or the problem was absent or less of a problem. When the professional directs attention to the client's past successes instead of his or her failures and failings, a positive expectation is generated: Clients begin to see themselves or the situation in a more positive light.

The Client Defines the Goal of the Treatment

You invite me to dine at your house and you serve broccoli. I tell you honestly that I do not like broccoli, but you have no idea what vegetable (or other food) I do like. So when you invite me over a second time and serve another vegetable that you think I will like, it is possible that I will not like that vegetable either. I wonder if, in that case, you would invite me to dinner again. You probably think: "She doesn't like anything!" Had you asked me directly what vegetable I do like, I would have been able to tell you, and our relationship would not have suffered.

If the professional does not know where he or she is headed with his client, he or she will probably end up in the wrong place. The task of the solution-focused professional is to look, together with the client, for a realistic goal. It is important to obtain from the client a detailed description of what life will look like when he or she has reached his or her goal. Research shows that the chance of success is greater if clients believe that they have some personal control over their future (W. R. Miller, 1983; W. R. Miller & Rollnick, 2002).

Van Tongeren (2004) cited Aristotle's favorite example in describing moral intelligence: the archer. Archers understand their task if, first, they know what target they want to hit and, second, they are aware of all the circumstances affecting the situation in which they have to shoot. They assess the force of the wind, the length of the arrow, the tension of the bow, and so forth. Aristotle viewed the intelligent human being as a kind of archer, someone with knowledge of the goal and the means to achieve it. Aristotle also referred to the virtue of striving, for if one knows the goal but is not intent on realizing it, then one's knowledge of the goal is worthless. This again serves to emphasize the importance of a sound goal formulation and of the motivation to change

Do this exercise in pairs. The other person says: "I'm too embarrassed to talk about my problem, but I need help now, because things can't go on like this any longer!" You respond, "Suppose there was a solution," to which you then add, "What difference would that make for you?" or "How would you know?" or "How would that help you?" This exercise shows that it is not necessary to know what the problem is to help a person examine his or her goal and possible means of achieving it.

one's behavior. Chapter 2 revisits the subject of motivating behavior change.

Much solution-focused literature talks about treatment goals (plural). I prefer to speak of the treatment goal (singular), because there is, in my view, but one goal the client wants to reach. Yet one can come up with many means of bringing the client closer to the goal (i.e., subgoals). It has been my experience that if one asks a client for goals (plural), it is likely that he or she will list means rather than the actual goal, which is potentially limiting if it turns out that a means is not attainable.

Reality Is Defined by the Observer, and the Solution-Focused Professional Participates in Creating the Reality of the System He or She Is Working With

Einstein argued that our theories determine what we observe. What you want to see is what you get. A psychoanalytic therapist will probably see unresolved conflicts and psychological "deficits." It is impossible for professionals *not* to have a theory. A solution-focused professional is a coauthor who helps the client rewrite his or her story. To use a metaphor offered by de Shazer (1984), the solution-focused professional must play tennis on the same side of the net as his or her client. In this metaphor, the professional plays alongside the client and does not stand opposite him or her or on the sidelines of the tennis court.

There Are Many Ways of Looking at a Situation, All Equally Correct

There are no definitive explanations for or descriptions of reality. Professionals mustn't be too wedded to the models that they most prefer. Emile Chartier, a French existentialist philosopher who lived from 1868 to 1951, said in this respect: "Nothing is more dangerous than an idea when it is the only one you have" (qtd. by O'Hanlon, 2000, p. 53). Even solution-focused interviewing is not a panacea.

De Shazer (1985) described how, in putting together his team, it was by no means his objective to have everyone think or do the same thing. He encouraged different approaches because he wanted to find out exactly what everyone did to make treatment effective. Bateson (1979), too, described how different ideas may actually be beneficial (see Chapter 8).

THEORY

Solution-focused interviewing has much in common with social constructionism (Cantwell & Holmes, 1994). This theory claims that the individual's notion of what is real—including his or her sense of the nature of problems, abilities, and possible solutions—is constructed in daily life in communication with others. In other words, people confer meaning on events in communication with others, and in this process language plays a central role. Shifts in client perceptions and definitions occur within frames of reference, within society; conferring meaning is not an isolated activity. Individuals live within ethnic, familial, national, socioeconomic, and religious contexts. They adjust the way in which they confer meaning under the influence of the society in which they live.

As early as the third century B.C., the ancient Greeks understood the distinction between observing and defining reality. On the one hand, there were the Stoics, who learned to follow reason alone, to banish the passions, and to disregard suffering. Imperturbability in the face of pain, suffering, and difficulties was the highest good: The goal was *not to be unhappy*, which one could achieve by not being affected by emotions. Epicureans, on the other hand, believed that culture and the exercise of virtue were the highest good: The goal was *to be happy*, which one could accomplish by having positive emotions.

The social constructionist perspective can be used to examine how the professional and conversations with him or her may contribute to the creation of a new reality for the client. The client's capacity for change is related to his or her ability to begin to see things differently. These shifts in the perception and definition of reality occur first and foremost in the solution-focused conversation about the preferred future and exceptions to the problem.

The questions that are asked are meant to map out the client's goal and solutions, which are usually assumed already to be present in his or her life. Solution-focused questions—important interventions in solution-focused interviewing, hence the title of this book—are invitations to the client to reflect on what the future could look like and what steps he or she can take to reach his or her goal.

The questions that make a difference inquire into how clients are managing despite their problems, what they think is already going well in life and would like to maintain, and what has already improved since they made their first appointment. Questions about goal formulation, questions about exceptions, questions regarding the client's proximity to his or her goal (scaling questions), and competence questions draw out the relevant information. They tap another "layer" of the client that usually remains underexposed. The solution-focused professional is not a technical expert who has all the answers; he or she lets him- or herself be informed by the client, who constructs his or her own goal and solutions.

Solution-focused brief therapy can be viewed from different perspectives. My preference is to view solution-focused brief therapy as a form of cognitive behavioral therapy (Bannink, 2005, 2006c). I explore this further in Chapter 13.

I would like to put forward two suppositions that invite further research. My first supposition concerns recent neurobiological insights and current knowledge about the functioning of the two cerebral hemispheres (Siegel, 1999). The right hemisphere mainly hosts processes that concern nonverbal aspects of communication, such as seeing images and expressing primary emotions. It is also involved in understanding metaphors, paradoxes, and humor. Reading stories activates the right hemisphere more than reading scientific texts, which principally activates the left hemisphere. The left hemisphere mainly hosts processes concerning the verbal meaning of words, also called digital representations. The left hemisphere deals with logical analyses (cause-effect relations). Examples of linear processes that take place in the left hemisphere are reading the words in this sentence, aspects of attention, and discovering the sequence of events in a story. Our language-based communication is therefore dominated by the left hemisphere. Some authors are of the opinion that the right hemisphere sees the world more as it is and has a better overview of context, whereas the left hemisphere divides the world into bits of information. The left hemisphere sees the trees; the right hemisphere the forest. My supposition is that solution-focused interviewing, which makes frequent use of the imagination, for example, by means of "mental rehearsal" and hypothetical questions as well as drawing techniques (see Chapter 7), predominantly draws on the nonverbal and holistic capacities of the right hemisphere. It does not only address the left hemisphere through language, as is the case in analytic problem-focused interviewing. How is it that if a client responds that he or she doesn't know the answer to a question and the professional subsequently asks the hypothetical question "Suppose you *did* know?" the client in 9 cases out of 10 does come up with an answer? The manner in which both hemispheres of the client's brain are addressed may (in part) explain the success of solution-focused interviewing.

My second supposition concerns the way in which Lang's bio-information model can be applied to solution-focused interviewing (C. W. Korrelboom & ten Broeke, 2004). According to Lang's theory, changing one's emotional reaction to certain occurrences and situations implies changing the associative networks upon which those emotional reactions are based. The knowledge coded in one's memory must be altered. As response codes are the prime determinant elements in those networks, one can make the biggest gains by influencing precisely those responses. In concrete terms, this means that behavioral change generally appears to be the best way to change emotional knowledge. But as knowledge cannot simply be undone, new knowledge must be added; additional learning is required (see also Brewin, 2006). That is why counterconditioning is applied and the client learns to connect different behavioral tendencies to given stimulus constellations. Homework suggestions in solution-focused brief therapy often make use of counterconditioning: The client practices part of the desired behavior or may pretend that the desired behavior already occurs, which is also what happens in cognitive therapy (J. S. Beck, 1995).

EMPIRICAL EVIDENCE

Many have cited the importance of evidence-based research into various kinds of treatment. The important question to ask is: whose "evidence"? Is the evidence that of the therapist or the researcher, or is it the evidence of the client?

Kazdin (2006) has noted that outcome studies of therapies look at statistically significant differences between groups. What statistical significance says about the influence of a therapy on a client's daily life remains unknown. Significance does not always mean relevance. If a client scores a few points

Listen to some music that you enjoy first with only your left ear, then with only your right ear. What differences do you perceive? Various studies have shown that most (right-handed) people prefer to listen to music with their left ear (which is linked to the right hemisphere), rather than with their right ear (which is linked to the left hemisphere). Listening to music with the left ear produces a more holistic sensation, a sense of "floating with the flow of the music" (Siegel, 1999, p. 153), while the sensation of listening with only the right ear is completely different. Incidentally, the reverse is true for professional musicians. One explanation may be that they listen to music with a more analytical ear than others do.

higher on a scale or test, does that mean the problem has actually been solved and that real change has occurred in his or her life? Besides statistical significance, one also uses clinical significance as a measure of success. In that case, the researcher defines the areas in which the client must exhibit change in order for a treatment to be designated successful. This too is an arbitrary gauge, because the client does not him- or herself determine what constitutes an important change. For this reason, clinical significance should be complemented by clinical relevance. In assessing the effectiveness of a therapy, one should consider not simply progress on a measuring instrument but also improvement in areas that the client him- or herself deems relevant. Statistics can then no longer obscure the fact that a client has not benefited from a treatment.

Wampold and Bhati (2004) argued that the persona of the therapist is of much greater significance to the success of a treatment than the treatment itself, and that evidence-based research concentrates on less consequential matters (i.e., the treatment itself). Their research indicated that the therapeutic relationship is 7 times as important as the treatment itself. Aspecific variables such as offering hope and the professional's faith in his or her own method appear to be more significant than the methodology that the professional employs.

Solution-focused brief therapy is the subject of an increasing number of outcome studies. De Shazer (1991) carried out a follow-up study into the success of solution-focused brief therapy. Earlier research was conducted by Watzlawick et al. (1974). De Shazer found a success rate of 80% (Watzlawick et al., 72%) after an average of 4.6 sessions (Watzlawick et al., on average 7 sessions). After 18 months, the success rate had risen to 86%, and it was noted that having 3 sessions (rather than 2 or 1) increased the chance of success to some extent.

De Jong and Berg (1997) asked whether the treatment goal had been reached to conduct a study of success rates: 45% said the goal had been reached, 32% said they had made progress (77% combined), and 23% said there had been no progress. The average number of sessions was 2.9. This rate of 77% is higher than the often-cited 66% of clients who report progress after problem-focused therapies, and, what's more, the number of sessions is smaller (the median is 2 rather than 6 sessions). This pertained to clients with both Axis I disorders (clinical syndromes) and Axis II disorders (developmental and personality disorders) as defined by the *DSM-IV* (American Psychiatric Association, 1994).

S.D. Miller, Hubble, and Duncan (1996) found that 40% of patients in a psychiatric hospital could be discharged 3 days after implementation of the solution-focused method, as opposed to 14% before the reorganization, and that the costs per hospitalization decreased considerably. The rate of relapse among patients did not increase after the reorganization.

De Jong and Berg (1997) gave clients a self-assessment questionnaire on their first visit. Among the problems listed on the questionnaire were depression, suicidal thoughts, eating disorders, work-related problems, parent-child problems, domestic violence, alcohol and substance abuse, sexual abuse, death of a loved one, self-confidence issues, and multiple domestic problems. With the exception of a few problem areas (individuals experiencing panic attacks and health problems), it turned out that over 70% of clients had made progress since they started therapy.

Gingerich and Eisengart (2000) provided an overview of 15 outcome studies of solution-focused brief therapy, distinguishing between statistically well-controlled and other less well-controlled research. One of the statistically well-controlled studies showed that solution-focused brief therapy produces results that are comparable to those of interpersonal psychotherapy among depressed students ($N = 40$). Other well-controlled outcome studies with positive results for solution-focused brief therapy pertained to a group of parents who had conflicts with their adolescent children ($N = 42$), the rehabilitation of orthopedic patients ($N = 48$), recidivism in a prison population ($N = 59$), and the alleviation of antisocial behavior among adolescents in a group home ($N = 40$). A variant of solution-focused brief therapy is well-being therapy (Fava et al., 1998), a brief psychotherapeutic strategy that covers, among other things, personal growth, life goals, autonomy, self-acceptance, and positive relationships with others. Fava et al.'s study into the treatment of affective disorders (depression, panic disorder with agoraphobia, social phobia, generalized anxiety disorder, obsessive-compulsive disorder) showed that well-being therapy and cognitive behavioral therapy both offered a significant reduction of residual symptoms. Fava et al. (1998) established that well-being therapy produced a markedly better result than cognitive behavioral therapy.

Stams, Dekovic, Buist, and de Vries (2006) published an outcome study of solution-focused brief therapy in which they compared 21 international studies in a meta-analysis. Whether the treatments in these studies contained enough elements to qualify as solution-focused is unclear. They reported:

> The results show a modest effect of solution-focused brief therapy. Although the effect of solution-focused brief therapy is no greater than that of conventional treatment, it does have a positive effect in less time, and the client is placed at the center, which may better safeguard the client's autonomy than more traditional forms of therapy do. (Stams et al., 2006, p. 90)

Macdonald (2007) has also provided an overview of outcome studies. One of his conclusions is that solution-focused brief therapy works better than traditional forms of therapy for clients from lower socioeconomic backgrounds. He also concluded that solution-focused brief therapy can be mastered fairly quickly and produces an improvement of morale among professionals. De Jong and Berg (1997) have developed protocols for solution-focused brief therapy that may facilitate further research.

INDICATIONS AND CONTRAINDICATIONS

There is copious literature on the solution-focused treatment of adults with a variety of problems, such as alcohol abuse (Berg & Miller, 1992), posttraumatic stress disorder (Bannink, 2008b; Berg & Dolan, 2001; Dolan, 1991; O'Hanlon & Bertolino, 1998), and personality disorders and psychoses (Bakker & Bannink, 2008; O'Hanlon & Rowan, 2003; van der Veen & Appelo, 2002). People have written about solution-focused brief therapy with "therapy veterans" (Duncan, Hubble, & Miller, 1997; Duncan, Miller, & Sparks, 2004), with children and adolescents (Bannink, 2008a; Berg & Steiner, 2003; Metcalf, 1995; Selekman, 1993, 1997), in group therapy (Metcalf, 1998), in the care of developmentally disabled people (Roeden &

Bannink, 2007a, 2007b, 2009; Westra & Bannink, 2006a,b), in management and coaching (Cauffman, 2003), in organizations (Stam & Bannink, 2008), in education (Goei & Bannink, 2005), and in mediation (Bannink, 2006a,b; 2008a,d,e,f,g,h; 2009a,b,d,e,f,g; 2010a,b; Haynes, Haynes, & Fong, 2004).

The solution-focused model of interviewing can be applied to "all kinds of clients" (Cladder, 1999); what matters is that the client has a goal (or is able to define one over the course of the sessions) that he or she is willing to work toward. The number of sessions is not predetermined, but an average of three to four conversations appears to be sufficient for most clients.

In my opinion, there are also a number of contraindications for solution-focused interviewing. In addition to situations in which the client does not have or cannot come up with a goal over the course of the sessions, situations in which solution-focused interviewing is contraindicated include those in which interaction with the client is impossible, such as in the case of acute psychosis, deep depression, or a severe intellectual disability. In some instances, medication may make solution-focused conversations possible at a later stage (Bakker & Bannink, 2008). Solution-focused interviewing is also contraindicated with clients for whom a well-executed form of solution-focused interviewing yielded no or insufficient results in the past. In exceptional cases, the client may experience the solution-focused model as too positive. In that case, a more problem-focused approach may be considered.

Two other contraindications concern not the client but the professional or the institution. If the professional is not prepared to change his or her stance from that of an expert who diagnoses and dispenses advice to one of leading from one step behind the client, solution-focused interviewing will not work well. Finally, some institutions appear not to want to get rid of their (financially beneficial) patient waiting lists. If the professional or the institution puts a premium on maintaining a waiting list, solution-focused interviewing is contraindicated, as it effects a quicker flow-through of clients.

THE PRACTICE OF SOLUTION-FOCUSED INTERVIEWING

The Solution-Focused Decision Tree

De Shazer (1988) proposed the following solution-focused decision tree:

1. Has there been any improvement between the time when the appointment was made and the first session? If so, inquire about it. If not, go to 2.
2. Can any exceptions to the problem be found, that is, situations in

EXERCISE 6

Do the following exercise with another person.

- For 5 minutes, talk to the other person about a problem, worry, or annoyance you are experiencing. Ask the other person to respond in a problem-focused way. This involves questions such as: "How long have you experienced this? How severe is it? How much does it bother you? What else is troubling you? In what other areas of your life does this problem affect you? Have you experienced this before as well?"
- Talk to the same person for another 5 minutes about the same problem, worry, or annoyance and ask the other person to respond in a solution-focused manner. This involves questions such as: "How does this present a problem for you? What have you already tried to do about it and what helped? When is the problem absent or less pronounced? How do you manage that? What are you doing differently then? If you experienced a similar problem in the past, how did you solve it at the time? What do you know about how others would address this problem?" You may also ask a question about goal formulation: "What would you like to have accomplished by the end of this conversation so that you can say that it has been of use to you and that it was meaningful?"
- With the other person, note the differences between the two conversations. You may sense a lighter tone and be in a more optimistic mood when you talk about the more positive experiences, whereas a certain heaviness often accompanies problem-focused conversations. It is also possible that you have already solved your problem or that you know what to do to reach your goal.
- Reverse roles: Now you listen while the other person talks about a problem or annoyance. For the first 5 minutes, respond in a problem-focused way, and then for the next 5 minutes in a solution-focused way. With the other person, note the differences again.

which the problem did not occur or was less of a problem? If so, inquire about it. If not, go to 3.
3. Can the client describe in behavioral terms what would be different if the problem had been solved (to a sufficient degree)?

When is the client able to see glimpses of the future he or she desires? If these positive exceptions have manifested themselves, the professional can solicit more information about them. If they have not yet appeared, but a goal can be formulated at this point, the professional can inquire about that.

If that is not the case, the problem can be analyzed. It is only necessary to shift to a problem analysis if no improvement has occurred before the first session, if no exceptions can be found, and if no goal can be formulated in behavioral terms by means of, say, the miracle question (described later in this chapter). In most cases, one can immediately begin working toward a solution without elaborately mapping the problem first (de Shazer, 1985).

It is easier and more useful to design solutions than it is to analyze and solve problems. A number of clients turn out to have already taken steps in the right direction after making an appointment, which one can build on during the intake. They succeed in finding exceptions to the problem, times when the problem is less of a problem, or parts of the goal that they have already attained. Solution-focused professionals pay attention to those very exceptions; they are always looking for the difference that makes a difference. If the exceptions are deliberate, the client himself can make them happen again. If the exceptions are spontaneous, the client can discover more about them, for example, by trying to predict the exceptions. I refer here to exceptions to the rule of the problem. If these are magnified by the professional and the client, they can bring the client closer to his or her goal. They can be repeated until they constitute a new rule. One does not need to dig deep to find exceptions: They lie at the surface but are usually overlooked by the client. It is the job of the professional to notice these hidden successes and to invite the client to view them as valuable. If the client wants to do homework in the time between sessions, the professional can assign tasks, which are always adapted to the client's motivation and wishes (see Chapter 5).

De Shazer (1994) viewed solution-focused interviewing as a "tap on the shoulder." The solution-focused professional does not need to push or pull but stands one step behind the client and looks in the same direction. A tap on the shoulder helps to direct attention toward the client's preferred future. This stance is also called *leading from one step behind*. Solution-focused questions are that tap on the shoulder. The solution-focused professional's stance is also referred to as the *stance of not knowing*. It is the stance of the shabby TV detective Columbo. Time and again he managed to solve the crime, as his somewhat befuddled style of not knowing put the murderer on the wrong track and invited others to help him.

Six Important Types of Questions
The six most important types of questions in solution-focused interviewing are discussed here.

The question about change prior to the first session
"What has changed since you made the appointment?" Many clients report progress since they made the appointment. Then one may ask: "How did you manage that?" and "What is needed so that this will happen more often?" This is consistent with the supposition that everything is subject to change and that the point is not to find out *whether* change takes place but *when* change takes or has taken place.

The question about the goal
"What is the goal of this conversation for you?" or "What must be accomplished by the end of this session (or these sessions) in order for you to be able to say that it has been meaningful and that your goal has been reached?" or "What would indicate to you that you do not need to come back anymore?" One may also ask: "What would you like to see instead of the problem?" or "What do you hope for? What difference would that make?" The miracle question is another path to goal formulation: "Suppose you're asleep tonight and a miracle happens. The miracle is that the problem that brings you here has been solved (to a sufficient degree). You are unaware of this, however, because you are asleep. How would you first notice tomorrow morning that the problem has been solved? What would be different tomorrow? What would you be doing differently? How else would you notice over the course of the day that the miracle has happened? How else? How would others notice that the miracle has occurred? How would they react?" One may also ask: "At what point can we stop seeing each other?"

The question "What else?"
Questions about details are key. "What is needed so that that will happen? Suppose it happens. What would you be doing differently? And what else?" It is important to keep inquiring about everything that looks like a success, a resource, or something that the client values in him- or herself. Moreover, the question implies that there *is* more and that all that the client needs to do is find out what it is.

The question about exceptions
"When has a small part of the miracle already occurred for a short period of time?" or "When have you caught a glimpse of the situation you want to arrive at? How could you tell? What was different then? How did you do that? How was it different from now?" One can also inquire about the times

when the problem has been absent or less of a problem, or when it has ceased to be a problem for awhile: "What is different about those times?" The client often overlooks the times when the problem is absent or is less of a problem, because, to his or her mind, the problem is always present ("everything is beige").

Wittgenstein wrote: "The aspects of things that are most important for us are hidden because of their simplicity and familiarity (one is unable to notice something—because it is always before one's eyes)" (1953/1968, p. 129). Consequently, one does not need to dig deep to find exceptions: They lie at the surface, but the client passes them over.

Scaling questions

Scaling questions focus on progress, motivation, and confidence. They can be asked at the end of the session (Duncan, 2005), when one has looked for exceptions or discussed the miracle (and, by extension, the client's goal). Sometimes it can be useful to ask the client whether he or she is familiar with the use of scales in order to explain in brief what a scaling question is. An often-used scaling question is:

> If the miracle (or the goal you would like to reach) is a 10 and the moment when things were at their worst (or the moment when you made the appointment) a 0, where on that scale are you now? How did you manage to come to this number? What would 1 point higher look like? What would you be doing differently? How would you be able to move up 1 point? What is needed for you to do that? What else?

It can also be useful to ask the client where he or she wants to end up; a 10 is often unnecessary as well as unattainable. Most clients are very satisfied with a 7 or 8. Consider for yourself: How often are you at 10? In solution-focused literature, scaling questions are used in different ways. One mostly works with a scale from 0 to 10, sometimes with a scale from 1 to 10—the latter presumably to exclude the worst situation, the 0, because the fact that the client is visiting a professional already implies some improvement. I believe that clients give a higher rating if the scale goes from 10 to 0 rather than from 0 to 10, which improves their self-perception. For that reason, I always ask scaling questions using a scale of 10 to 0.

One of the basic solution-focused questions is: "What is already working in the right direction?" (see Chapter 3). And then: "And what else?" These days, I choose to ask these questions before I ask the client to give a rating—contrary to the standard methodology, according to which one first asks for a rating and subsequently inquires what the rating means. It has been my experience that clients give higher ratings if they are first asked what is already working in the right direction. This has to do with cognitive dissonance: If the client gives a low rating, for example, he or she cannot name much that is working in the right direction afterward.

Questions about skills (competencies) the client already has
Competence questions are: "How do you do that? How do you manage to . . . ? How do you keep going? How come things aren't worse?" It is again important to ask about small, positive details. If the client has an undesired way of coping, for example, a tendency to scream at the other person during an argument, one might say: "You must have a good reason to raise your voice. Please tell me about how screaming helps you." This question shows that the client's suffering is being *acknowledged*. The question also makes it easier for him or her to formulate a response. Afterward, one can ask what other (more desirable) ways the client has of achieving the same effect.

In *Winnie-the-Pooh on Success*, the wise and, yes, in part solution-focused Stranger tells the animals how they can become successful.

> "What does the success formula taste like?"
> "It's not that kind of formula, Silly Bear," said The Stranger. He took a sheet of paper out of his case and began writing on it. When he finished, he turned it around and showed it to his friends. This is what he had written:
>
> Select a Dream
> Use your dreams to set a Goal
> Create a Plan
> Consider Resources
> Enhance Skills and Abilities
> Spend time Wisely
> Start! Get Organized and Go
>
> "It spells Suchness!" shouted Piglet.
> "Close, Piglet," said The Stranger. "It spells Success." (Allen & Allen, 1997, p. 17)

EXERCISE 7

Think back to a period in your life when you had a problem. How did you resolve the problem back then? Think of at least three things you did that helped you at the time. If you currently have a problem, which of those strategies could you apply again (or are you already applying) to solve the current problem? What do you know about the ways in which others have solved similar problems?

Walter and Peller abandoned the distinction between problem and solution altogether. They talked about "preferences," because they believed it allowed them to converse more creatively with their clients. "Our basic research question changed from 'how do we construct solutions?' to 'how can we create a space of dialogue and wonder where purpose, preferences, and possibilities can emerge and evolve?'" (Walter & Peller, 2000, p. xii). De Bono also argued that "designing" a desired outcome often bears no relation to the conflict itself. He did not use the term "solutions" either: "I do not even like saying design 'solutions,' because this implies that there is a problem" (De Bono, 1985, p. 42).

Solution-Focused Interviewing via the Internet

Technological developments in the last few years have given us the ability to conduct electronically supported conversations. Online therapy is the way of the future. Using solution-focused protocols for the first and subsequent sessions outlined in the following chapters offer a solid structure in this respect. Experiments in which solution-focused brief therapy is conducted online are ongoing in the Netherlands; there is, for example, a Web site called Praten Online where teenagers between the ages of 12 and 20 can chat anonymously with a solution-focused professional. The results are promising.

SUMMARY

- Finding solutions is different from solving problems; solution-focused interviewing does not focus on the problem but asks: "What would you like to see instead of the problem? What is your goal? What is already working in the right direction?" In principle, the solution-focused professional asks questions and does not give advice (Smock, Froerer, & Bavelas, personal communication, 2009; Tomori & Bavelas, 2007).

TABLE 1.1
Differences Between Problem-Focused and Solution-Focused Interviewing

Problem-Focused Interviewing	Solution-Focused Interviewing
Focus is on feelings/emotions.	Focus is on seeing (meaning) and doing.
Looking for faults is important.	Designing solutions is important.
The client's view is no good.	The client's view is validated (which makes letting go of a point of view easier).
Whose fault is it?	What does the client think should happen?
Motivation is called into question.	Motivation is sought and used.
The past is important.	The future is important.
The professional confronts.	The professional accepts the client's view and asks: "In what way does that help?"
The professional persuades the client.	The professional lets him- or herself be persuaded by the client.
Big changes are needed.	A small change is often enough.
Resources must be acquired.	Necessary resources are already present.
The problem is always present.	The problem is not ever always present.
Theory-determined conversation is used.	Client-determined conversation is used.
Insight into or understanding of the problem is a precondition.	Insight into or understanding of the problem comes with or after the change.
Theory of change is the professional's.	Theory of change is the client's; the professional asks: "How will this help you?"

- The gaze is directed not at the past but at the future. The client is viewed as capable of formulating his or her goal, coming up with solutions, and executing them.
- A brief history of solution-focused interviewing based on 10 principles was provided in this chapter.
- Theoretical backgrounds, research, and indications and contraindications were outlined.
- The practice of solution-focused interviewing was described by means of six important types of solution-focused questions.
- Table 1.1 provides an overview of the differences between the problem-focused and the solution-focused models of interviewing.

CHAPTER 2

· · · · · · · · · · · · · · · · ·

Motivation and the
Cooperative Relationship

If you want to build a ship
Don't drum up the men to gather wood
Divide the work and give orders
Instead, teach them to yearn for the vast and endless sea
—Antoine de Saint-Exupéry, *The Wisdom of the Sands*

MOTIVATION FOR BEHAVIOR CHANGE

Motivation for behavior change refers to the client's willingness to change his or her own behavior in order to reach the goal. In theory, the fact that the client visits the professional doesn't say anything about the client's willingness to change his or her own behavior. Often the client secretly hopes that the professional will deliver the solution or, in the case of relationship therapy or mediation, point to the other person as the one who needs to change. Metcalf put it as follows: "If you are not part of the solution, you are part of the problem" (1998, p. 5).

This chapter discusses how the client's commitment to the treatment and his or her motivation for behavior change can be gauged at the start of the sessions and explores the way in which this commitment and motivation for behavior change can be enhanced. Professionals too often claim that they do not even start a treatment if there is, in their view, insufficient motivation. Many a time they appear to be at their wits' end if the client is not immediately prepared to change his or her own behavior. Schippers and de Jonge had this to say on the subject:

> Unwilling, unable, or not the right time: these are ways of saying that someone is not motivated. It is not as easy to come up with a defini-

tion of motivation for behavior change, however. It is definitely not simply the outcome of a sum of positive and negative consequences of one's behavior. After all, the client's point of view determines what are positive and negative consequences, and this doesn't necessarily coincide with what the professional deems important. (2002, p. 251)

Appelo has argued that it is a misconception that clients are willing to change:

Therapists who feel annoyed with clients who fail to show effort and who do not change would do well not to concentrate too much on external behavior. It is much more advantageous to look at the biological, cognitive, and social motives for the absence of the willingness to change. (2009, p. 73)

"Biological motives" refers to the fact that our brains are predisposed to automatization. And mental programs, once formed and automatized, remain stored in our memories forever. They can always be reactivated and take over the regulation of our behavior. That is why successful behavioral change is often followed by relapse, according to Appelo. Cognitive factors, on the other hand, allow one to ignore suffering or to believe that personal effort is unnecessary or impossible. This involves limiting one's goals, not submitting any, or keeping them vague, which obviates any unfavorable comparison with the here and now. Another trick is to devalue the preferred situation, telling oneself that things aren't all that bad right now. Both tricks serve to prevent or cancel out cognitive dissonance. Yet another trick is to attribute failures to external factors, which precludes the motivation to change oneself. Finally, the single most determining factor in repeating, consolidating, and automatizing one's behavior is social reinforcement. People like to belong to groups, which often serve to reinforce undesired behaviors; this is why many people do not even think about changing their behavior, unless they are willing to seek new sources of social support.

One of the principles of motivational interviewing is unconditional acceptance (W. R. Miller & Rollnick, 2002). The professional develops a relationship with the client based on collaboration, individual responsibility, and freedom of behavioral choice. Miller and Rollnick argued that the prerequisite of approaching problem behavior in a non-moralizing way makes it difficult for professionals who are not willing or able to suspend their own (prejudiced) ideas about problem behavior to engage in motivational interviewing. The professional reacts empathetically, avoids discussion, and strengthens the client's self-efficacy. Miller and Rollnick used the term "change talk," which is a way of communicating that draws out a person's own reasons for change and the advantages of making those changes. Change talk facilitates change. One method of eliciting change talk that they identified is asking evocative questions, for example, "In what way would you like things to be different from now on? What would you like your life to look like 5 years from now? Where do you find the courage to change, if you want to do so?"

Prochaska, Norcross, and DiClemente (1994) developed a theory about the stages of behavior change. When a person adopts an indifferent or unknowing attitude (the attitude of what is called a "visitor"), the emphasis is on providing information and on establishing a link between the behavior to be changed and the worries or problems that others experience. In the next stage, with someone who is contemplating change (the attitude of what is called a "complainant"), the emphasis is on deciding on and initiating the desired behavior. This is followed by the stages of change action, behavior maintenance, and (possibly) relapse. The stages of Prochaska et al. can be broadly compared to the configuration of the therapeutic relationship in solution-focused interviewing.

Orlemans, Eelen, and Hermans (1995) and Bannink (2007a) have pointed out that stable behavior change is attained if the extrinsic reinforcement gradually turns into an intrinsic one:

> Extrinsic reinforcement means that the reinforcement artificially succeeds the behavior, while an intrinsic reinforcement is naturally connected with the action; the action leads to satisfying consequences of its own accord. Usually the two appear in combination, but it is clear that extrinsic reinforcement alone offers little guarantee that the action will endure. If a child learns to play the trumpet solely because it gets candy after practice, the behavior remains under extrinsic control and is extinguished when the reward ceases. It is not for nothing, for instance, that popular melodies are taught early on in music lessons, which can intrinsically strengthen the practice behavior. (Orlemans et al., 1995, p. 111)

By inviting the client to talk about his or her skills and successes and to look for exceptions, the solution-focused professional can encourage a visitor or a complainant to become a customer. Compliments and positive character interpretations are examples of extrinsic reinforcements of desired behavior that the professional can provide. Competence questions prompt the client to talk about his or her successes and give self-compliments. In this way, the professional can help the client achieve a stable behavior change that lasts after the sessions have ended.

Solution-focused professionals do well to carefully tailor their questions during the session and any homework suggestions to the client's motivation for behavior change. Chapter 5 discusses this at length.

The professional's challenge, then, is to turn visitors and complainants into customers. This is not always successful. Interventions by the professional that are directed at behavior change will not be accepted by the client as long as the latter thinks either that he or she does not have a problem (visitor) or that someone or something else (e.g., partner, health, housing, work) needs to change (complainant). The solution-focused professional is trained to compliment the existing motivation and motivate behavior change. The professional pays attention to motivation not only at the beginning of the sessions but throughout the entire process. After all, a customer can always revert to being a complainant, for example, if the professional has a different or larger goal than the client, and may no longer be motivated to change his or her own behavior.

The literature on solution-focused interviewing distinguishes between voluntary and involuntary clients. A client sent by others, in a visitor relationship, is considered an involuntary client: It is the referrer, after all, who thinks the client should consult the professional. The client him- or herself does not have a problem. In that case, it is useful to ask the client about his or her perceptions of the referrer's motives.

Lastly, it is important to bear in mind that what matters is the relationship among the client, the professional, and the goal. This means that the relationship varies not only by client but also by goal, especially in the case of clients who have been referred to the professional. *The solution-focused professional is an expert at motivating behavior change in clients.* This is particularly important if the client has been referred or thinks that another person is to blame for the problem and needs to change. Solution-focused interviewing may improve the pessimistic or barely hopeful attitude of some professionals, thanks to a number of interventions that enhance the client's commitment and motivation.

CASE 1

Two concerned parents take their 15-year-old daughter to a solution-focused therapist. They are very worried about her weight: She weighs 88 pounds and is continuing to lose weight. She has also been missing school. The family doctor has spoken to them about hospitalization. The father surreptitiously butters her sandwiches to smuggle in some fat. They are at their wits' end: "Please, do something about this!" The daughter, however, feels that she does not weigh too little at all, that she is still too heavy, in fact. The parents (i.e., the referrers) are complainants here: Their daughter needs to change and the therapist has to make sure it happens. The daughter is a visitor: She is not experiencing her weight and her eating as a problem. The therapist compliments them all on showing up, especially the daughter; she can undoubtedly think of something more fun to do than spend time with a therapist and her worried parents. When she's asked about her goal (as long as she's here), she says she would like for her parents to leave her alone a bit more. The therapist asks what she thinks would need to be different about her behavior (at a minimum) in order for her parents to be able to take a step back and to leave her be a little more. "If I were to go to school more often," she replies. She turns out to be willing to attend school more often so that her parents will leave her alone more and is, therefore, as far as that goal is concerned, a customer. Only at a later stage will it be possible to discuss her weight and eating.

THE COOPERATIVE RELATIONSHIP: VISITOR, COMPLAINANT, AND CUSTOMER

Research shows that a cooperative relationship is crucial to the outcome of the sessions. Client factors contribute 40% to the result, relationship factors 30%, hope and expectancy 15%, and methods and techniques 15% (Duncan et al., 2004). Wampold and Bhati (2004) have claimed that a positive therapeutic relationship explains as much as 60% of a treatment's success, the professional's faith in his or her own method 30%, and the method itself only 10%. It is important to listen to the client's theory of change and to accept his or her goal. Listening to what the client thinks will help and needs to happen is of primary importance. It is also useful to ask how change usually occurs in his or her life and what has already helped. Duncan et al. developed the SRS (Session Rating Scale), which has since been validated and increases the effectiveness of sessions because it allows the professional to obtain direct feedback about them. The scale is a short list of four topics that allow the client to evaluate the session (see Appendix E). For children there is a variant with emoticons. The four evaluation points are:

- *The relationship.* I felt heard, understood, and respected.
- *Goals and topics.* We talked about and worked on what I find important.
- *Approach or method.* The therapist's approach is a good fit for me.
- *Overall.* Overall, this session was right for me.

It is useful, then, to ask the client to rate the cooperative relationship on a scale of 10 to 0 at the end of each session. Questions about the rating are the logical next step: If the client gives the collaboration a rating of 5, for example, the professional can ask how they managed to reach 5 together, what a 6 would look like, and what the professional needs to do differently to see to it that the client rates the next session higher. The SRS scale (see Chapter 11) is primarily intended to get a conversation going about the collaboration between the professional and the client.

As early as the first session and in all subsequent sessions, the solution-focused professional pays attention to his or her relationship with the client: Does it constitute a visitor, a complainant, or a customer relationship?

In a visitor relationship, the client has been referred by others (e.g., judge, partner, insurance company, probation office, school, parents) and does not identify a problem to work on. There is no appeal for help. Others are worried about the client or have a problem with him or her. There is no motivation for the client to change his or her own behavior. The professional can try to create a context in which an appeal for help is made possible. What matters is finding out what the client would like to achieve through his or her relationship with the professional. For example, the latter might ask what the referrer would like to be different in the future and to what extent the client is prepared (at a minimum or maximum) to cooperate in the process. How the client has ended up with the professional is an important question, as the referrer has usually indicated what he or she believes must (at a minimum) be achieved (e.g., the client must cease using violence). With respect to a visitor relationship, the following guidelines can be provided:

- Assume that the client has good reasons for his or her thinking and behavior. Assume that an involuntary client is often on the defensive; after all, it wasn't his or her idea to come to the session.
- As a professional, suspend your own judgment and empathize with the perceptions of the client that make his or her cautious and sometimes defensive attitude understandable (unconditional acceptance).
- Ask the client what he or she would like (because the client is here now) and accept the answer.
- Acknowledge the fact that the client would rather not be sitting here with you. Questions such as "What needs to change in order for you not to have to come back?" and "How can we make sure that you're here for as little time as possible?" are indicated.

In a complainant relationship, the client does provide information about the problem, he or she is often experiencing a great deal of suffering, and there is an appeal for help, but the client does not yet see him- or herself as part of the problem or the solution. It is also possible that the client was at one point a customer but isn't anymore. Someone or something else is to blame for the problem and needs to change, not the client him- or herself. There is no motivation for the client to change his or her own behavior; what the client would like is for the other person to change his or her behavior or for something else to change with the help of, for example, a pill, a miracle, or the professional. The solution-focused professional acknowledges the client's pain ("How do you manage to keep going?") and may suggest that the client observe the times when the problem is absent or is less of a problem, reflect on what is different then and on what he or she is probably doing differently then, or observe the times when the problem ceases to be a problem for a short period of time. The professional can also ask clients to pay attention to the moments when they catch a glimpse of what they are striving for (the goal), to what is different then, and to what they are probably doing differently then. By asking these questions, one invites clients to talk no longer about the problem but rather about the goal and solutions.

In a customer relationship, the client *does* see him- or herself as part of the problem or the solution, there is suffering and an appeal for help, and the client is motivated to change his or her own behavior. The client uses the word "I" or "we" in his or her appeal for help: "What can I do to solve this problem?" or "How can we make sure that we reestablish a good relationship?" Customer relationships are a minority upon clients' initial contact with the professional. Yet for most professionals they are the icing on the cake. Successful sessions with clients in a customer relationship are vital because they constitute a form of positive reinforcement for the professional. However, the main challenge for the professional lies in increasing motivation for behavior change in clients in visitor and complainant relationships.

CASE 2

A classic example of two complainants: Husband and wife show up for relationship therapy. The wife says: "If my husband showed his emotions more and talked about himself more, I would definitely want to have sex with him more often." The husband says: "If my wife wanted to sleep with me more often, I would certainly show more emotion."

Although this classification always pertains to the relationship of the professional with the client and not, therefore, to a personal trait of the client, for the sake of convenience, one often talks about "visitors," "complainants," and "customers." Flemish solution-focused professionals prefer a classification based on a shopping metaphor: A "visitor" becomes a "passerby"; that is, he or she stands in front of the professional's shop window and looks at what is on sale. A "complainant" becomes a "browser"; that is, he or she has entered the store and is looking around. And a "customer" becomes a "buyer" (Le Fevere de Ten Have, 2002). How the passerby has ended up in front of the professional's shop window is not fleshed out in the metaphor.

In sessions with two or more people, different relationships may coexist; for example, one client may be a customer, the other a complainant. At the start of relationship therapy or mediation, one often finds a constellation in which both clients are complainants: They concede that there is a problem, but each thinks that the other has caused the problem and thus needs to change. The visitor-complainant-customer trichotomy is considered a continuum; each client position is validated and accepted. The fact that the client has shown up for a session makes him or her a visitor; after all, the client could have not shown up. The solution-focused professional should always compliment him or her on that. Direct compliments, positive character interpretations, and questions about the client's competencies (indirect compliments) are powerful, motivating interventions. They enhance the positive tenor of the conversation and invite the client, or clients, to look at him- or herself, or each other, in a more positive way. Chapter 3 revisits this topic.

Experience has shown that when there is negative countertransference (the professional feels irritation, discouragement, insecurity), it is often because the professional views the client as a customer—and devises interventions accordingly—when the client isn't one (yet).

CASE 3

During a divorce mediation, the solution-focused mediator compliments both clients on their having shown up and their willingness to examine how mediation can help them come up with a sound custody agreement. The mediator notes that both parents must care deeply about their children to visit a mediator (positive character interpretation). The woman is complimented for indicating that she does not want to rush the process; she wants to tackle this thoroughly and properly. The man is complimented because he would like everything to get settled quickly yet manages to muster the patience not to force matters.

SOLUTION-FOCUSED QUESTIONS FOR VISITORS AND COMPLAINANTS

Some solution-focused questions for visitors are:

- "Whose idea was it for you to come here?"
- "What do you think about what should be discussed here today?"
- "What does the referrer think you should do differently?"
- "What, at a minimum, would the referrer say you have to do differently?"
- "Do you agree with the concerns the referrer has about you?"
- "What does the referrer think you should do here?"
- "What is needed in order for you not to have to come back?"
- "What do you have to do to convince the referrer that you do not have to come back here?"
- "If you decided to do that, how would things change between you and the referrer?"
- "Is that something you could or would want to do? How would you be able to motivate yourself to do that?"
- "What, at a minimum, would you say you could do differently?"
- "When was the last time you did that? If you decided to do that again, what would be the first small step that you would take?"
- "In what way would your life change if you were in charge?"
- "Suppose that the miracle happened. What would be the first small step that you would take?"
- "How will you be able to tell that you've done enough?"
- "What would happen in your life that isn't happening now?"
- "Suppose you did have a goal. What might it be?"
- "What are your best hopes? What difference would that make?"

See who in your caseload may have been referred (a visitor). Think about which of your clients have indicated that they wanted something out of their sessions with you. Does the client him- or herself want to achieve something by coming to you? Or are others who want something from the client involved? If the answer to the first question is no, your client has no goal. If your client says someone else is forcing him or her to come, you have an involuntary client, a visitor.

- "You must have a good reason to . . . Please tell me about it."
- "What is happening that gives you the sense that this problem can be resolved?"
- "What would happen if these sessions didn't continue?"
- "What should and shouldn't I do based on your experience with previous professionals?"
- "Is there anything else that you're curious about that we could look at together?"
- "What do you think could happen here that makes you think, 'That, never'?"
- "In addition to all the reasons you have for not wanting that, do you perhaps also have any thoughts as to why you might want it, how it could work or solve something?"
- "What would have to be put on the agenda so that you would be able to say: 'This has been meaningful to me after all'?"
- "How would you know that coming here today was a good idea after all?"
- "You say: 'These things are not in my hands.' What can you exert influence over?"
- "What happens if you do nothing?"
- "What is the worst that could happen if you do nothing?"

Some solution-focused questions for complainants are:

- "How is this a problem for you?"
- "How can I best work with you?"
- "When is the problem absent or less of a problem?"
- "When has the problem not been a problem for a short period of time?"

- "How do you cope?"
- "What are your best hopes? What difference would that make?"
- "If you can continue to do that, would you have accomplished what you came here for?"
- "What gives you the sense that this problem can get resolved?"
- "What doesn't need to change and should stay as it is?"
- "What should definitely not change?"
- "What have you been holding on to that it might be time to let go of?"
- "In what area would you like to see the most improvement?"
- "What have you considered doing but not yet tried?"
- After the scaling question: "How do you manage to stand strong at that number?"
- "How do you manage to . . . with everything you've been through?"
- "What has seen you through until now?"
- "Could things be worse than they are? How come they aren't?"
- "Suppose you did want to change something about yourself. What might it be?"
- "Suppose that a change that you desire occurs (e.g., a person changes, you get a new job or a new house, an illness is cured). What would you do differently?"
- "Suppose the other person or thing doesn't change. What will you do?"
- "Suppose the other person were to do the things you would like him or her to do. How would he or she say you treat him or her differently?"
- "What would you like to achieve at the very least?"
- "What difference would it make for you if the other person were to change in the way you wish for? What would be different between the two of you? And how might that help you?"
- "Suppose the two of you did have a joint goal. What might it be?"
- Following the reply "I don't know": "Suppose you did know. What would you say?" (See Chapter 7.)
- "Suppose the other person respected your need to . . . What would be different between the two of you?"
- "What should and shouldn't I do based on your experience with other professionals?"
- "How do you rate your chances of finding a solution? Use a scale of 10 (a very good chance) to 0 (no chance)."

- "What do you need from the other person in order to (re)establish a good relationship?"
- "What is the least you could offer the other person in order to (re)establish a good relationship?"
- "What do you need from the other person in order to split up amicably?"
- "What is the least you could offer the other person in order to split up amicably?"
- "Suppose the other person were to offer you what you need in order to (re)establish a good relationship. What would you do differently then?"
- "Suppose the other person were to offer you what you need in order to split up amicably. What would you do differently then?"
- "You have talked a lot about how you don't want things to be. What do you want?"
- "What would you like instead of the problem?"

Some questions for visitors can also be asked of complainants. Chapter 10 provides 1,001 solution-focused questions.

Walter and Peller (1992) described four strategies that may be used if clients point to someone else as the problem. These clients are complainants who do not see themselves as part of the problem or the solution, but who identify someone or something else as the cause of the problem or as the person or thing that needs to change. It has been my experience that the third strategy in particular, whereby the professional asks about what would happen if the other person changed in the desired manner, yields good results.

- "I wish I could help you with this, but I am not a magician. I do not believe that anyone is capable of changing anyone else. How else can I help you?"
- Investigating the future if the other person doesn't change: "What do you want to do now?"
- Investigating the future if the other person does change: "Suppose the other person were to change in the manner you desire. What would you do differently? When has that already happened? And when it has happened, what did the other person do differently? What difference did that make for you?"
- Finding out the intention or the goal behind suggested and attempted solutions: "What do you eventually want to achieve

Choose someone to join you in this exercise. Ask your partner to talk about someone he or she would like to change. (Make sure that you yourself are not that someone!) Now practice with the questions of the four strategies, and note the differences. Reverse roles. In the role of client, you will be able to learn a lot from the different types of questions you are asked.

together? What will have changed for you once the other person has solved his or her problem? How do you know that he or she has to do that him- or herself and that you are not responsible? How do you manage to leave that responsibility to the other person, even though it may be hard for you to do so?"

RESISTANCE DOES NOT EXIST

Walter and Peller wrote: "Clients are always cooperating. They are showing us how they think change takes place. As we understand their thinking and act accordingly, cooperation is inevitable" (1992, p. 200). The notion that the professional knows what is best for his or her client derives from the medical model. If the client puts the expert's ideas aside or does not follow his or her advice, it is usually attributed to the client's own character flaws or to a deep-rooted pathology. In the medical model, the expectation is that the professional will make the client better through his or her interventions. If it works, the professional feels proficient in his or her work and receives credit for the progress made. If there is no progress, the blame is frequently assigned to the client, which allows the professional to distance him- or herself from any responsibility.

In his article "The Death of Resistance," de Shazer (1984) argued that what professionals view as signs of resistance are, in fact, unique ways in which the client chooses to cooperate. For example, a client who does not do the assigned homework does not show resistance; rather, this is his or her way of cooperating and telling the professional that the homework is not in accordance with how he or she does things. De Shazer assumed that clients are capable of finding out what they want and need as well as how they can achieve it. It is the professional's task to help the client discover these abilities and guide him or her in creating a satisfying and productive life.

De Shazer has offered the pleasing image of the relationship between the client and the professional as that of a tennis team:

With resistance as a central concept, therapist and client are like opposing tennis players. They are engaged in fighting against each other, and the therapist needs to win in order for therapy to succeed. With cooperating as a central concept, therapist and client are like tennis players on the same side of the net. Cooperating is a necessity, although sometimes it becomes necessary to fight alongside your partner so that you can cooperatively defeat your mutual opponent. (1984, p. 85)

The professional is on the court and plays alongside the client; he or she does not stand on the other side of the net as an opponent, nor does he or she stand on the sidelines of the tennis court. Here the opponent is the problem. This view is in line with the narrative approach, in which externalizing the problem, turning the problem into the enemy, is a much-used intervention (see Chapter 7).

In his overview of the 10 principles of solution-focused interviewing (see Chapter 1), Selekman also noted that resistance is not a useful concept:

Resistance implies that the client does not want to change and the therapist is separate from the client system he or she is treating. De Shazer has argued convincingly for therapists to approach each new client case from a position of therapist-client cooperation, rather than focusing on resistance, power, and control. (1993, p. 25)

O'Hanlon (2003) provided 26 ways to respectfully dissolve the client's resistance, for example, by validating and accepting where the client is and simultaneously challenging him or her to change. In this way, he went one step beyond the unconditional acceptance of the client, which prevails in client-centered therapy. Another method he identified is using "Yes, and," as described later in this chapter.

Leary's Rose

Problems are primarily determined by how people respond to each other. Leary (1957) developed a practical model to categorize social relationships: the so-called Leary's Rose. He distinguished two main dimensions: on the one hand, power and influence ("above") or the lack thereof ("below") and, on the other hand, personal proximity and sympathy ("together") or distance ("opposed"). These two dimensions govern how people interact with each other. People with a great need for power position themselves above others.

They are quick to engage in battle and tell others what they have to do. People at the other end of the power spectrum take a subservient or dependent position. If the division of influence is equal, the relationship is symmetrical. If it is unequal, the relationship is complementary. Some people only feel happy if they can work with others. Cooperative behavior, such as providing support and help, suits them. People at the other end of the spectrum are associated with behavior that creates distance and implies opposition.

On the basis of these dimensions, Leary came up with four communication positions: below and together, above and together, below and opposed, and above and opposed. The client or professional often assumes a preferred position within one of these four quadrants. There may also be a varying preference for two (or more) quadrants. The communication position taken by one person prompts in the other person a supplemental (complementary) or an opposite (symmetrical) interactional position: Above elicits below, down elicits below, together invites opposed, and opposed provokes together. Communication behavior and, hence, interactional disruptions proceed according to these rules. The professional quickly identifies this behavior on the basis of his or her own reactions and on the interactional position that is, as it were, forced upon him or her. The professional can also help the client change positions, for example, from below and together to above and together, by means of the solution-focused stance of not knowing (the Columbo stance) and by regarding the client as competent and as an expert.

The four main positions are:

- Above and together: I adopt a position of leadership and solidarity and command cordial docility from the other person.
- Below and together: I adopt a dependent and cordial position in relation to the other person and command him or her to benevolently take the initiative.
- Below and opposed: I adopt a dependent and suspicious position in relation to the other person and command him or her to ignore me (contrary and complaining toward the other person).
- Above and opposed: I adopt a superior and oppositional position in relation to the other person and command him or her to stand in awe of me.

In the medical model, the professional adopts the above and together position (he or she is the expert), which automatically puts the client in the below and together (or opposed) position. In solution-focused sessions, the profes-

Think about what your preferred position in Leary's Rose is in your professional capacity, and in which sessions you succeed—even temporarily—in adopting a different position. What difference does that make for you and your client?

sional takes the below and together position as much as possible (the stance of leading from one step behind and not knowing), which causes the client to move, seemingly automatically, to the above and together position, in which the client is the expert. The professional can enhance the cooperation, commitment, and motivation of the client by paying attention to the preferred position of the client and by shifting from his or her own position above and together to below and together. Inquiring about the client's competencies produces equal cooperation between the professional and the client as well.

A client who is a customer is in the together position, and a client who is a complainant is (still) in the opposed position as far as behavior change is concerned. Solution-focused questions and the professional's invitation to talk about his or her own capacities may help the client move to the together position. If the professional notices him- or herself becoming irritated, insecure, or discouraged, there is negative countertransference, that is, a negative reaction by the professional to the client's behavior. In practice, this usually occurs because there is a visitor or complainant relationship, but the professional—mistakenly—considers the client a customer.

The Difference Between "Yes, But" and "Yes, And"
The expression "Yes, but" is often used to indicate that one disagrees with the other person. When used by the client, it is often interpreted by the professional as a form of resistance: "Of course you're right, but . . . ," "Yes, but I see it differently . . . " An utterance like "Yes, but" drains energy from the conversation, which soon turns into a discussion that revolves solely around who is right. "Yes, but" is actually an indirect form of "No, because" (the opposed position in Leary's Rose).

It is better to use "Yes, and," which creates new possibilities and vastly improves cooperation. "Yes, but" excludes others' positions; with "Yes, and," they complement one another. Clients (and professionals) who often use "Yes, but" can for the most part be classified as complainants, which carries the usual implications as far as the interviews and homework suggestions are concerned.

Explain the difference between "Yes, but" and "Yes, and" to a group. Ask someone to make a random announcement (e.g., about the weather or the news) and ask another person to follow up with "Yes, but . . ." A third person does the same, and so on. Let this go on for 5 minutes; then ask the group whether they are getting anywhere in this manner. You will notice that the discussion goes around in circles and that the members of the group look for ways to convince each other that they are right. The mood will soon turn increasingly negative.

Do the same exercise and replace "Yes, but" with "Yes, and." After 5 minutes everyone will notice that the atmosphere is more positive and open and that new themes have come to the fore. The "Yes, and" exercise is an excellent technique for improving cooperation.

SCALING MOTIVATION AND CONFIDENCE

Asking scaling questions about motivation and confidence is another way to find out how motivated the client is to change his or her own behavior and how much confidence he or she has that the goal can be reached. It can also help enhance the client's motivation and confidence. The professional may ask him- or herself the same questions about motivation and confidence as well. Some solution-focused questions for scaling motivation for behavior change are:

- "I would like to ask you a scaling question about how motivated you are and how hard you're willing to work to solve the problem that brought you here. If a 10 means that you're willing to do anything to reach your goal and 0 means that you are merely waiting for something to happen by itself, where on that scale are you?"
- If your client comes up with a high rating, you can ask: "Where does your willingness to work hard at this come from?" You can then compliment your client on being so motivated to get closer to his or her goal.
- If your client provides a low rating (e.g., a 2), you can ask: "How do you manage to be at 2, and how come you're not at 0 or 1?"
- A question that may follow is: "What would a score that is 1 point higher look like?" And then: "What is needed for you to get to a score that is 1 point higher?" or "Who or what can help you reach that score?"

It can be useful to ask how much confidence the client has that he or she will reach his goal, especially early on in the treatment. One may do so, for instance, during the first session after the goal has been formulated and exceptions have been sought. Also, the client may have already volunteered that he or she has little confidence in the sessions or the professional. Even in that case it is a good idea to ask a scaling question to seriously explore that statement. Frequent use of scaling questions with the client and with important people in the client's life can provide good calibrations to assess the client's progress, motivation, and confidence.

Some solution-focused questions for scaling confidence are:

- "If a 10 means that you are very confident that you can reach your goal and 0 means that you have no confidence at all, what rating would you give yourself?"
- If your client comes up with a high rating, you may compliment him or her by saying: "Are you the kind of person who, once he or she has decided to tackle something, is very confident that that he or she will succeed?" or "Where does that confidence that you will reach your goal come from?"
- If your client gives a low rating (e.g., a 3), you can ask a competence question: "How do you manage, given your current situation, to be at 3?" and "What would a score that is 1 point higher look like? What is needed for you to reach that score?" or "Who or what can help you get 1 point higher on the scale?"
- "How will I know that you have enough confidence that we can end these sessions? How will I notice that?"
- "How much confidence do you have that you can maintain your current rating for the next 6 months?"

CASE 4

During the very first session of his treatment, a man says that he has little confidence that this course of therapy, his fourth, will succeed. He didn't make much headway in the previous three. The overly optimistic therapist does not explore the man's remark, although the latter repeats that he has little confidence that he will ever do better. The conversation soon runs aground and the conversation turns tense. The therapist tries harder; the man becomes increasingly passive.

The therapist would have done better to explore the man's low confidence by asking scaling questions and by acknowledging his disappointment with previously provided help. Doing so probably would have offered an opening to increase the man's confidence and to formulate a goal. The therapist also might have asked how the man had managed, despite negative experiences in the past, to start another course of therapy.

OFFERING HOPE

There are two situations that may lead to feelings of hopelessness: One may feel insecure because one fears that things will change in an undesired way, or one may feel that change is exactly what is needed but be afraid that nothing will ever change. In both situations, there is an overarching sense that one has lost control over the future.

S. D. Miller, Duncan, and Hubble (1997) and Duncan et al. (2004) demonstrated the importance of offering hope and creating a positive expectancy of change during interactions with the client. According to them, it is often the assumptions, the attitude, and the behavior of the professional him- or herself that lead to "hopeless cases." They identify four ways in which professionals may bring about failure, which are described in Chapter 9. They also offer an example of how hope can make a difference:

> In a small hospital a man was dying. The doctors had given up any hope for his recovery. They were unable to ascertain the cause of his illness. Fortunately, a famous diagnostician was coming to visit the hospital. The doctors told the man that they might be able to cure him if this famous doctor could diagnose him. When the doctor arrived at the hospital the man was near death. The doctor looked at him briefly; mumbled, "Moribundus" (Latin for "dying"); and walked over to the next patient. A few years later the man, who did not speak a word of Latin, managed to find the famous doctor. "I would like to thank you for the diagnosis. The doctors had said that if you could diagnose me, I would be able to get better."

The mere willingness to take part in sessions with a professional generates hope and a positive expectancy. These are strengthened if there is a ritual that draws and holds the client's attention, such as taking a break and giving feedback, and if the client's attention is directed toward his or her options rather than limitations. When the professional steers the client's attention to his or her previous successes instead of failures, a positive expectancy is generated. It allows clients to see themselves and their situations in a more positive light.

It is vital that the professional have faith in his or her own procedures and approach and take an interest in their outcome. The procedures and the approach must also be credible in the eyes of the client and must be based on, connected to, or drawn out of a previous experience in which the client experienced success. The focus needs to be on the future. The notion of the client's personal control is emphasized and the client's problems are placed outside the client, which serves to "de-blame" him or her.

In the five-session model, the emphasis is on treating demoralization (Stoffer, 2001). One asks who is demoralized and what the nature of that demoralization is (the professional, too, may be demoralized). According to the model, people seek professional help not because they have a problem but because they no longer know how to deal with a problem. Lessening or lifting demoralization is, to my mind, the same as offering hope, only formulated in negative terms. In line with this, Frank (1974) speaks of "the restoration of morale."

Tips for Offering Hope

Duncan et al. have sometimes referred to people who have already received a lot of help but weren't helped by it as "veterans of impossibility":

> Veterans of impossibility are sometimes overwhelming in their presentations of problems. These problems seem, at times, to fill the session so full that the therapist feels smothered, gasping for air. The much needed oxygen and breath of fresh air for both client and therapist come when the problem is connected to a description that states or implies that the presenting complaint is changeable. (1997, p. 64)

One should take note of signs of hope during the sessions with the client when he or she fantasizes about the future that he or she desires and begins to work toward making that fantasy or dream come true. The professional may invite the client to reflect on earlier periods in his or her life when the client did have hope and ask: "What was that like? What did you do then? What exactly did you hope for then?" These hopeful thoughts can then be carried into the present, allowing the client to regain hope. After all, he or she has done it before: The client is the expert as far as his or her life is concerned. One small difference can be important in helping the client acquire more hope; hope is not about moving mountains but about moving loose rocks one by one. If the client has made one small difference, he or she has taken a step forward and experiences more control. As a homework suggestion, one may ask clients to observe what occurrences give them the hope that they might be able to reach their goals.

CASE 5

During a solution-focused therapy session, a woman says she might be happy if she lost 65 pounds. The therapist asks her: "What difference will it make in your life when you have lost the first the first 1 or 2 pounds?" The woman replies that she might feel slightly better and that she would cautiously begin to believe that losing more weight was possible. The therapist asks her what difference that slightly better feeling and that bit of hope would make in her life. She says that she would go outside more and would also be a bit nicer to her children and her husband, because her mood would be improved. The woman's vision of her desired future is further magnified, which increases the chance that she will take the first step.

Because there are multiple ways of gaining hope, the client can experiment. What works for one person may not be suitable for another. It helps if there is room for humor, because laughter can reduce tension and often puts things into perspective. The client may also come up with something that reminds him or her of times of hope, so that he or she can think about or look at it every now and then.

Hope usually grows slowly. The client might predict his or her behavior for the following day and discover that exceptions to the problem can be found and that more control can be exerted than he or she probably thought. Professionals can augment the client's hope by asking questions about it and by stimulating the client's creativity. The next chapter expands on the importance of hope.

Some solution-focused questions about hope and how hope may increase are:

- "What are your best hopes? What difference would that make?"
- "What has kept your hope alive during this prolonged period of difficulty?"
- "How has your hope influenced your decisions recently?"
- "Suppose you had more hope. How would your life (or your relationship) change?"
- "How would (more) hope help you reach your goal?"

- "What is the smallest difference that would increase your hope?"
- "How would you be able to tell that you had enough hope?"
- "When did you feel hopeful and how did you manage that?"
- "When you think of hope, what does it conjure up?"
- "If you had a painting on your wall that reminded you of hope when you looked at it every morning, what would that painting look like?"
- "What smell, color, song, or sound reminds you of hope?"
- "What rating do you give yourself on a scale of 10 to 0, where 10 = lots of hope and 0 = no hope?"
- "How do you manage to be at that number?"
- "What would 1 point higher on the hope scale look like?"
- "How could you move up 1 point?"
- "Can you tell me about a period in your life when you had a lot of (or more) hope?"
- "If you were to examine your problem, which aspects of the problem would give you more or less hope?"
- "What would someone who did have (more) hope do in your situation?"
- "What occurrence or person can make your hope increase or decrease?"
- "What can you do to make hope visible at a time when you see no hope?"
- "If you wanted your hope to increase by the next session, what would you do or like me to do before we see each other again?"
- "What in our conversation has given you more hope, even if only a little?"
- "What indicates that you are on the right track to solve this problem?"
- "Suppose the positive moments were to last longer. What difference would that make for you?"
- "How has going up 1 point given you hope?"

If the professional has no confidence in his or her own ability to help clients reach their goals and has lost the hope of a favorable outcome, the professional can examine what is needed for him or her to regain hope (see the discussion of scaling motivation and confidence earlier in this chapter). He or she may also halt the sessions and turn them over to a colleague.

The solution-focused model works for the professional, too: It can prevent or cure burnout symptoms because the atmosphere of the sessions is positive and the professional is able to help the client reach his or her goal.

SUMMARY

- The distinction among visitor, complainant, and customer in the cooperative relationship between the professional and the client is essential in determining the questions that the professional asks and the homework suggestions that he or she provides.
- The solution-focused professional knows how to complement and enhance the client's motivation for behavior change. Resistance is not a useful concept and needlessly turns the client into the enemy.
- Ways to advance the conversation include questions about motivation and confidence, flexibility in the professional's position (Leary's Rose), the use of "Yes, and" instead of "Yes, but" by the professional and the client, and solution-focused questions and tips as a means of offering and increasing hope.

CHAPTER 3

The First Session

If you don't have a dream,
how you gonna have a dream come true?
—*South Pacific*

THE OPENING

In the first solution-focused session the professional devotes attention to:

- Giving information about the structure of the session (deciding whether or not to make time for a short break and possibly a conference with colleagues) and the duration of the session. The professional also explains to the client that he or she works in a solution-focused way. I find that transparency about the session model that the professional employs is important. Clients and colleagues often think that the "problem-focused game" is the only game one can play, and pointing out the possibility of playing a new, solution-focused game may help shift the focus from problems to solutions. Alternatively, the client him- or herself is allowed to choose between problem- and solution-focused therapy (Bannink, 2009f).
- Establishing and building rapport (a positive working relationship) by asking the client about, for example, his or her work, relationships, and hobbies; by inquiring what the client is good at or enjoys; and by paying the client compliments about those things. Moreover,

the professional obtains valuable information in doing so. What qualities or resources does the client already possess to help him or her reach the goal? What might be added?

It is, in principle, unnecessary to acquaint oneself with the problem when one is conducting solution-focused interviewing, even if advance information about it is available. Case files need not be read beforehand and diagnoses need not be known in advance. After all, if the referrer refers to a case as "exceedingly difficult and complex," for instance, there is a risk that the professional's positive expectancy and hope could be negatively influenced. Should it become apparent during the sessions that one needs to have certain information about the problem at one's disposal, one can still apprise oneself of it. Appendix A contains two protocols for the first session.

Duration

In my experience, a solution-focused session with one client optimally lasts 45 minutes, and one with two or more clients an hour and a half. That is enough time to make the client's acquaintance, establish rapport, explain the structure of the session, define the goal, ask about exceptions, ask scaling questions, and examine whether the client is a visitor, complainant, or customer. It also allows one to take a short 5-minute break, if desired, after which one may provide feedback with homework suggestions and ask the client to offer some feedback about the session, too. Incidentally, not all solution-focused professionals adhere to this sequence: Some do not take a break and only discuss homework suggestions at the end. Compliments and competence questions have come up enough throughout the session and need not be repeated during the time reserved for feedback (feedback is discussed in detail later in this chapter). If the client so wishes, a new appointment can be made.

EVERY SOLUTION-FOCUSED SESSION IS, IN PRINCIPLE, THE FINAL SESSION

In theory, every session is considered the final session. Solution-focused interviewing does not start from a predetermined, fixed number of sessions, unlike the five-session model or treatments that require that 10 appointments be made at the beginning. At the end of the first session, one asks the solution-focused question, "Is it necessary or would it be useful for you to come back?" If the client wants to come back, the next question is: "When would you like to come back?"

To the extent possible, the solution-focused professional lets the client determine the amount of time between sessions. If the client wants to come back soon, the professional can compliment the client on his or her obvious motivation to reach the goal. Should the client prefer to take more time in between sessions, the professional can compliment the client on his or her apparent willingness to take the time to practice other behavior or to carefully observe certain situations.

In a number of cases—and more often than you might think—no subsequent session will be required, because the client believes he or she can take it from here now that he or she is on the right path and the goal has become clear. In my view, the client often returns because the professional thinks it important or necessary, because he or she does not feel entirely confident yet that the client can get along alone. The solution-focused professional sees him- or herself as a tugboat—or, better yet, a push tug (leading from one step behind)—that helps the stranded client get his or her grounded boat back into the deep. He or she does not need to sail along all the way to see whether the client safely reaches harbor. Experience has shown that once clients have a concrete, positive, and realistic vision of their goals, they can often get along on their own and take the requisite steps to reach their goals. These steps and their sequence may, if so desired, be designed and guided during the sessions. With an average of three to four sessions of 45 minutes each, most solution-focused interactions can be brief and hence cost saving.

COMPUTER MODEL OF THE FIRST SESSION

De Shazer (1988) designed a model of the first session, offering the following questions:

Is There a Complaint?

If there isn't, the client is still a visitor, in which case the professional only pays compliments, goes along with the client's worldview, and makes a new appointment if the client so wishes. If there is, the client is a complainant, perhaps even a customer. In that case, the professional looks for exceptions to the problem (times when the problem is absent or is less of a problem) together with the client. Incidentally, if multiple clients are present, as in relationship therapy or in mediation, one of the two clients may be a customer and the other a complainant, or both may be complainants. Alternatively, one client may be a complainant and the other a visitor. It is vital to the success of the sessions that the professional make this distinction as quickly as possible, because subsequent interventions and any homework suggestions must be attuned to it.

Are There Exceptions?

If there aren't, the professional can help the client construct hypothetical solutions by asking the miracle question, and together the professional and the client can explore the difference between the miracle and the problem. If there are, the professional and the client look for differences between the exceptions and the problem, and they examine the extent to which the client him- or herself has control over the occurrence of the exceptions. Appendix A contains two protocols for the first session.

Are There Exceptions or Is There a Hypothetical Solution?

If so, a goal can be formulated and one can offer the following homework suggestion: Continue with what works, do more of what works, do the easiest thing that might work, predict the seemingly coincidental exceptions and explain the result, or learn more about these seemingly coincidental exceptions. Appendix B is the protocol for goal formulation. If a sound hypothetical solution cannot be found because the goal remains vague, the professional can suggest as a homework assignment that the client observe what he or she would like to keep the way it is, what need not be changed, so that he or she can talk about it the next time. The solution-focused professional can also explore and analyze the complaint together with the client. De Shazer, it should be noted, does not even list the latter option in his computer model anymore.

Walter and Peller (1992) put together a map for developing solutions (see Figure 3.1), which covers the following areas:

- From wish or complaint to goal: And what would you like to change about that?
- Are there exceptions to the problem (yet)?
- If so, can they be repeated? Do more of what works.
- Are there only spontaneous exceptions? Learn more about them.
- Are there no exceptions, but there is a goal? Do a (small) piece of it.

Whenever possible, wishes and complaints are phrased as goals, that is, as something about which something can be done. The questions that are asked lead to three types of homework suggestions. If usable exceptions can be found, the miracle question (the hypothetical solution) is usually unnecessary.

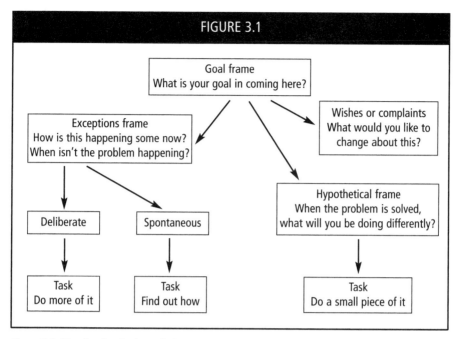

FIGURE 3.1

| | Goal frame
What is your goal in coming here? | |

Exceptions frame
How is this happening some now?
When isn't the problem happening?

Wishes or complaints
What would you like to
change about this?

Hypothetical frame
When the problem is solved,
what will you be doing differently?

Deliberate

Spontaneous

Task
Do more of it

Task
Find out how

Task
Do a small piece of it

Figure 3.1. Map for developing solutions. From Becoming Solution-Focused in Brief Therapy (p. 125), by J. L. Walter and J. E. Peller, 1992, New York: Brunner/Mazel. Copyright 1992 by Brunner/Mazel. Adapted with permission.

FEEDBACK

The feedback at the end of each solution-focused session is not the same as the feedback given during an intervention in a problem-focused session. In the latter case, the professional uses the information he or she has acquired about the nature and the severity of the problem to decide what actions will most benefit the client. The professional undertakes these actions or offers advice that the client is encouraged to follow (as homework). These actions (interventions) are intended to bring about positive changes. The interventions are designed by the professional based on the information he or she has gathered as an expert, and on his or her analysis, and are founded on theoretical grounds. Consequently, it is the professional who brings about change.

In solution-focused sessions, the feedback at the end of the session is not considered more important than the other components of the process. It is the client, not the professional, who brings about change. During the session, clients provide information about themselves and their situations. The feedback organizes and underlines aspects of the information that are useful to

Think about what opening sentence you usually start a session with. You may opt for a problem-focused question: "What is the problem?" or "What's the matter?" You may choose a neutral question: "What brings you here?" You may opt for a question that implies that you will work hard: "What can I do for you?" Or you may choose a solution-focused question about the goal of the session: "What is the purpose of your visit?" or "What needs to be accomplished by the end of this session (or these sessions) so that you can say that coming to see me was useful and meaningful?" or "What do you hope to accomplish by the end of this session (or these sessions) so that you do not have to come back again?" or "How would you be able to tell that you do not need to come back again, because you have reached your goal (to a sufficient degree)?" or "What would you like to see instead of the problem?" Or you may ask the miracle question: "Suppose that while you're asleep tonight a miracle happens. The miracle is that the problem that brought you here has been solved (to a sufficient degree). When you wake up, you are unaware that the miracle has occurred because you were asleep. How would you first notice tomorrow morning that the miracle has happened? What would be different and what would you be doing differently? What else? After you, who would be the first to notice that the miracle has happened? How would that person be able to tell? How would that person react? And what would that be like for you? And how would you, in turn, react to that? And how else would you notice over the course of the day that the miracle has happened? What else would you be doing differently? How would others react to that?" And, if applicable: "How would your relationship change? And what else?" Or you may ask: "What are your best hopes? And what would be different if those hopes were realized?"

Try out all the possibilities and note the differences in your clients' reactions and the differences in the mood of the sessions.

clients in the realization of their goals. Before the feedback section, the solution-focused professional may schedule a short break of about 5 minutes to think about the feedback he or she will give. Clients may also be asked to reflect on the session so that they can say something about it after the break if they so wish, or they may complete the Session Rating Scale (see Chapters 2 and 11 and Appendix E).

The professional and the client may remain in the same room during the break, or one of them can move to a different room for awhile. If the professional wants to formulate feedback together with a colleague or a team of colleagues, he or she may do so away from or in the presence of the client.

It is my experience that the latter constitutes an extraordinarily powerful intervention, because it allows clients to hear firsthand everything they are already doing well (compliments) and what else they could do to get closer to their goals (homework suggestions).

It should be noted that taking a break and giving feedback is not imperative. Some professionals find it useful and pleasant, and so they always do it; others, myself included, do not. The latter experience the format as a sudden change in style: Before the break the professional has a stance of not knowing; after the break he or she is the expert telling the client what to do. It is also possible to offer compliments and homework suggestions in a different, somewhat more informal way during the session itself. It is recommended that you try both formats to find out which best suits you and the circumstances in which you work.

Some solution-focused questions for feedback formulation by the professional are:

- "Is there a well-defined goal? What is it?"
- "Are there exceptions? What are they?"
- "Are the exceptions deliberate or spontaneous?"
- "What type of relationship is there between the professional and the client (i.e., visitor, complainant, or customer)?"

The feedback has a fixed structure and consists of three components:

- Compliments. Compliments are forms of positive reinforcement; they affirm what the client finds important and confirm his or her successes and competency.
- Bridge. Also called "rationale," the bridge connects the compliments to the homework suggestions and tasks. The bridge often begins with "and because . . ."
- Homework suggestions. The third feedback component is the assignment of one or a few tasks to the client. They fall into two categories: observational tasks and behavioral tasks. Chapter 5 provides an in-depth description of these tasks.

If the professional wants to use a break, he or she does well to announce it at the start of the session and to ask clients before the break whether or not they would like a homework suggestion. A client does not always need to be assigned a task; often the session has already produced a change in his or her thinking about the problem. Before the break one may also ask the client whether there is anything else that the professional should know that has not been addressed yet (de Shazer, 1994).

With an observational task, the professional suggests that the client pay attention to a certain aspect of his or her life that is likely to bring him or her closer to the goal. The client may, for instance, take note of the times when the problem is absent or is less of a problem, of what is different then, or of what he or she is doing differently then. The client may also look at times when the goal appears a little closer for awhile and how that happened. If clients wish to, they can write those moments down so that they can talk about them during a subsequent session.

Behavioral tasks are tasks that involve actions that the client thinks can bring him or her closer to the goal. Behavioral tasks, like observational tasks, are based on data the client has provided and should, therefore, be meaningful to him or her. An example of a behavioral task is the suggestion that one continue with a certain behavior if it has helped before.

CASE 6

During a solution-focused session, an inpatient with a mild intellectual disability says his girlfriend has ended their relationship and that his life no longer has meaning. He is deeply unhappy and the team of counselors is concerned: Can he stay in the open ward if he wants to die? The therapist acknowledges his grief and asks about his goal: What would he like instead of all that sadness? The client says that he would like to be cheerful again, in response to which the therapist asks what that would look like, what he would do then. The client says he would sing a lot and be happy. The therapist asks him what music he puts on to sing along to and whether he would like to play the music he likes for her. One thing leads to another: The client starts to sing along softly, and then louder. He relaxes and a smile appears on his face. The therapist compliments the client on his beautiful music and his singing, and on knowing that this is what helps him feel better. It is agreed (with the team of counselors) that if he feels down in the coming days, he will play the music again and sing along. This is an example of a behavioral task: Go on with or do more of what works.

The feedback for visitors, complainants, and customers differs. In each case, the solution-focused professional first pays compliments. The compliments and positive character interpretations establish a good relationship with the client (rapport) and strengthen the client's sense of competence and hope for change. When one is dealing with two or more clients, another positive effect of compliments is that each client gets to hear the compliments that are directed at the other, which may make him or her see the other in a more positive light.

It is important that no homework suggestions be given to visitors. Complainants only receive suggestions for observational tasks. To customers one may give suggestions for both observational and behavioral tasks. If in doubt about whether a client is a customer yet, the professional does best to choose interventions that suit the position of complainant. If in doubt as to whether a client is a complainant, he or she does best to opt for interventions that suit the position of the visitor. If there are two or more clients, the professional may start with interventions that fit the position of the client who is least prepared to change; he or she usually needs the most attention. One can also address all levels of motivation, as in this example.

CASE 7

Twenty people attend an in-company training session. The majority are customers: They are interested in learning something new and finding out how they can apply what they learn in practice. Some are complainants: They experience problems at work as a result of the high pressure to meet production standards, but they feel that that is something for management to solve; they do not (yet) see themselves as part of the problem or the solution. There are also a few visitors: They have been sent by management, they do not have a problem, and nothing bothers them. At the end of the first day of training, the solution-focused trainer offers the following homework suggestions: "Between now and the next day of training, I would like to ask those of you who already want to do something to read the literature and to practice part of what was discussed today (behavioral task). Alternatively, you could also examine what you think is going well in your job and would like to keep the way it is, so that you can tell me about it the next time (observational task). And if you don't want to do anything in between training days, that's fine, too."

Experience has shown that when one begins to work with a group in which there are people who want to change their own behavior (customers), members of the group who are complainants and visitors often become motivated to do something at a later stage; they do not want to be left behind. And if visitors and complainants do not become customers, they probably have good reasons not to, which they can discuss when they are invited to do so.

I see motivation as a continuum. All client positions are fine and do not necessarily need to change. This makes the collaboration with clients easier and more positive.

During the next conversation you have that lasts over 5 minutes, pay the other person at least three compliments and pay attention to how the mood of the conversation changes. Direct compliments can be about something the other person said, made, or did, or about his or her appearance. Indirect compliments use solution-focused competence questions to elicit self-compliments from the client: "How did you succeed in . . . ? How did you manage that? How did you come up with that fine idea?" Compliments may also take the form of positive character interpretations: "You must be very resolute to . . . Please tell me more" or "You must have a great sense of responsibility to . . ." or "So, if necessary, you are someone who is willing to fight for . . ." or "You must love your children very much to . . . Please tell me more about that."

Many clients indicate that they really value feedback. Sometimes they also express their appreciation of the fact that the professional takes time during the break to think about what has been said (and sometimes confer with a colleague or team) and they note that they like to be able to give feedback about the sessions themselves. I know of no clients who have thought it strange that a break was scheduled. Nonetheless, it is useful to set forth the structure of the session at the very beginning. The professional says: "After a half hour, I would like to take a 5-minute break to think about the session. I would like to invite you to do the same, because I think it's important that I hear your thoughts about the session. I will then leave the room for awhile. You can stay right where you are. After 5 minutes, I'll come back to hear your ideas and to tell you what my ideas are and what you might be able to do to reach your goal."

In exceptional cases, the client may object to the fact that all the feedback is positive. It may not seem "real" to him or her. Sometimes the client deems it necessary to delve deep into the problems to find a solution or to understand *why* the problem exists. In such cases, it can be useful to precede the positive feedback with "You will probably consider this too positive, but . . . "

To an exceedingly problem-focused client one can also explain that the solution-focused professional mainly focuses on what works. If that proves insufficient, one may devote more time to the problems. One might ask clients how they think talking about the problems will help them reach their goals. The professional can also work with the narrative therapy model or refer the client to a colleague who works in the problem-focused vein. Transparency of the professional's method is important to clients and colleagues alike. Appendix D is the protocol for formulating feedback.

FOUR BASIC SOLUTION-FOCUSED QUESTIONS

Chapter 10 of this book contains 1,001 solution-focused questions. In the spirit of keeping things simple, here are four basic solution-focused questions:

1. "What are your best hopes?"
2. "What difference would that make?"
3. "What is already working in the right direction?"
4. "What would be the next sign of progress? What would the next step be?"

Hope Theory

The first question asks what the client hopes for. As stated earlier, hope and expectancy play a role in the therapy's success. The question is not whether the client hopes for something, but what his or her best hopes are. And what else does he or she hope for? And what else?

The professional continues to ask "what else" questions until the client indicates that it's been enough. The question about hope offers the professional a clear image of the "roads to Rome."

Since the 1950s, doctors and psychologists have pointed to the role of hope in people's health and well-being. In his address to the American Psychiatric Association, Menninger (1959) said that hope was an untapped source of power and healing. Menninger believed that hope is an indispensable factor in psychiatric treatments and psychiatric training.

The interest in hope in psychotherapy was initially aimed at reducing despair rather than increasing hopeful thoughts. Given the link between despair and suicide, A. T. Beck, Weissman, Lester, and Trexles focused on combating hopelessness. Their definition of hopelessness was: "a system of cognitive schemas whose common denomination is negative expectations about the future" (A. T. Beck et al., 1974, p. 864).

Reducing hopelessness is not the same as increasing hope, however. Compare offering hope to its negative formulation: lifting demoralization (Stoffer, 2001). Frank (1974) spoke of "the restoration of morale." Bakker and Bannink (2008) contended that it is crucial in crisis interventions to offer hope, for example, by asking the client what his or her best hopes are and what difference that would make, which brings the client's preferred future into view.

During the 1990s, Snyder conducted research on hope. In his hope theory, he proposed a cognitive model of hope with a focus on goal attainment. Motivation and planning, which are required to reach a goal, are also taken into consideration. Snyder et al. defined hope as "a positive emotional state that is based on an interactively derived sense of successful (a) agency and (b) pathways (planning to meet goals)" (1991, p. 287).

Hope can be viewed as a journey. Three things are needed: a destination (goals), a map (pathways), and a means of transportation (agency). The first component of hope is formulating goals. Setting goals with an average degree of difficulty generates the most hope. When goals are seen as too difficult or too easy, people no longer try their best to reach them. Snyder made a distinction between hopeful people (high-hope people) and non-hopeful people (low-hope people). Compared with the non-hopeful people, whose goals are often vague and ambiguous, hopeful people usually formulate their goals more clearly.

The second component of hope is pathway thinking, which pertains to devising ways to reach one's goal, to drawing up a "mental road map" of solutions. Athletes' performances are shown to improve, for instance, when they visualize the steps that are needed in order for them to do well. Here, too, there turns out to be a distinction between hopeful and non-hopeful people. The former have more skills to draw a detailed road map. They are also better at coming up with alternative solutions, so that they may still reach their goals if the original route is blocked. In addition, they are better able to anticipate difficulties that may present themselves, which gives them more resilience. Lastly, they find it easier to break a large goal up into a number of smaller subgoals.

The final component of hope is agency thinking. Formulating goals and devising routes does not produce the desired result if one is insufficiently motivated. This component comprises thoughts about one's ability to set oneself in motion and advance in the direction of the goal, impediments notwithstanding. Snyder's research indicated that hopeful people show a greater predilection for positive self-expressions, for example, "I will succeed" or "Yes, we can," than non-hopeful people, Hope, therefore, is not just something you have but is mainly something you do.

These three components of hope are so intricately linked that drawing out just one of the three exerts a positive influence on the whole process of hopeful thinking.

What Difference Would That Make?

The second question asks about difference. Bateson (1979) touched on the difference that makes a difference—not in the eyes of the professional, but in the eyes of the client. The question is: What difference would it make if what the client hopes for were to come true? And what other difference would it make? And what else? And what difference would it make for important people in the client's life? And what difference would it make to the client's relationships with these people?

Questions about difference bring not the roads to Rome into view but rather Rome itself.

What Is Already Working In the Right Direction?

The third question asks what is already working in the right direction. The road map, as described in hope theory, is composed of the road already traveled and the road yet to be traveled. Research shows that it is useful to regularly look back at the road already traveled, not merely ahead to the road one still has to travel. Questions such as "What is already working in the right direction? How did you manage that? What else is working in the right direction? And what else?" elicit many exceptions, positive emotions, and motivation to take the next steps.

It has been my impression that if a client first answers these questions and is then asked a scaling question, he or she will give a higher rating on the scale. This may have to do with cognitive dissonance. If one gives a low rating, one cannot go on to name much that is working in the right direction. Giving a higher rating on the scale leads to even more hope and confidence that the rest of the road can also be covered, and the motivation to do so. This is different from what most solution-focused literature proposes, that is, first asking the client a scaling question and then asking what the rating represents, which may limit his or her answers.

What Would Be the Next Sign of Progress?

The fourth question asks about subsequent signs of progress. Walter and Peller (2000) described how they keep an eye out for indications or signs of progress in their sessions with clients. For example, the professional could ask: "What might be a few indications that you are more relaxed? What would be a sign that you are doing better? What other signs might there be that things are going the way you'd like? And what else might be a sign?" These questions leave aside who is going to make sure that things get better. Therefore, it may be useful to add, "What would be your next (small) step?"

which makes clear that it is up to the client him- or herself to bring about change.

OTHER POINTS OF CONSIDERATION
FOR THE FIRST SESSION

Distinction Between Goal and Means

It is important to distinguish between the goal and the means. The goal is the situation where the client wants to end up; the means are the ways of achieving it. Rome is the goal; the roads to Rome are the means. "What are your best hopes?" often reflects the roads to Rome, and the subsequent question, "What difference would that make?" brings Rome itself—the client's preferred future—into view. The client often names means when asked for his or her goal. If the professional accepts a means as the goal, the goal is usually ill defined and it becomes unclear where the sessions need to lead in order for them to be considered successful. I repeat the view I put forward in Chapter 1 that it is better to talk about *a* goal (singular) than goals (plural), which is prevalent in solution-focused literature. Experience has shown that if one asks a client for goals (plural), he or she will mostly list means. "To become more assertive," "to process the past," "to gain insight," and "to find a job" are all examples of means. The goal emerges when the professional asks: "Suppose that some time from now you are as assertive as you would like to be. What difference would that make in your life? What is different now and what are you doing differently?" The same goes for the other cited means of reaching a goal in the future. It is recommended that one work with positively formulated goals: so-called stretch goals. This term is derived from Snyder's hope theory (2002). In addition to solving the problem, the client can "stretch beyond" to a richer and happier life and experience greater well-being. In other words, solution-focused brief therapy goes beyond reducing symptoms, unlike most traditional therapies.

Some solution-focused questions about goal formulation are:

- "What is the purpose of your visit?"
- "What would you like to see instead of the problem?"
- "What are your best hopes? What difference would that make? What would you need to have accomplished by the end of this session (or these sessions) in order to be able to say that it was a success or that it has been meaningful and useful?"
- "Suppose a miracle happens tonight; for example, the problem that brings you here has been solved (to a sufficient degree), but you

are unaware of it because you are asleep. What will be the first thing you notice tomorrow morning that tells you that the miracle has taken place? What else?"

- "How will you be able to tell that you do not need to come back to see me anymore?"
- "What will be different (in your relationship) when the problem has been solved?"
- "What would you like to be different as a result of these sessions?"
- "When can we stop seeing each other?"
- "What would you like to accomplish here regarding . . . (e.g., your relationship, your children, your company)?"

By way of addition and illustration, the professional can use a whiteboard, a flip chart, or a piece of paper to visualize the goal and the means. This technique is described in Chapter 7.

If more than one person is present during the sessions—for example, in relationship or family therapy, group therapy, team coaching, or mediation—it is important that a collective goal be formulated. The goal is often framed as a situation in which the (cooperative) relationship has been mended. It may concern a personal relationship between partners, parents, or neighbors, or a professional relationship between employer and employee, among colleagues, or within teams. The shared goal may also be that a cooperative relationship be terminated in as positive a way as possible.

Again, there are many means of reaching the collective goal. To find out what the collective goal is, the professional can ask the clients what will be different between them when the desired situation has been attained. Clients often respond that their relationship will be (sufficiently) sound again or can be brought to an end. Clients provide their own interpretation of goals and means: Together they determine what Rome looks like and how they can reach it. In principle, they are assumed to be competent and capable of formulating their collective goal.

In group therapy, where each participant has his or her own individual goal, the others serve as "supporters" (Furman & Ahola, 2007).

CASE 8

At a session regarding problems with a 14-year-old boy, the father and mother (who are divorced), the mother's boyfriend, and the boy's guardian are present. There are divergent views about what needs to happen and what the right approach is for the boy. Everyone tries to convince the others of the rightness of his or her vision, which leads to ever-growing irritation. In such a case, it may be helpful to carry the conversation into the (distant) future. The solution-focused therapist asks all those present how they see the future: What kind of person would they like the boy to be when he is grown up and leaves home? There turn out to be marked similarities of vision: He must be independent and sociable and have a diploma and a network of friends, and so forth. All can find themselves in this collective goal. They then look at what is required to reach this collective goal. Everyone indicates where he or she is on a scale of 10 to 0, where 10 means that the collective goal has been reached in full, and 0 that no part of the goal has been accomplished; what a higher rating would look like; and how he or she can reach a higher rating. Questions from the interactional matrix are asked; for example, the mother is asked: "What do you think the guardian would say is needed to go up 1 point?" Unfortunately, the son is not present during the session. Otherwise, he could have joined in the conversation and talked about his own ideas, and he would have been able to hear the others' goal for him. He probably would have been surprised at so much positivity and unanimity.

Benefits of the Miracle Question

Some professionals ask the miracle question at virtually every first session, whereas others have reservations about doing so. Reasons for the frequent use of the miracle question are:

- It is a useful way to find out with the client where he or she wants to end up and what that will look like in concrete terms. To this end, one may of course ask other questions about goal formulation, too.
- In describing the miracle, the client may react nonverbally as if the miracle is already taking place. This brings the preferred future closer and makes the step to making the miracle actually happen smaller.
- The miracle question affords a good starting point when one is inquiring about exceptions, because one can ask: "When has a small part of the miracle already manifested itself?" The professional can also inquire what will be different in the client's life after the miracle.
- Asking the miracle question and looking for times when a small part of the miracle has already occurred for a short period of time facilitate conversations about progress instead of stagnation and retrogression.

"I Don't Believe in Miracles"

Most clients react to the miracle question with surprise. With children, one can also use the image of a magic wand instead of a miracle and inquire what they would ask for if they had a magic wand and were granted three wishes. If the client says he or she does not believe in miracles, the professional can still attempt to obtain a description of the desired outcome by asking one of the following questions:

- "Suppose that no miracle occurs, but when you wake up tomorrow morning, the problems you've described have indeed disappeared. What would be different in your life?"
- "There is no need to believe in miracles, but suppose you did believe in them. What would the miracle look like?"
- "Suppose a miracle were to occur nonetheless. What would be different in your life?"
- "Naturally, miracles don't happen. But may I conduct a thought experiment with you? Imagine that the problems that bring you here have disappeared by tomorrow. What would tomorrow look like?"
- "I understand that you have both feet firmly on the ground. What, then, would your ideal day look like?"

It may help to introduce the miracle question by saying something like, "I am going to ask you a slightly odd question. Suppose a miracle happened in the middle of the night." One may also ask the client whether he or she has a good imagination; a client who does will probably enjoy the miracle question.

Creating a "Yes Set"

Creating a "yes set" is a hypnotic technique that good salespeople often use, often without realizing it. One runs things by the client in a manner that leads him or her always to answer with a yes. After awhile he or she is inclined to say yes to somewhat less self-evident suggestions. The idea is to create a positive context. Yes sets are mainly created in solution-focused interviewing before the miracle question to maximize the chance that the client will react positively to the miracle question.

For instance, the miracle can be introduced as follows: "After this, maybe you will go home or somewhere else (yes), at the end of the day you will have a bite to eat (yes), and tonight you will go do something you had planned or maybe you will just stay home (yes). At the end of the night you go to bed (yes), and at some point you fall asleep (yes) and while you're asleep, the house is completely quiet (yes), and in the middle of the night a miracle happens (yes) . . ." This hypnotic parlance ensures that the client is at his or her most attentive and invites cooperation.

A Balanced Session

When more than one client is present, as in relationship, family, or group therapy, it is important that an equilibrium be maintained during the session. All clients need to receive approximately the same amount of attention, acknowledgment, and compliments. If the professional speaks with one client for a certain length of time, the others need to know that their turns are coming. For example, the professional might say: "I would like to ask you some more questions so that your goal is completely clear to me. In a minute, I will ask the others the same question, because I think their opinions are equally important."

The balance of power between clients deserves attention as well. The professional does well to realize that power imbalances occur. In fact, there is generally an asymmetry in relationships because there is usually a difference in the levels of suffering. This needn't be an obstacle, however. A perceived imbalance of power can be addressed and the professional can ask the clients whether it constitutes a problem and if so, how. One may then proceed to look at how the sessions can help the clients reach their shared goal.

Talking About the Problem

Some clients like to have the opportunity to talk about the problem, not least because they think that that is the intent of the sessions or the therapy (the aforementioned problem-focused game). The professional may briefly let them talk but does not ask for details so that there is no positive reinforcement of problem talk. With the question "How is that a problem for you?" one can often begin to talk about the problem in a different way. Providing information about the solution-focused method is important, too. It makes clear that another therapy game is being played: a game about possibilities, not impossibilities. It is important to validate the client's point of view: "You must have a good reason to . . . Please tell me more" In this way, the professional shows that he or she respects the client's opinions and ideas. At the beginning of the session, the professional can also give the client one opportunity "to say what really needs to be said," before resuming the session in a solution-focused way. This has also become a proven method in solution-focused mediations (Bannink, 2008d,e,f,h,g).

Hypotheses Are Unnecessary

In many types of therapy it is common for the therapist to develop hypotheses about the source of the complaint or problem or the reason for its perpetuation. In psychoanalytic forms of therapy it is even considered an essential part of the therapy. The problem-focused cognitive behavioral therapist develops analyses and hypotheses, too. In formulating these hypotheses, the therapist usually decides where he or she thinks the client should end up. In other words, the therapist determines the treatment goal and the means of reaching that goal, thus limiting the client's options. If a client suffers from a panic disorder, the psychoanalytic therapist will look for its cause in the client's past and generate hypotheses about the roots of the panic disorder—for example, it probably goes back to his relationship with his disapproving mother, the therapist thinks, and so the client is expected to tackle his fear of rejection by women.

Sometimes problem-focused therapists formulate an explanatory hypothesis, the idea being that the hypothesis provides points of departure toward an attainable and hopeful treatment goal. In his model for brief psychotherapy, Rijnders (2004) considered the core of the treatment to be the improvement of overview and perspective, which enables the functional reutilization of one's own solution skills. To that end, an explanatory hypothesis is developed that highlights the client's view of the relationship among complaint, circumstances, and personality traits.

Not only professionals turn out to be fond of hypotheses and puzzles; clients frequently occupy themselves with hypotheses related to their complaints or problems, too. They often have the notion that if they only knew how everything fit together, the complaint or problem would disappear of its own accord. Unfortunately, this is by no means always the case. Therefore, if a client voices a hypothesis, the solution-focused professional will listen respectfully but will not ask questions about it.

In stark contrast to the alleged importance of hypotheses as therapy aids stands the following assertion by de Shazer: "If you feel a hypothesis coming on, take two aspirin, go to bed, and hope it's gone tomorrow" (personal communication, 1998). What he meant is that not only is formulating hypotheses unnecessary when one is searching with the client for his or her goal and the means to reach it, but it may even have the opposite effect, because possible solutions outside one's field of vision go unnoticed if the professional indicates in which direction the client should look.

Using Metaphors

Minutes into the description of their problems, clients often use a metaphor. The client's use of figures of speech can be helpful to the professional during goal formulation and when he or she is asking scaling questions. Clients might say: "I'm not comfortable in my own skin," "I am at the end of my rope," "We want to pick up the thread," or "I want to be my old self again." The professional can then ask for a detailed description of the preferred future; she can ask, for example, what the client's life will look like when he is "his old self" again, what he would be doing differently from what he is doing now, and who would notice the difference. Then she might ask a scaling question: "Suppose a 10 means you are completely your old self again, and a 0 signifies the moment when you realized you were no longer your old self. Where are you now?" The customary follow-up questions to the scaling question follow. The "clean language" technique (Tompkins & Lawley, 2003) can be applied to find out how clients use metaphors and to examine how they can change them in order to gain a different view of the world.

Open Questions

Instead of closed questions, ask as many open questions (*how*, *what*, and *when* questions, but not *why* questions) as possible. An example of an open question is: "What is the purpose of your visit?" A closed question is: "Do you have a purpose?" Another example of an open question is: "When are things already going better?" Another closed question is: "Have there been times when things are going better?" Open questions are more congruent with the professional's stance of not knowing and put the client in the role of expert. Open questions ensure that control and responsibility lie with the client, not with the professional. It is likely that a client will respond with a mere yes or no if he or she is asked a closed question. This will certainly be the case with a visitor or a complainant, as he or she will not feel encouraged to reflect. It is always the professional's turn then, and he or she will have to keep coming up with new questions, which often causes the session to proceed awkwardly. Open questions invite an active attitude, reflection, and more elaborate responses on the client's part. It should be clear by now that the way in which solution-focused questions are asked often determines the answer.

Normalizing and Neutralizing

It is advisable, whenever possible, to normalize and neutralize both the problem itself and the ways in which the client and his or her environment respond to it, for example: "Of course you were angry when you heard that" or "It is understandable that you should have thought so." Neutral language is essential; accusations, threats, hurtful speech, and other words with negative emotional connotations must be avoided as much as possible. Normalization puts the client at ease, changes the moral judgment of and by the other person, and encourages greater understanding from and of the other.

It is also important to always keep in mind that the client him- or herself *is* not the problem, but that the client is a person who *has* a problem. Labels like "depressed" and "borderline" are not used in solution-focused interviewing. After all, the client is much more than his or her problem or diagnosis! Instead of saying, "Henry is depressed," one might say: "He is Henry and he suffers from depressive episodes." O'Hanlon and Rowan have also emphasized the importance of distinguishing between person and illness and of examining the effects of the illness on the person: "Ask not what disease the person has, but rather what person the disease has" (2003, p. 49).

Ignoring Problem Talk and Paying Compliments

The professional ignores talk about problems as much as possible (in the language of learning theory, administering punishment of problem talk). Talking about the goal and the solutions, on the other hand, is at all times encouraged (in the language of learning theory, offering positive reinforcement of solution talk). Sometimes the client proffers subtle invitations to talk in a problem-focused way. On a nonverbal level, one should pay as little attention as possible to problem-focused expressions by not explicitly heeding them, by not looking at the client at those moments, and by not nodding. Positive reinforcement occurs when the professional pays particular attention to desired behavior and talk about the desired outcome, gives compliments and positive character interpretations, and asks competence questions. Positive reinforcement also means that the client sees the professional add more notes to the case history when the sessions deal with things the client wants and sees him or her taking fewer notes when they deal with things he or she does not want. De Groot (2004) also underlined the import and potential of positive reinforcement. Bringing variation to positive reinforcement is critical as well; it is recommended that professionals bring variety to the compliments they pay their clients.

Verbiest (2004) conducted research on the language of compliments. She distinguished two types of compliments: the solidarity compliment and the encouragement compliment. By praising something that the other considers praiseworthy, the compliment giver can indicate how connected the speaker and the listener are, how much they share the same values. The solidarity compliment often occurs between social equals, especially between women on the subject of appearance. The encouragement compliment is less straightforward in approach and execution and more diffuse because of its varying effect on the recipient. This type of compliment mainly occurs between people of unequal status, such as parents and children, employers

EXERCISE 16

This is a listening exercise that you can do with a team of colleagues or in family or group therapy.

One person tells the others about a recent success, something he or she is proud of or happy about. The others are asked to respond by giving a number of compliments. They can take the form of direct compliments, competence questions, or positive character interpretations. The storyteller him- or herself is then asked what compliments pleased him or her the most.

Then the same person or a different group member is asked to tell the others about something vexing that recently happened to him or her. The others are again asked to respond with a number of compliments. And the storyteller is again asked what compliments spoke to him or her the most.

This exercise allows you to ascertain how much harder it often is to give complainants compliments. (However, a person who talks about an unpleasant occurrence is not always, in a complainant relationship.)

and employees, and professionals and clients. This type is mostly given from "high to low," because the reverse (i.e., from "low to high") is often perceived as flattery. These compliments are not about externals but are usually about achievements, work, and the like. Verbiest (2004) contended that in paying such a compliment, the giver in a sense "guides" the receiver. For the receiver, the compliment may constitute an inducement to display a desired behavior. Praising a toddler for quickly clearing his or her plate, for example, may very well ensure that the meal goes just as smoothly tomorrow. Men handle compliments differently than women do. The effect a compliment has, for men, on the power relations between the interlocutors is important. He who gives the compliment is in a position of judging or evaluating the other. Thus, compliments result in a (temporary) inequality of status.

Arts, Hoogduin, Keijsers, Severeijnen, and Schaap (1994) found not only that the systematic use of compliments in psychotherapy guarantees a positive cooperative relationship between the professional and the client, but that the psychotherapy outcome improves by no less than 30% compared with psychotherapy in which no compliments are paid.

Little Details, the Beginning, Then Always a Step Further
Asking about minor details is instrumental in amplifying desired behavior, for example, "How exactly did you do that?" or "That sounds like a big miracle. What would be the first little thing that would indicate to you that things

were beginning to get better? What would be the easiest step you could take?" Client responses can always be taken one step further: "What else? And what else?" The professional can also inquire about *signs* that would make a difference: "What would be a (small) sign that you are on the right track? What would be the smallest sign that tells you that you are on the right track?" (Walter & Peller, 2000, p. 93).

Paraphrasing

It is useful to paraphrase the client's statements in order to turn impossibilities into possibilities. Verb tenses can play a role in this respect: Talk about problems in the past tense, about possibilities in the future or present tense, avoiding the use of the conditional tense.

- "I can never ask a girl out" becomes "So far you have not managed to ask a girl out."
- "I can't lose weight" becomes "You haven't managed to lose weight yet."
- "If I get out of my depression, I can resume my hobby" becomes "When you come out of your depression, you will be able to resume your hobby."
- "It would be great if I would find a job" becomes "It'll be great when you find a job."
- "I'm depressed" becomes "Depression has held you in its grip for some time now."

Tentative Language and the Use of Key Words

Tentative language and hypothetical questions should be used as often as possible: "Suppose the other person were to change (a little) in the manner that you want. What would you do differently?"

The professional also repeats the client's key words and adapts his or her language as much as possible to the client. Needless to say, this especially relevant if the professional works with clients with a developmental disability (Roeden & Bannink, 2007a and 2007b; Westra & Bannink, 2006a and 2006b) or with children.

Summarizing

Summarize what the client has said. Summaries promote understanding of the client's frame of reference and thus contribute to a strong cooperative relationship with the client. They also check the professional's tendency to

Suggest the following to your client: "Suppose you were to write a story about your life and you called it Chapter 2. You can leave out your current problem. What would be different from the current Chapter 1, that is, the story of your life including the problem? What people would you omit and what people would you add? What ideas from Chapter 2 could you use between now and the next time we see each other to make the problem less of a problem?"

make evaluations while listening and help keep his or her attention on the session.

Clients Have to Work Harder Than the Professional

If the professional works harder than the client, he or she is doing something wrong and had better lean back and ask more open questions. It is also possible that the professional wants to reach the goal more than the client does or that the client's goal isn't clear yet. Or the client may be a complainant, whereas the professional assumes he or she is a customer, or the professional may be pursuing a goal of his or her own. In that case, the professional should go back to square one and start anew, using the protocol for the first session. It should not be the case that the professional is too tired at the end of the day to do anything fun while the client is fine to do so! It is best if both still have some energy at the end of the session.

Expressing Emotions

If clients are fearful, angry, or disappointed, one does well to keep in mind that these emotions may indicate a desire to be taken care of, respected, appreciated, and loved. It helps to be conscious of the fact that there are two sides to emotions—not just the one side that is shown.

It is the professional's task to treasure and emphasize (with a compliment or positive character interpretation) signs that point to thoughtfulness and consideration on the client's part—and thus to cultivate hope, for instance by illuminating the positive side of the problem. The professional may provide a favorable new label; for example, anger can be designated a sign of concern or sensitivity. He or she may also ask: "What do you know that indicates to you that things could get better again?" or "What do you know about this relationship that indicates to you that you can get along better than you do now?" Clients often respond by describing moments when things were going better. One may then proceed to ask about earlier successes, how they came about, and what is needed to repeat them.

In addition to validating and normalizing clients' emotions ("Of course you're angry, that's understandable"), the professional may compliment clients on coming to the session. After all, it shows that they have not given up—fear, anger, or disappointment notwithstanding.

In some problem-focused models of interviewing, talking about the problem and expressing emotions is considered an essential strategy (as in the psychoanalytic notion of catharsis, which means "cleansing," or "purification"). In many psychotherapeutic settings one can still find a box of Kleenex on the table—an indirect suggestion that expressing emotions (crying) benefits the therapy outcome.

Frijda (1986) argued that emotions constitute changes in a person's willingness to act. Expressing emotions alone does not mean that the purpose of the emotion has been reached. The goal of expressing grief (crying) is to ask for help and care. Solution-focused interviewing focuses on the goal of the emotion, not on the expression of the emotion itself. Expressing emotions is not viewed as an important means of solving the problem, nor is crying or expressing anger encouraged. The solution-focused professional does not keep a box of Kleenex on the table. He or she may ask, however, how expressing emotions can help clients reach their goals. Nonetheless, it is important for the professional to acknowledge the (emotional) impact the problem has on the client.

At the beginning of the sessions, for example, in mediation, it may be useful to invite the client, once, to briefly "say what absolutely needs to be said" in order to reduce the risk that emotions keep "feeding back."

Psychotherapy mainly devotes attention to negative emotions. After all, there are more negative than positive emotions. Think, for instance, of the four basic emotions: anger, fear, sadness, and happiness—only one is positive; the other three are negative. In the psychological literature of the last 30 years of the 20th century, 46,000 articles about depression were published, but only 400 about happiness (Myers, 2000). The broaden-and-build theory introduced by Fredrickson (2003) focuses on positive emotions.

Negative emotions have immediate survival value; think, for instance, of fear triggering a flight-or-fight response. Positive emotions do not have immediate survival value, but they lead to creativity and the undertaking of new behaviors, which builds skills. In addition, research has shown that positive emotions have an *undoing effect* on negative emotions; negative emotions wane or disappear when the emphasis is placed on positive emotions.

This is consistent with solution-focused interviewing and its focus on solution talk about the client's preferred future, exceptions, and competencies. Paying indirect compliments also fosters positive emotions in the client.

Offering Acknowledgment

Solution-focused interviewing is impossible if the usually negative impact a problem has on the client goes unacknowledged. The client is often in great distress because of the problem or complaint and generally wants to make that known during the session. The professional respectfully listens to the client's story and shifts to a solution-focused conversation as quickly as possible.

It is a misconception that there can only be sufficient acknowledgment if the problem or complaint is wholly dissected and analyzed or if the client is afforded every opportunity to expatiate on his or her view of the problem. Utterances by the professional such as "I understand that this is an unpleasant situation for you (both)" and "I can imagine how annoying it must be for you to realize that you are not getting out of this deadlock (together)" offer that acknowledgment just as well and take up considerably less time than having a client describe the entire problem. Furthermore, the mood of the session can remain positive if the focus remains on the preferred future. It can be useful in this respect to explain to the client right away that the sessions will be solution focused and what the sessions will look like. The client may be under the impression that he or she is (yet again) expected to talk about the problem with the new professional. After all, most professionals still work in the problem-focused vein. The client may therefore think that he or she is doing what a client is supposed to do by talking about the problem as much as possible.

The professional may also give the client the option by asking: "Would you like to conduct these sessions in a solution-focused or a problem-focused way?" In this context, Appelo (2009) has spoken about a focus on enhancement of strengths and resources instead of symptom reduction. It has been my experience that clients who are customers, who are motivated to do something about their problem themselves, often choose solution-focused sessions, the strength-focused approach. Clients who are complainants may choose problem-focused sessions, the complaint-focused approach (Bannink, 2009f). I believe they make that choice because it does not require them to take action yet. After all, preceding any behavioral change, the problem must first be analyzed and explored or insight must be gained into the source of the problem or the reason for its perpetuation.

Some solution-focused questions that you can use to offer acknowledgment are:

- "How do you cope?"
- "How do you ensure that the situation isn't worse than it is? How do you do that?"
- "I can tell that this is a problem for you and I understand that this is an unpleasant situation for you. What would you like to be different?"
- "How is this a problem for you (both)?"
- "Unfortunately, it seems you agree that things will not go back to the way they were. Is that correct?"
- "I see what's important to you. What solutions would fulfill your wishes?"
- "Suppose you were given one opportunity to say what absolutely needs to be said before we proceed. What would you say?"

SUMMARY

- In the first session, attention is paid to getting to know each other, formulating goals, looking for exceptions, and asking scaling questions. Professionals can establish rapport by asking competence questions and paying compliments. At the end of the session, feedback tailored to the client's position as a visitor, complainant, or customer is given.
- Each solution-focused session is, in principle, the final session, unless the client finds it necessary or thinks that it would be useful to come back. In that case, the client determines when he or she wants to come back.
- De Shazer's computer model and the protocol for the first session provide a clear structure for solution-focused interviewing.
- There are four basic solution-focused questions that one can use to conduct the first (and each subsequent) session.
- The list of additional points of consideration may help the professional conduct the first session in a pleasant and solution-focused way.

CHAPTER 4

The Subsequent Session

Insanity is doing the same thing over and over again
and expecting different results.
—Albert Einstein

THE GOAL OF THE SUBSEQUENT SESSION

According to de Shazer (1994), the goal of the second and each subsequent session is:

- To ask questions about the time between the sessions in such a way that one can definitely discern some progress: If one looks carefully and creatively, one can (virtually) always find improvements
- To see whether the client feels that what the professional and the client did in the previous session has been useful and has given him or her the sense that things are going better
- To help the client find out what he or she is doing or what has happened that has led to improvements so that he or she will know what to do more of or more often
- To help the client work out whether the improvements have caused things to go well enough that further sessions are not necessary
- To ensure that the professional and the client will not do more of what doesn't work, if the client does not see any improvement, and to find a new approach.

THE OPENING QUESTION OF EVERY SUBSEQUENT SESSION

The opening question that the solution-focused professional asks the client in each subsequent session is: "What is better?" The question implicitly suggests that something *is* going better and that one only needs to pay attention to *what* is going better. Therefore, the question is fundamentally different from "What went better? How are you?" or "How have things been since our last session?" With this opening question about the client's progress, the professional determines the answer he or she receives.

The client usually reacts to the question with surprise, because he or she does not expect it. Sometimes clients initially respond with "Nothing," because that is, in fact, what they experience from their point of view; they have not given any thought to anything better. In that case, the professional can ask very thorough questions about the recent past and look for times when the problem was absent or was less of a problem. Working on the assumption that one can always find exceptions if one only looks for them, the professional asks questions not about *whether* there are exceptions but about *when* there are or have been exceptions.

It has been my experience that if the professional opens every session with this question, the client begins to anticipate it and starts to reflect on the answer prior to the session.

In each subsequent session one may also ask the four basic solution-focused questions presented in Chapter 3. They may pertain to each individual session (e.g., "What are your best hopes for this session?") or to the entire therapy, or even to the client's entire life.

De Jong and Berg (1997) developed the acronym *EARS* to distinguish the activities in subsequent solution-focused sessions. *E* stands for *eliciting* (drawing out stories about progress and exceptions). *A* stands for *amplifying*. First, the client is asked to describe in detail the differences between the moment when the exception takes place and problematic moments. Afterward, one examines how the exception took place, especially what role the client played in it. *R* stands for *reinforcing*. The professional reinforces the successes and factors that have led to the exceptions through the meticulous exploration of the exceptions and by complimenting the client. *S*, finally, stands for *start again*. One can always go on with the question: "And what

---

EXERCISE 18

Begin the next 10 or, better yet, 20 sessions with the opening question: "What is (going) better?" Dare to ask that question! You will notice that your clients begin to anticipate it and think about what is going better prior to the next session in order to tell you about it.

else is going better?" Appendix F is a protocol for the use of EARS in subsequent sessions.

FOUR POSSIBLE RESPONSES

Selekman (1997) argued that the client can provide four different kinds of responses in subsequent sessions to the question as to what is going better. How well the client is doing and whether the homework suits him or her determine whether the professional should continue on the same path or should do something else. Professionals must always carefully tailor their questions and homework assignments to the relationship they have with the client (i.e., whether he or she is a visitor, complainant, or customer). It is important to keep in mind that the client wants the problem solved, however pessimistic or skeptical he or she may be. For that reason, it is important to listen closely and to examine *how* the client wants to change. In subsequent sessions, it is vital to optimize the relationship with the client and to retain the progress already made and build on it. In addition, one needs to verify whether the homework has been useful and meaningful, and any possible regression must be caught. The four possible responses are: "Things are going better," "We disagree" (if there is more than one client), "Things are the same," and "Things are going worse."

Things Are Going Better

If things are going better, one can generally tell by the client's appearance. He or she usually looks better and often identifies many things that have changed. The professional does well to ask for details about the improvements, to emphasize the difference from how things were before, and to pay compliments.

Some solution-focused questions for clients who report that things are going better are:

- "How did you make that happen?"
- "How do you manage to . . . ?"
- "How did you manage to take such a big step?"
- "How did you come up with that fine idea?"
- "What did you tell yourself to help you do it that way?"
- "What do you have to keep doing so that that will happen more often?"
- "How is that different for you?"
- "Suppose we see each other again in a month. What additional

changes will you be able to tell me about then?"

- "How do I know that you have enough confidence to halt the sessions now?"
- "What ideas do you now have (e.g., about yourself) that are different from the ideas you had before?"
- "What would you have to do to go back to square one"?
- "Can you indicate on a scale of 10 to 0, where 10 means that things are fine the way they are, where you are today?"
- "How will you celebrate your victory over the problem?"
- "Who will you invite to this party?"
- "What will you say in the speech that you give at the party?"

At the end of the session, one asks again: "Is it necessary or would it be useful for you to come back?" If so: "When would you like to come back?" If the client does not have a preference, the professional can gradually increase the time between sessions, to indicate his or her confidence that the client will work things out him- or herself.

Some solution-focused homework suggestions for clients who report that things are going better are:

- "Go on with what works (better)."
- "Do more of what works (better)."

Clients Disagree

If there are multiple clients and they disagree about the progress they have made or are concerned that they have not made enough progress, it is good to normalize matters. The professional can make it clear that one often makes progress by taking three steps forward and then taking one or two steps back.

In any case, it is a good idea to begin by taking a look, together with the clients, at what *is* going better, even if it is only going better to a very small degree. Those differences can be amplified and the professional can pay compliments. Moreover, he or she can point out that small differences may lead to significant changes later on.

A solution-focused question for clients who disagree is: "Suppose we see each other again in four weeks. What changes would you like to have achieved by then?" If any of the clients remain concerned, one may ask competence questions (especially with complainants who often use "Yes, but" phrases):

- "How come things aren't worse for you?"
- "What steps have you taken to ensure that things don't get worse?"
- "What else helps to ensure that things don't get worse?"
- "And what difference does that make?"

The solution-focused professional can ask him- or herself the following questions:

- "Are the clients customers, complainants, or visitors?"
- "Is there a goal and has it been formulated well?"
- "What homework suggestions would suit these clients best?"
- "Can I present the clients with a number of homework suggestions to choose from?"

Some solution-focused homework suggestions for clients who disagree are:

- If a client tries to undermine another client's attempts to achieve a desired behavior, one can suggest an observation exercise. For a week or longer, each of the clients observes what desired behavior the other clients display and makes a note of it. Clients bring their notes to the next session. They are not allowed to go over the notes together before the session.
- If the homework suggestion was helpful, but if one or both of the clients did not find it a pleasant or useful exercise, the professional can examine together with the clients how the suggestion may be improved.
- If more exceptions are needed, the professional may propose the surprise task, a playful way to challenge a person's fixed ideas. It is agreed with all clients that they will do something (either subtle or highly noticeable) to surprise the other in a positive way. What that might be is left to each client. The other may then guess what the surprise was and talk about it at the next session. Children and adolescents in particular take great pleasure in surprise tasks.
- If both clients are stuck in a pattern of negative interaction, one may also propose the do-something-different task. Here, too, the clients themselves decide what they will do differently in the upcoming period. What they do is immaterial; the purpose is to break a fixed pattern. For example, during a course of family therapy,

there has been frequent mention of serious arguments because the adolescent son and daughter did not follow the parents' rules. During the next argument, both parents lie down on the floor and stop speaking. The children are so shocked that they come along to subsequent sessions because they're worried about their parents.

- Another possibility is the pretend-the-miracle-has-happened task. All the clients are instructed to pretend for a day or two (or for a shorter period of time if that proves too ambitious, e.g., part of a day or an hour) that the miracle has happened. They are asked to pay attention to the difference that the task makes. Everyone may guess on what days the others chose to pretend that the miracle had happened. They keep their findings to themselves and do not share them until the next session with the professional. As it turns out, they may well guess the wrong day!
- One may also suggest the prediction task: Every day, the clients predict what the following day will look like. This task is intended to supply information about what works. Afterward, the clients examine whether the prediction has come true and what contributed to this. In a variant of this homework suggestion, the client may predict each morning whether or not he or she will be successful at fulfilling the prediction.

It is important to distinguish between behavioral tasks for customers and observational tasks for complainants. The do-something-different task and the pretend-the-miracle-has-happened task are behavioral tasks, whereas the prediction task is an observational task. In the latter instance, clients (complainants) do not have to change their own behavior yet (see Chapter 5 for homework suggestions).

Things Are the Same

The client may feel that nothing about the situation has changed. In that case, it is useful to find out when small improvements in the situation have been noticeable nonetheless. The client can use every exception that is found to create solutions by making that exception happen again or more often. Sometimes remaining stable is a great result in itself; progress is not always attainable.

Some solution-focused questions for clients who report that things are the same are:

- "How did you manage to remain stable?"
- "Suppose I were to ask someone who knows you well what is going a little better. What would that person say?"
- "On a scale of 10 to 0, how would you rate your current situation?"
- "What is needed for you to maintain that rating in the time to come?"
- "Who among the most important people in your life is most worried about you?"
- "On a scale of 10 and 0, how worried is that person?"

It may be useful to expand the sessions to include an important person from the client's life to help find a solution to the problem. If the client stays negative and fails to name exceptions, one can ask more competence questions, such as: "How do you cope? How do you manage to go on with these sessions?"

The solution-focused professional may ask him- or herself the following questions:

- "Is the client a customer, complainant, or visitor?"
- "Do we need to revisit the goal?"

Some solution-focused homework suggestions for clients who report that things are the same are:

- If the do-something-different task has not yet been assigned, it can be introduced as an experiment, especially if the client is stuck in a rut.
- The pattern of interaction can be changed through the addition of a new element or through deliberate exaggeration of the pattern.
- If the client indicates that he or she cannot exert any control over the problem, he or she can be asked to externalize the problem. One may also use creative nonverbal visualization techniques or assign drawing tasks. These techniques are described in Chapter 7.

Things Are Going Worse

The client who says that things are going worse often has a long history of failure or has contended with big problems for years. If the professional is too optimistic, he or she will usually be unable to help that client. This client often needs a lot of space to tell the story of the problem, including any (negative) experiences with previous professionals. In that case, one may apply the "Greek chorus" technique (Papp, 1983). Anyone who has seen Woody

Allen's 1995 film *Mighty Aphrodite* will remember that the Greek chorus warns of potential dangers between scenes. With the Greek chorus technique, the professional always adopts an attitude in favor of change, whereas the team of colleagues adopts an attitude against change. If the professional works alone, he or she can apply the technique by introducing a pessimistic supervisor. The client is then invited to work with the therapist to prove the team of colleagues or the supervisor wrong (Selekman, 1993). Some models make use of the Greek chorus not just with pessimistic clients (complainants), as in the solution-focused model, but with all clients, regardless of whether they are visitors, complainants, or customers.

CASE 9

An 18-year-old client smokes a couple of joints every day. He would like to break the habit; he cannot see himself finishing school if he does not, and he would like to pass his final examination. The therapist introduces a pessimistic colleague, who predicts that he will undoubtedly relapse if he stops smoking marijuana. This upsets the client: He knows what he is getting into, and once he has made his decision he will certainly stick to it. At the next session he reports having barely touched a joint. The therapist offers compliments and positive character interpretations: He must be a truly determined man! The client blossoms as he shares, when asked, that this is not the first time in his life that he has shown such determination.

The professional may ask "pessimistic" questions of clients who report that things are going worse:

- "How do you manage to go on under these circumstances?"
- "How come you haven't given up by now?"
- "How come things aren't worse than they are?"
- "What is the smallest thing you could do to make a minimal difference?"
- "How can you make the same thing happen to a very small extent right now?"
- "What can others do for you?"
- "What can you remember about what used to help that you could try again now?"
- "What would most help you climb back into the saddle and face these difficulties?"
- "How did you manage to get out of bed this morning and make it here?"

It is useful to put this client in an expert position and ask him or her, as a *consultant*, what his or her treatment should look like. Some solution-focused questions for the expert client are:

- "What did professionals you worked with previously miss?"
- "Of all the things that these professionals did, what did you find most disagreeable?"
- "How could I be of greater assistance?"
- "What qualities would your ideal professional have, and what would he or she do?"
- "What questions would your ideal professional ask you, and what, in your opinion, would be the best course for him or her to follow?"
- "If I worked with other clients who were in the same boat as you, what advice would you give me that would allow me to help them?"
- "What question can you think of that would allow me to help you the most?"

The solution-focused professional may ask him- or herself the following questions:

- "Is the client a customer, complainant, or visitor?"
- "Do we need to revisit the goal?"

Here are some solution-focused homework suggestions for clients who report that things are going worse:

- It may help to have the exceedingly pessimistic client predict in detail when and how the next crisis will take place. As a result, the crisis may fail to occur or the client may discover better ways to deal with it.
- The client can also be asked to exaggerate the problem. This is a paradoxical assignment: As a result, the gravity of the problem may immediately decrease, as the client does not feel like carrying out such an assignment. If the client does exaggerate the problem, he or she will likely experience more control than he or she first thought.
- One may also examine the client's earlier successes in solving problems to see what strategies he or she can try again.

With this group of clients one may deploy the same strategies as with clients who report that nothing is going better. If the professional works alone, it may be useful for him or her to invite a colleague to sit in and give feedback. With this group of clients, the professional might also apply the technique of externalizing the problem (see Chapter 7). Lastly, the solution-focused professional may discharge him- or herself in a final rescue attempt if all other strategies have failed. The professional can explain to the client that he or she apparently does not understand the client and therefore cannot help. He or she says it would be best for the client to enlist the help of another professional, who may have fresh ideas. The client may agree with this proposition. He or she may also begin to formulate more realistic expectations, after which cooperation may be possible.

Relapse

Relapse prevention contributes to the client's road map. The client is encouraged to think about ways to maintain the gains of the therapy. The therapist may also ask the client to imagine a future relapse and consider how his or her skills could be used to deal with it. Snyder's research has shown that hopeful people are able to come up with more alternative routes than non-hopeful people if the original route is blocked. Discussing ways to tackle future problems serves as a means to develop alternative solutions before these difficulties present themselves. This builds coping strategies and enhances pathway thinking, which further diminishes the risk of relapse. If relapse occurs, one does well to normalize it: Progress often means taking three steps forward and one or two steps back (and it would be a shame to give up even a single step). The professional may also give a positive slant to the relapse; after all, a relapse offers an opportunity to practice getting back on one's feet. As Milton Erickson has said, "If you fall on your face, at least you are heading in the right direction" (2000, p. 192).

In solution-focused interviewing it is not necessary to dwell on the cause of the relapse and its consequences. The professional does well to offer acknowledgment by showing that he or she understands how frustrating the relapse is to the client. Following this, it is most important to explore how the client has managed on previous occasions to get back on the right track after a relapse. If the client remains disconcerted in the wake of the recent relapse, he or she and the professional can consider what steps he or she can take to get back on the right track.

The session can also deal with relapse in a lighter, more playful manner. One may ask what it would take for the client to obtain a low rating or go

back to square one as quickly as possible. This immediately indicates what
the wrong approach is and often lends the conversation a light-hearted tenor.

SUMMARY

- The opening question at the beginning of a session plays a part in
  determining the client's response.
- There are four possible responses to the question as to what is
  going better: "Things are going better," "We disagree" (if there is
  more than one client), "Things are the same," or "Things are going
  worse." There are specific solution-focused questions and homework suggestions, and questions the professional may ask him- or
  herself, for each answer.
- A protocol for subsequent sessions (EARS) was outlined in this
  chapter.

CHAPTER 5

Homework Suggestions

Only a small change is needed.

—Steve de Shazer

At the end of each session, the solution-focused professional gives the client feedback. The feedback consists of several fixed components: compliments, perhaps a bridge or rationale, and homework suggestions. Whereas Chapter 3 dealt with giving feedback, this chapter explores possible homework suggestions in general and for specific cases. One may also solicit the client's feedback: How does the client evaluate the session and what does he or she want to take away from the session? The Session Rating Scale, which is described in Chapters 2 and 11, is very useful in this respect. For solution-focused questions to ask at the end of the session, please refer to Chapter 10.

GENERAL SUGGESTIONS

At the end of each solution-focused session, one has the option to offer the client homework suggestions (as part of the feedback and after the break, if one is taken). These are intended to direct clients' attention to those aspects of their experiences and situations that are most useful in finding solutions and in reaching their goals. If the professional complements the client on his or her motivation, there will always be cooperation (Walter & Peller, 1992). In offering the client suggestions, the professional will find it important to keep the following three questions in mind:

- Does it concern a visitor-, a complainant-, or a customer-relationship?
- Does the client have a well-defined goal?
- Are there spontaneous or deliberate exceptions related to the client's goal?

In a visitor relationship, no assignments are given. After all, the problem has not yet been defined, nor is there any talk of a goal or related exceptions. It may be that people from the client's environment have a problem with him or her or feel concern. In that case, the environment itself is often the complainant. The professional goes along with the client's worldview; extends acknowledgement, compliments, and positive character interpretations; and proposes another appointment to continue to find out with the client what would be the best thing for him or her to do.

In a complainant relationship, only observational tasks are assigned. To a complainant who cannot name exceptions or a goal or who has vague complaints, one may assign one of the following observational tasks:

- "Pay attention to what happens in your life that gives you the sense that this problem can be solved."
- "Reflect on what you would like to accomplish with these sessions" (Walter & Peller, 1992).
- "Pay attention to what is going well and should stay the same" (de Shazer, 1985) or "Pay attention to what happens in your life that you would like to continue to happen."
- "Observe the positive moments in your life so that you can talk about them next time."
- "Pay attention to the times when things are going better so that you can talk about them next time."
- If a scaling question has been asked: "Observe when you are 1 point higher on the scale and what you and (significant) others are doing differently then."
- "Pay attention this week to what gives you hope that your problem can be solved."

The use of an observation task implies that the exceptions can occur again and can contribute to the client feeling more hopeful. Observation tasks also indicate that useful information is to be found within the client's own realm of experience (de Jong & Berg, 1997).

De Shazer (1988) has found it useful to add an element of prediction. He believes that the value of such a task derives from its suggestive power. If there are exceptions already, a prediction task suggests that they will occur again, maybe even sooner than the client imagines. If the client predicts a better day, he or she will be more inclined to look for signs of confirmation (a positive self-fulfilling prophecy). A complainant who is able to describe spontaneous exceptions receives a prediction task:

- "Predict what tomorrow will be like, find an explanation for why the day turned out the way it did the following evening, and then make a new prediction for the following day."
- "Pay attention to exactly what happens when an exception manifests itself so that you can tell me more about it: What is different then, and what are (significant) others doing?"
- With a complainant who thinks the other person is the problem: "Pay attention to the times when the other person does more of what you want, to what is different then, and to what he or she sees you do then that is helpful to him or her."
- "Pay attention to what the other person does that is useful or pleasant and to the difference it makes so that you can talk about it next time."

In a customer relationship, behavioral *and* observational tasks are assigned. If the customer is able to clearly formulate his or her goal (or the miracle) and find exceptions, you can make the following suggestions:

- "Continue with what works and pay attention to what else you're doing that is helpful that you hadn't noticed before," (a combination of a behavioral and observational task)
- "Continue to find out what works best for you," (a combination of a behavioral and observational task)
- "Do more of what works."
- "Do the easiest thing that works."
- "Think about what else might help."
- "Do a piece of the miracle or the goal." (as an experiment)
- "Discover more about seemingly coincidental exceptions."
- "Predict the seemingly coincidental exceptions and explain the result."

If the customer seems motivated but does not have a clear picture of the miracle or the goal and is unable to find exceptions, or if there is a power struggle between two or more clients, suggest that the client or clients "Do something else, preferably something unexpected, and note the difference it makes."

If the customer does have a clear picture of the miracle or goal but is unable to find exceptions, you can give the following homework suggestions:

- "Pretend the miracle has happened. In the coming week, pretend for a day (or part of a day) that the miracle has happened and pay attention to the differences it makes."
- "In the coming week, pretend for one day that you are 1 or 2 points higher on the scale and pay attention to the differences it makes. Pay special attention to the reactions of people who are important to you."

The Value of Homework Suggestions

Some clients struggle with the words "homework" and "task." They remind people of their school days and not everyone has positive memories of doing homework. Instead of saying "homework" and "task," the solution-focused professional can speak of "suggestions for something to do between now and the next appointment," thus avoiding any possible negative associations. Presenting a task as an "experiment" or even a "small experiment" may also make it easier for the client to try it, because it alleviates the pressure for the client to be successful at accomplishing the task. Before the break and feedback formulation, it is useful to ask the client whether he or she wants to receive homework suggestions. If clients say that they don't have any need for them, there is probably a good reason: Perhaps they don't consider it necessary or useful, or maybe they don't have any time before the next session. In those instances, the professional needn't come up with suggestions.

The use of homework in cognitive behavioral therapy is no longer deemed useful in solution-focused interviewing. According to de Shazer,

> We found that we could get as much information when the client did not perform the task as when the client did perform the task. Not only that, we also found that accepting non-performance as a message about the client's way of doing things (rather than as a sign of

"resistance") allowed us to develop a cooperating relationship with clients which might not include task assignments. This was a shock to us because we had assumed that tasks were almost always necessary to achieve behavioral change. Thus, we became more successful with more clients in a fewer number of sessions. (1985, p. 21)

As a result, solution-focused interviewing prevents unnecessary battles (referred to as "resistance" in problem-focused therapy) between the professional and the client. If a client hasn't done the agreed-upon homework, the problem-focused professional will talk to the client about the importance of doing his or her homework and will want to know why the client failed to do the homework. The solution-focused professional will be more inclined to say that he or she thinks it's fine that the client hasn't done the homework, as the client undoubtedly had a good reason not to; he or she probably did something that worked better and the professional can invite him or her to talk about that. In this way, cooperation with the client is improved.

It is important that the homework suggestions that the client receives be doable and realistic. The key is to keep it simple. Offering one or at most two suggestions is sufficient. In order to remember what the suggestions are, the client can write them down before the end of the session. It goes without saying that the same applies for the professional. The homework suggestion is often concluded with the phrase "So that you can tell me what's going better next time" (with behavioral tasks for customers) or "So that you can tell me something about it next time" (with observational tasks for complainants). In other words, the professional implies that the client will have something to relate at the next session.

Baseline Measurements

Cognitive behavioral therapy makes frequent use of baseline measurements. In problem-focused behavioral therapy, baseline measurements are mostly concerned with the gravity and frequency of complaints and problems. In solution-focused brief therapy, baseline measurements—if assigned at all—deal exclusively with desired behavior (and hence also with desired functional cognitions and positive emotions) and with the situation that the client wishes to attain in the future. The desired behavior and the preferred future are defined in positive, concrete, and achievable terms. For instance, the registration may cover the degree of relaxation rather than the degree of tension, or the times when the client already manages to be in a somewhat better mood or not to display undesired behavior (e.g., using alcohol) despite instigation. It is concerned not with the reduction of the complaints but with the increase of desired behavior and with progress toward the preferred future. If the registration pertains to frequency, it is concerned with how often the desired behavior (or a desired functional cognition) occurs. For instance, how often does the client manage to remain calm or calmer in stressful situations? How does he or she already manage to have functional cognitions in these situations? This may be followed by additional competence questions, for example, "How did you succeed in doing that?" In other words, the objective is to find exceptions. If the registration concerns intensity, it asks the client to rate the positive feeling associated with the desired situation or behavior instead of the negative emotion associated with the undesired behavior.

CASE 10

An employee has been sent to a solution-focused coaching session by his superior. Both agree that the employee isn't performing well, especially if one compares his current performance with his performance a year ago or more. The relationship with the client quickly turns into a customer relationship, especially when the professional offers acknowledgment of the fact that the supervisor has insisted on a coaching trajectory, as a result of which the employee now finds himself where he is. As a homework suggestion, the client is asked not only what he himself would be willing to do in order to do well again at and outside work, but also what he thinks his supervisor would like to see go better and what the latter thinks the client should do in order to do well again. In this way, it is as if the supervisor is present in the room. By carrying out his own ideas for improvement and the ideas that he thinks his superior has, the employee manages after a few sessions to get back on track and perform well.

SPECIFIC SUGGESTIONS

De Shazer (1985) described how he developed "skeleton keys," keys that fit different locks. De Shazer's formula tasks are examples of skeleton keys, as are questions about goal formulation and about exceptions, scaling questions, and competence questions. Having a different key for each lock is unnecessary, and there is no need for the lock be analyzed first; interventions can initiate change even when the professional does not know in detail what the problem is. The only thing the interventions need to ensure is that a new behavioral pattern can emerge. De Shazer provided the following examples of skeleton keys.

The write, read, and burn task is used if the client is plagued by obsessive or depressive thoughts. De Shazer described a client who was obsessed with her ex-partner months after breaking off the relationship. She felt guilty and kept asking herself what she had done wrong. The thoughts had even grown into nightmares. After normalizing the problem, de Shazer gave the client the following task in order for her to move on with her life. At the same time every day, she was to retire to a comfortable place for at least an hour and no more than an hour and a half. During that time, she had to focus and, on all odd-numbered days, write down all her good and bad memories of her ex-partner. She had to keep writing the entire time, even if it meant that she ended up writing some things down more than once. On even-numbered days, she had to read her notes from the previous day and then burn them. If the unwanted thoughts came to her at times other than during the scheduled hour, she had to tell herself, "I have other things to do now and I will think about it when the scheduled hour has arrived," or she had to make a note to remind herself to think about it at the scheduled time. After just a few days, the thoughts had largely disappeared.

The structured-fight task is used if clients complain that their arguments never lead anywhere. This task consists of three steps: (1) A coin is flipped to determine who gets to go first; (2) the winner may berate the other person for 10 minutes, without interruption; (3) and then the other person may do the same, also without interruption. Ten minutes of silence follow before the next round is begun with another coin toss.

The do-something-different task is used if the client complains about another person and claims to have "already tried everything." Solutions involve doing something that is different from what didn't work before. De Shazer offered the following example: A 10-year-old boy was apprehended for prowling around his school. He had broken in to get his homework, which he'd forgotten; however, he refused to answer the policeman's questions. Once the policeman had tried everything to get him to talk, he threatened to hold his own breath until the boy explained why he had broken into the school. This proved too much for the boy. He revealed that he had broken in to retrieve his homework so as not to get a failing grade.

The "pay attention to what you do when you overcome the urge" task is used to help the client find and use exceptions to the rule. It can be used as an alternative to the do-something-different task. Although the client will often say that the problematic behavior (e.g., drug use, gambling, nail-biting) always occurs, there are often circumstances under which the problematic behavior does not manifest itself. These are exceptions on which one can build, because they are already part of the client's repertoire. This task presupposes that the client definitely conquers the urge every now and then and that he or she may be doing something different in order to overcome the urge. The client's attention is directed to his or her behavior, not to any interior sensation. In some cases, it may also be useful to draw attention to what other people do in comparable situations.

The first session formula task is used to shift the client's attention from the past to the present and the future, and to increase the expectancy of change. This task implies that the professional has positive expectations. The professional says: "Between now and the next time we see each other, pay attention to what happens in your life (e.g., your family, marriage, relationship) that you would like to continue to see happening." The word "if" is not used: The professional assumes that there are things the client wants to maintain.

De Shazer drew the following conclusion: Solution-focused brief therapy does not require the client to learn or add anything. Unlike in problem-focused therapy, the professional does not tell the client what he or she needs to do differently, nor does the client learn new techniques. Nonetheless, solution-focused interviewing has an enormous impact because it demonstrates how a small difference can make a big difference. Solution-focused professionals do examine with their clients how they can improve certain skills, but that is different from learning skills that clients do not already possess. My suggestion is not to use the word "learning" in solution-focused interviewing and to opt instead for "becoming better at." The word "learn," which is often used in youth welfare work, detracts from what the client has already accomplished, that is, the road already traveled (see Chapter 3).

Problem of Choice

If a client has multiple options and is unable to choose, an observation task may be useful.

- Suggest that the client observe what happens that gives a clearer indication of what he or she should do so that you can talk about it together the next time.
- The client can flip a coin and pretend. Every night before going to sleep, the client flips a coin and the next day he or she carries out what has been agreed upon on the basis of the coin toss. Heads

may mean that the client pretends to have made one decision, for example, to stay with his wife, and tails means he pretends to have made the other decision, that is, to leave his wife. This may bring the client more clarity so that he can reach a decision. This task is a behavioral task.

- With problems of choice, projection into the future can be a useful technique as well: The client imagines how he or she will be doing in the future (in 1 year, 5 years, or 10 years) if he or she decides to do a or b (or even c). The client can also look back from the future to the present and examine what helped him or her make a decision. Chapter 7 describes a number of techniques for projection into the future.

Emotions

If there are strong negative emotions involved that cause nothing to change, the professional may propose the following to the client as an experiment.

- "When you are angry, pretend you are not. Observe the difference and see what happens."
- "Pretend you feel differently (e.g., on odd-numbered days)."

These too are behavioral tasks, which require motivation on the client's part (i.e., the client must be a customer).

Tasks for Groups

Metcalf (1998) has described how she helps group members develop a task. If the goals of all the clients in the group have been identified, the professional can encourage them to work toward their goals in between group sessions. For instance, he or she might say: "You all have good ideas about the moments when the problem is less of a burden to you. Now let's talk about what you could do until the next meeting to keep the problem under control" (behavioral task). If the goal is not yet clear, the professional can motivate the clients to make good use of the time between sessions: The clients are invited to closely observe their daily activities until the next meeting and to pay attention to when the problem does not bother them quite as much (observational task). The goal is for the clients to keep track of exceptions so that they can describe them during the next group session. I find it noteworthy that Metcalf, in describing both cases, used negative terminology and did not first ask what the clients would like to see instead of the problem.

At the end of the first group session, Metcalf gives the clients a six-page binder titled "Solution Notes." The binder outlines externalization techniques (see Chapter 7). It also asks the following questions:

- "If a 10 means that you have control over your life and a 1 means that the problem has control over you, where on that scale would you say you are today?"
- "Where on the scale would you like to be when our group reconvenes?"
- "What did you learn about yourself in group today that can help you reach that number?"
- "Does anyone have a suggestion for anyone else?" (In my view, "What suggestions do you have for each other?" would be preferable because it is an open question and it encourages the group members to reflect more.)

The clients take the binders home. At home they then keep track of times when they have more control over their lives.

Tasks for Children and Families

Berg and Steiner (2003) listed a number of tasks that can be divided into two categories: do-more-of-what-works tasks, which are the more prevalent, and do-something-different tasks, which are suggested only under extreme circumstances, especially where teenagers are concerned. Proposing a homework assignment or experiment carries the therapy into the client's (the child's and possibly his or her parents') real life outside the therapy room. They provided a few guidelines and principles for assigning homework:

- The experiment must be related to what the client wants, as discussed during the first session.
- The experiment must be doable and should usually involve a small step toward the client's goal. It is important to take things slowly.
- The main purpose of the experiment is to elicit different reactions from those who play an important role in the child's life. The experiment or the homework alone rarely makes a difference; what matters are other people's responses to the child's execution of the experiment. If the child's new behavior is known solely to the child, it has but a limited effect. It is important to generate a ripple effect

that involves the observations and reactions of the people who are important to the child.

- If you cannot think of an idea for an experiment, do not force yourself to come up with one; often a mere compliment is sufficient to bring about new behavior.
- Most experiments fall into the category of doing more of what works.
- The number of do-something-different tasks that the child is asked to carry out should be extremely small. These exercises are useful for breaking a chronic pattern that has everyone frustrated.

Some experiments that Berg and Steiner discussed are:

- ***Flipping a coin.*** When the child wakes up, he or she flips a coin. If the child throws tails, he or she engages in a secret new activity. If the child throws heads, it will be an ordinary day and the child does nothing different. The parents then have to guess which way the coin landed each morning, but the child has to keep this information secret. At the next session with the professional, the parents can compare notes with each other and with the child.
- ***Surprise task.*** Together with the child, the professional finds out what the child could do that would really surprise the parents (making breakfast, cleaning his or her room), which then becomes a surprise the child can carry out him- or herself. The child is asked to pay attention to the others' reactions.

  A surprise task is sometimes referred to as a technique of pattern disruption. Parents who claim that they have "already tried everything" often make progress by carrying out a surprise task. The predictable way in which parents react to their child's behavior can be disrupted if the parents do something different, for example, give a surprise kiss or do something kind instead of becoming angry.

  The surprise can also come out of a "wonder bag." The child and the parents each write down five wishes, each on a separate piece of paper. The wishes are placed in separate bags and the bags are exchanged. Each week each family member pulls a wish from the bag he or she received in the exchange, and each individual has a week to make the wish come true. What we have here, then, are (fulfillable) wishes—for example, for the parents to read the child a story, for one of the parents to go along to a sports activity, for the child to clean his or her desk—rather than assignments.

- **Pretend the miracle has happened.** After one has discussed what the miracle looks like, the child is asked to choose a day or part of a day for the miracle to occur. On that day the child is to pretend that the miracle has occurred. The child then pays attention to who has noticed that he or she is acting as if the miracle has happened and what he or she is doing differently.

- **General observation task.** This task can be assigned to the child and parents. The professional can tell the child: "Pay attention to the expression on your mom's face each time you start your homework without having to be told to." He or she may tell the parents: "Pay attention to the times when things are going well at home" or "Observe the times when things are going well and do not need to change."

  The parents and the child can make a list of things that the other party does that are agreeable or impressive. Every time the child carries out a task assigned by the parents or the child engages in a desired behavior, the parents can put a marble in a glass jar. In the evening the parents and the child can briefly discuss what each marble signifies and what went well that day. When the jar is full, the child receives a reward. Doing something fun with the child is a nice way to positively reinforce the desired behavior.

Berg and Steiner (2003) described three additional activities. For the first activity, called "magic 5 minutes," parents spend 5 minutes with the child every day, regardless of how the child has behaved. The child gets to determine how the 5 minutes are spent. The second activity that they suggested is horsing around with the child every day, and for the third, the parents ask the child to take on a "big responsibility," for example, preparing meals or running errands. This allows the child to feel important and make a positive contribution to family life.

Berg and Steiner (2003) believed that parents and teachers have a "treasure box" full of tricks at their disposal, even if they are often unaware of this. It is often enough, therefore, to do more of what works. They also named a few techniques from hypnotherapy that parents and children can use:

- The hand-on-your-hand technique is a hypnotic form of cue conditioning, whereby the child carries a positive feeling from a previous situation into a situation where that positive emotion is needed. A connection is established between that positive feeling and a touch of the child's wrist. The parent demonstrates this to the child by touching the child's hand with his or her own. The goal is for the child to be able to conjure that positive emotion by him- or herself in the future by briefly touching his or her own wrist.

- Concentration techniques, such as rubbing thumb and index finger together or placing one's hands on one's head, can be used by children to pay attention in class, for example.
- Imagining a safe place with the child is a technique that offers the child a feeling of security. It can be an existing or dreamed-up place that the child can visit in his or her mind whenever he or she needs to feel safe and relax.

I would like to add a homework suggestion—making a compliment box— to the aforementioned techniques. To make a compliment box, each day all members of the family put a note with a compliment for each of the other family members into a box. This encourages them to take a positive view of each other. At dinner, the family members remove the compliments from the box and read them to each another. Experience has shown that even if not every member of the family is a customer yet, even those who initially do not want to play along often will later on when they notice how it improves the atmosphere among the others.

One can also make a compliment box during group therapy with children—and with grown-ups too. At the end of the session, each group member puts a note with a compliment for each of the other group members in the box. These notes are read aloud during the next session. The compliments may be given anonymously or signed.

CASE 11

A variant on the compliment box is the success box, which is used in group therapy. First, the participants make or buy a beautiful box together. All group members are asked to anonymously submit three separate notes with solutions that have helped them successfully face or solve their problems. Examples of solutions are talking to a friend, taking a walk, going to coffee shops, and keeping a diary. When all the notes have been placed in the box, they are removed one by one and read aloud by the members of the group. Other group members can pick up one or two of these notes with solutions that are new to them and try them out so that they can talk about how the notes helped them at the next session.

Selekman (1993) described a number of other, sometimes paradoxical, tasks:

- **Solution enhancement task.** This task is comparable to the task de Shazer (1985) has described as the "pay attention to what you do when you overcome the urge to . . . " task. Selekman had the client write down helpful solutions on cards and asked him or her to carry these "solution cards" around with him or her in order to read them in difficult times.
- **Coin flip task.** At the start of the day, parents flip a coin to determine who will be in charge of the children's upbringing for the day. This task can help parents who disagree about how their children should be raised or punished. This technique can also be used in a team if the team members have conflicting views.
- **Habit control ritual.** This task works well with families that have experienced problems over a long period of time. The task is based on a technique from narrative therapy called externalizing the problem (see Chapter 7). Every day, family members observe what they do to confront the problem and make sure that the problem does not take control. They can also pay attention to the times when the problem gets the better of them. In the evening, the family discusses how the day went and can design strategies for improvement. One variation is the symbolic externalization ritual: Family members choose a symbol for the problem, describe their relationship to that symbol, what they would like to say to the symbol, and what they want to do with it once they have conquered it.
- **The secret surprise task.** The adolescent chooses one or two things with which to surprise his parents in a positive way in the course of one week. He is not allowed to tell his parents what the surprises are; it is up to the parents to find out. This is a fun way to magnify exceptions and changes, as it turns out that parents often guess wrong. This task can also be assigned in reverse, in which case the parents are in charge of the secret surprises and the child has to find out what they are.
- **Writing letters.** It can be useful, especially in a school context, to write a letter. Selekman offered the example of a conflict between a teacher and a student. He helped the mother write a letter to the

teacher in which she complimented him on his patience with and concern for her son and expressed her hope that things would go better for her son at school. She wrote to the teacher that she had given her son a task: He was to pay attention to the things he liked about the teacher, write them down, and tell her about them after school. This dramatically changed the relationship between the teacher and the student.

- ***Assigning ordeals.*** Erickson (1980) developed this therapeutic strategy as a last resort in order to make it as uncomfortable as possible for the client to maintain his or her problem. Selekman has used this strategy when the client reports that nothing is going better or that things are going worse. It involves the assignment of a very arduous task; for example, Erickson had a depressed client carry around a few pounds of bricks in a shopping bag for awhile as a symbol of the heavy burden of her depression.
- ***Predicting the next crisis.*** Selekman (1997) suggested this for exceedingly pessimistic clients who are often in crisis. The professional asks for many details about the next crisis: Who will be involved, where will it take place, what effect will it have on others? This may help break a pattern, as the therapist and the client can look for ways to withstand the crisis: How did the client solve a previous crisis, what worked before, what could be useful again?
- ***Exaggerating the problem.*** When a client exaggerates the problem, it sometimes becomes apparent that he or she can exert more control over it than he or she suspected. This task may offer a starting point for change.

Selekman (1993) described a formula for groups of parents of adolescents. The parenting group convenes six times, the time intervals between sessions progressively increasing as a sign of the professional's confidence in the group. Numerous solution-focused questions are asked during these parenting groups. At the end of each session, the following tasks are suggested to the parents:

- ***First session.*** "Pay attention to what is going well (at home, in the relationship with the adolescent, in the adolescent's behavior) and should remain the way it is."
- ***Second session.*** The parents are invited to observe what steps they

can take to reach their goals. The parents are also asked to observe how their child responds to this so that they can talk about it during the next session.

- **Third session.** "Do more of what works."
- **Fourth session.** "If something doesn't work, do something different; pay attention to what works and do more of it."
- **Fifth session.** "Do more of what works" or, for parents who do not report any progress, "Pretend the miracle has happened, and pay attention to how the child reacts to this."

At the sixth and final session, there's a celebration: There are snacks, the parents receive certificates declaring them to be "Solution-Focused Parents," the parents all give a brief speech in which they talk about how they've grown as parents, and they are invited to join the "Solution-Oriented Parents' Alumni Association," through which they can be invited to act as consultants to future parenting groups.

SUMMARY

- Homework suggestions are not always necessary or useful.
- A visitor does not receive homework suggestions, a complainant is assigned observation tasks, and a customer may be assigned behavioral and observational tasks. That way, there will always be cooperation.
- General and specific homework suggestions were discussed in this chapter, including de Shazer's formula tasks. Also included were homework suggestions for groups and for children and parents. Creativity and humor often play an important role in these tasks.

CHAPTER 6

• • • • • • • • • • • • • • • • • •

Concluding the Sessions

Remember not the former things, neither consider the things of old.

Behold, I will do a new thing; now it shall spring forth; shall you not know it?

I will even make a way in the wilderness and rivers in the desert.

—Isaiah (43.18.19)

"HOW CAN WE KNOW WHEN TO STOP MEETING LIKE THIS?"

De Shazer (1991) has stated that if the professional accepts the client's statement of his or her problem at the beginning of treatment, by the same logic the professional should also accept the client's declaration that he or she has sufficiently improved as a reason to end the treatment. This gave rise to the idea that the client's goal and solutions are more important than the problems the client has discussed. In this way, the distinction between problem and solution becomes clear.

There is no limit to the number of sessions a client attends in solution-focused brief therapy. However, the average number is about three. The sessions are discontinued if the client achieves his or her treatment goal (to a sufficient degree). After the second session, the time interval between sessions usually increases. One week between the first and the second session is generally a good amount of time (but it can be more if the clients so wishes). In principle, each session is viewed as the last session and just one session may even be enough if the client's goal has become clear. In a chapter titled "How Can We Know When to Stop Meeting Like This?" de Shazer (1991) described how the client's goal comes into view if during the sessions the client and the professional have been attentive to:

- The occurrence of exceptions and the presence of parts of the client's preferred future (the goal), which indicate that desired changes are taking place
- The client's vision and description of a new life
- The confirmation that change is taking place and that the client's new life has, in fact, begun

Contrary to what happens in many problem-focused conversations, discussion of ending the client's contact with the professional occurs as soon as the solution-focused sessions commence. This is evident from the questions the client receives about goal formulation: "What needs to change in your life in order for you to be able to say that these sessions have been worthwhile?" or "What would indicate to you that you're doing well enough that you no longer have to come here?" What the professional wishes to elicit here is a description of what the client would consider a successful result, in concrete and measurable behavioral terms. A clear and detailed description or picture of the preferred future situation can be of great help: "What do you do differently in that picture that tells me that that's the situation you would prefer?"

Discussing the desired outcome from the very beginning of the sessions creates an atmosphere of optimism and gives the client hope that the problem he or she wants help with can be solved (to a sufficient degree). That is why the importance of adequate goal formulation cannot be stressed enough. The professional should feel free to set aside a fair amount of time for it, for it has been my experience that when the goal has been formulated well, half the work is often already done and the client usually knows precisely what he or she needs to do to get closer to his or her goal. This relates to the image of the professional as a tugboat or, better yet, a push tug: As soon as the client is released from the shoal, he or she can sail on unaided. It is often unnecessary for the professional to travel farther along with the client.

The moment when the sessions can be concluded can also be revealed by means of scaling questions. After goal formulation, one can ask the client where he or she currently is on a scale of 10 to 0, and at what number he or she needs to be in order not to have to visit anymore. Experience shows that most clients are happy with a 7 or 8 and don't need to reach a 9 or 10 before they're content and able to finish the treatment. Sometimes the treatment can be concluded at a low rating, because the client has enough confidence that he or she can go it alone from there, toward the number where he or she would like to end up. In any case, it should be clear that in solution-focused interviewing the client decides when the treatment can be concluded, not the professional.

Selekman (1993) described the use of consolidating questions at the conclusion of the sessions as an effective means to get clients to talk about differences. A few of these questions, which can ensure that the achieved result becomes permanent, are:

- "What would you have to do to go backward?"
- "What would you have to do to prevent a major relapse?"
- "What do you have to keep doing to make sure that these changes keep happening?"

Selekman (1993) invited the client to use what he described as his imaginary crystal ball and the clear and detailed description or picture to tell him what changes he or she saw him- or herself making in the future. He expressed disbelief in the psychoanalytic hypothesis that clients are subject to a "flight from health" if they terminate treatment following rapid changes at the beginning of the therapy. He felt that the client must determine not only the goal of the therapy but also when to end it:

> As a Solution-Oriented therapist, I do not believe my job is to cure people, but instead, to help clients have more satisfactory life situations. If clients call to cancel future scheduled appointments because they feel things are better for the time being, I always let them know that I have an open door policy and if they need to schedule a future tune-up session, they may feel free to call me. (Selekman, 1993, p. 156)

This touches upon my sense that the solution-focused professional has a task comparable to the family doctor's. Often the patient doesn't visit the family doctor for years; sometimes he visits a few times in a row. It is not the family doctor's objective to make the patient healthy once and for all. Many professionals have a much loftier goal in mind than most clients do. If professionals were more in tune with the client's goal, treatments would become shorter and probably more successful. It is customary in problem-focused therapy to make appointments for sessions concerning relapse prevention and follow-up sessions. It has been my experience that this is rarely necessary in solution-focused brief therapy. It quite often seems that the point of these sessions is to reassure the problem-focused professional rather than to meet a need on the client's part. Chapter 4 describes how to deal with relapse prevention in a solution-focused manner.

SOLUTION-FOCUSED IDEAS FOR CONCLUDING THE TREATMENT

Solution-focused therapists are not only goal-oriented; they are often creative, too. The following list of ideas for concluding the treatment, brainstormed by some of my students a couple of years ago, illustrates that creativity.

Certificates

- The professional makes a valedictory certificate inscribed with a number of compliments.
- The professional makes a certificate or pamphlet on which the miracle is written down or drawn and hands it to the client upon their parting. In *Counseling Toward Solutions*, Metcalf (1995) offered examples of certificates that the professional can give to the client and that can be copied.

Celebrating Success

- At the beginning of the treatment, the professional asks how the client would like to celebrate when he or she has reached his or her goal. Children in particular find this highly enjoyable. At the last session, the professional comes back to this.
- The client celebrates the conclusion of the sessions with cake, flowers, and snacks.
- The professional asks how the client will celebrate his or her victory over the problem.
- The professional asks whom the client will invite to his or her victory party.
- The professional asks what the client will say in the speech that he or she will give at the party.
- The professional asks each family member to pay a compliment to the other members of the family.

Drawings or Letters

- The professional writes the client a letter outlining his or her goal, the steps he or she has taken toward achieving the goal, and his or her successes, and complimenting the client.

- The client makes a drawing of the situation at the beginning of the sessions and one of the situation at the conclusion of the sessions. The professional can ask the client whether he or she would like to save the drawing of the situation at the beginning of the sessions or, by way of ritual, burn it, for instance.
- The client frames a drawing that he or she makes of the miracle.
- The client makes a recipes-for-success booklet filled with descriptions of how the client has brought about successes in his or her life.

Symbols

- The professional gives the client a transitional object, for example, a cuddly toy, a mascot, a magic wand—something appropriate for the treatment. The client may choose one such object from a small assortment.
- The professional has the client choose a symbol for his or her victory over the problem and lets the client draw or make it.
- The professional or the client makes a small plaque with a maxim or motto on it that symbolizes the client's success.
- The professional gives the client a mug that says on one side: "Stop what doesn't work, do something different." The other side says: "Keep doing what works."
- The client comes up with a magic spell for things to continue to go well.

The Client's Expertise

- The professional asks what the most important tip is that the client has for the next client who experiences the same problems.
- The professional asks permission to consult the client as an expert if he or she finds him- or herself at a loss during a similar treatment.
- The professional asks what the client would have to do to ensure that things go badly for him or her again as quickly as possible (relapse prevention).
- The professional asks what the most important thing is that the client has learned about him- or herself and is therefore worth remembering.
- The professional asks what the client will have achieved in 1 year (5 years, 10 years) if he or she continues on the right path.

- The professional makes a follow-up appointment so that the client can come tell him or her what is going well and what is going better.

SUMMARY

- From the very first session, the solution-focused professional has the end of the sessions in mind and discusses it with the client: "When can we stop meeting like this? What must be achieved by the end of these sessions for you to be able to say that they have been meaningful and useful? What would indicate to you that you no longer have to come here because you're doing well (enough)?"
- Solution-focused ideas for concluding the sessions include making certificates and recipes-for-success booklets, enacting rituals, and celebrating the client's success.

·················

CHAPTER 7

Other Solution-Focused Skills

Focusing on the positive, the solution, and on the
future facilitates change in the desired direction.
Therefore, focus on solution-oriented talk rather than
on problem-oriented talk.
—John Walter

EXTERNALIZING THE PROBLEM

Externalizing the problem can help the client see the problem as something
that is separate from him or her—something that influences the client, to be
sure, but that doesn't always and everywhere control his or her life. This
intervention is borrowed from the narrative therapy of White and Epston
(1990). By externalizing problems, they gave their clients the freedom to
detach themselves from their problematic self-images. By asking clients how
a certain problem influenced their lives and relationships, they offered
clients the opportunity to gain more control. The problem can be perceived
as something that lies outside the client and usually has a negative influence
on him or her. In consequence, the professional and the client view the problem as the enemy that they can then fight together.

De Shazer (1984) used the metaphor of a game of tennis: As tennis players, the professional and the client (or clients) stand on the same side of the
net, and the problem is their opponent. One can also externalize the problem by drawing it or choosing a symbol for it. First, the problem is given a
name (X), for example, Depression, Anger, or (for a child with ADHD)
Hyper Monster. The question for the client is: "What do you call the thing

that troubles you?" Then one can look for times when X is absent or exerts no or less control (i.e., exceptions) and find out what the client is doing differently at such moments. One may also ask the client when X definitely manifests itself and how he or she deals with it. Depending on the client's needs, one can devote more or less time to the problem. In this way, the client's competence and confidence that it is possible for him or her to exert more control can be enhanced. It may also dissolve the need to blame others for the situation, as one can collaborate with others to gain more control.

Narrative therapy uses the phrase "unique outcomes" where exceptions are concerned and views the two terms as interchangeable. De Shazer (1991), however, noted a marked difference: A unique outcome happens only once, whereas exceptions are repeatable until the exceptions to the rule of the problem become the new rule.

Scaling Questions for Externalizing the Problem

At each session the client can indicate on a scale of 10 to 0 to what extent the problem has control of him or her. A 10 means that the client is in total control of the problem, and a 0 that the problem has complete control of the client. If there is more than one client, the scaling question can be put to everyone present. It goes without saying that, in most cases, the problem is less noticeable or even gone if the client's control has increased, though this is not spelled out in so many words.

Some solution-focused scaling questions that the professional can ask when externalizing the problem are:

- "Where do you now rate yourself on the control scale?"
- "What was last week's (or last session's) rating?"
- If the rating is higher than the previous rating: "How did you manage to reach a higher rating?"
- If the rating is the same as the previous rating: "How did you manage to maintain the same rating?"
- If the rating is lower than the previous rating: "What did you do before to get ahead again? What did you do in a comparable situation in the past that was successful?"
- "What have important others in your life noted about you this past week? How did that influence their behavior toward you?"

Additional solution-focused questions that the professional can ask when externalizing the problem (X) are:

- "What do you do when X has the upper hand?"
- "How does X manage to control you?"
- "What are you doing (differently) when you have X under control?"
- "How do you manage to get X under control?"
- "What do you do when you're planning to attack X?"
- "What weapons do you have at your disposal to do that?"
- "How have you recently been able to deceive X?"

Appendix G is a protocol for externalizing the problem.

PROJECTION INTO THE FUTURE

Dolan (1998) and Isebaert (2005) have described a number of ways to encourage clients to examine themselves in their current situations as seen from the future, including a letter from the future, advice from and reflection by the client's older and wiser self, reflection on the client's situation 1 year in the future, and the 5-year plan. Covey (1989) describes a technique in which he lets the client describe what the individual would like to hear other people say at his or her own funeral. Experience has shown that only customers—clients who are motivated to change their own behavior—are willing to imagine how they can influence their present lives from the future. For clients who are still visitors or complainants, other interventions are advised (see Chapter 2).

Letter From the Future

The client receives the following assignment:

> Write a letter from the future to your current self. Choose a time in the future that is relevant to you (e.g., 1 year, 5 years). Have your future self from that period of time write to your current self that you are doing well, where you are, and what you're doing. Provide a description of the most important things you've done to get to that point. Finally, offer yourself a wise and kind piece of advice from the future.

In my capacity as trainer of the Mental Health Team of Doctors Without Borders, I coached counselors in northern Sri Lanka. The counselors were working in the refugee camps that were established during the war between the Tamil Tigers and the Sri Lankan government. As part of the training, counselors wrote themselves letters from the future. One of the counselors began to cry as she was writing. Afterward, she said that writing the letter made her

Write a letter from the future to your current self and allow yourself to be surprised by the impact that writing such a letter can have.

realize that she had to continue to take care of her children even though her husband was missing and her house had been set on fire a month earlier. "I felt dead inside. Writing this letter makes me feel alive again," she said.

For clients in relationship therapy, writing letters from the future turns out to offer many starting points for improving the relationship.

One's Older and Wiser Self
A client can be asked to imagine that many years have passed and that he or she has become older and wiser; however, the client still has his or her health, looks good, and still enjoys all his or her intellectual faculties. The professional can ask the client the following questions:

- "As you look back on your life, what advice would you give your younger self?"
- "As you look back on your life, what pleases you most about the life you have lived?"
- "Is there anything you wish you had done more or done differently?"
- "Can you indicate on a scale of 10 to 0 to what extent you have realized those wishes at this point in time?"
- "What do you hope your children will remember most fondly about your life with them?"
- "What would be the smallest step you could take to reach a higher number?"

The client can also go for a virtual walk with his or her older and wiser self and ask for advice about finding solutions to his or her problem.

One Year Later
The client describes a day in his or her life 1 year in the future. The description of what the client does over the course of the day may be elaborate and detailed. If the client has trouble making a choice, this can be a good intervention, as the consequences of both choices can become more apparent.

Even if the professional has the impression that the client does not discern the consequences of a certain choice, it can still be a valuable intervention.

The 5-Year Plan

The client is invited to look further ahead than usual. He or she is asked to divide a large sheet of paper into fields. On the vertical lines, the client lists (sub)goals that he or she would like to reach, which may concern, for example, work, relationships, or money. On the horizontal lines, the client writes down for each goal that he or she would like to attain in 5 years' time. In the fields the client writes down the steps that he or she can take to reach the goal, for example, "If that's where I want to be in 5 years, how far do I need to have come 3 years from now? What should I have achieved by then? And in 2 years? And in 1 year? And in 3 months? And what can I start doing now?" The 5-year plan helps clients formulate realistic goals and lay them out on a time line to illuminate what steps can be taken to maximize his or her chances of reaching the goals in 5 years' time.

Attending One's Own Funeral

The client is asked to imagine traveling in time to a funeral that will take place in 3 years' time. It turns out to be the client's own funeral. Four people will deliver eulogies: a member of the client's family, a friend, someone from work, and someone the client knows through his or her social network (e.g., religious organization, sports). The client is asked, "What would you like these people to say about you at your funeral? What difference would you like to have made in their lives?"

USING THE INTERACTIONAL MATRIX

The interactional matrix (see Table 7.1) is used to conduct solution-focused sessions from an interactional point of view and to invite the client to examine differences in perspective. The matrix is good at illustrating "how difference in a question can make a difference" (Walter & Peller, 1992, p. 177). The first position on the matrix is that of the self—that is, the client is asked to answer questions from his or her own point of view. The second position is that of the "other"—that is, the client is invited to respond as if he or she is speaking for someone else. In sessions with couples, for example, the husband might be asked what he thinks his wife would say if she were asked what would help solve the relationship problem. Subsequently, the wife is asked what she thinks her husband would say. In order to respond to such a question, the client must set aside his or her own ideas for awhile and imagine what the other person would say. This often leads one to look for new and different information and gain a better appreciation of the other person's point of view. The third position is one of distance—that is, the client can imagine what a fly on the wall would observe or what a video recording of the situation would show: "Suppose I were to see a video recording of the moment when your goal has been reached and a recording of the current situation. What differences would I see? How would I be able to tell that it's the video recording of the future situation?" Each question and each point of view in the interactional matrix encourages the client to think differently about the problem. In this way, exceptions (in the present and the past) and new solutions are easier to detect. The client also acquires more insight into the influence that his or her behavior has on the other person, which is likely to make the client more inclined to change something about his or her behavior. Use of the interactional matrix is also recommended for groups, for example in relationship and family therapy; it often heightens mutual understanding and opens up new perspectives.

In the related technique of circular interviewing, which is used in systems therapy, others are also asked to answer for the client. Sometimes one asks the client's explicit permission to engage in this somewhat unusual form of inquiry.

TABLE 7.1 Interactional Matrix			
Position of Observation	**Goal**	**Miracle**	**Exception**
Self	"What is the purpose of your visit?"	"What will you be doing differently then?" "What will the other person be doing differently?"	"What are you doing differently then?" * "What is the other person doing differently?"
Other	"What would he or she say your goal is?"	"What would he or she say you would be doing differently then?"	"What would he or she say you're doing differently then?"
Video/fly on the wall (distance)	"What would I think your goal is?" "What would I think the other person's goal is?"	"What will I see you (both), or the other person, doing differently then?"	"What do I see you (both), or the other person, doing differently then?"

* These questions can also be asked in the present or past tense: "What are you doing differently?" or "What were you doing differently?"

CASE 12

At a relationship therapy session where it is the goal of both partners to have a good relationship again, the following questions are asked of the husband: "How would your wife be able to tell that as a couple you are starting to get on the right track? What would your wife say you're doing differently then? And how do you think your wife would react to that?" The wife is asked: "How would your husband be able to tell that as a couple you are on the right track to reestablishing a good relationship? What would your husband say is needed to make that happen?" They are both asked: "How do you think your children would be able to tell that things are going better between the two of you? What will I see the two of you doing differently when the relationship is going better again?"

Another benefit of using the interactional matrix is that those who are absent can nonetheless be present, as it were, during the sessions.

CASE 13

At a certain point during a divorce and custody mediation, the man wants to halt the sessions. The mediator asks him: "Suppose you did continue. What would be the first small step you could take to be able to go on?" The man says he doesn't know. The mediator then asks a question from the interactional matrix: "Suppose we were to ask your children. What would they say the first step could be?" The woman quickly replies that the children would clam up if they were asked anything. The mediator asks: "And suppose your children didn't clam up. What would they say the first step could be?" The man says they would reply that the four of them could go do something fun, like go to the park or get a burger. In fact, the man and the woman think this is a nice idea and, after some encouragement from the mediator, they arrange to go to the park and the playground for an hour that same week if it's nice out or, if the weather's bad, to go out for a burger with the children. The mediator asks both clients to keep the conversation light in the children's presence and, if that proves difficult, to pretend that things are going reasonably well between them (for the children's sake).

EXERCISE 21

Take a situation in which you have a problem with another person. Ask yourself all the questions from the interactional matrix or have someone else ask you the questions, in the order in which they appear, from the goal to hypothetical solutions (miracle) to exceptions. Note the difference in your reactions and pay attention to how it alters your personal movie, the image you form of your life. Go to each row with a different point of view and pay attention to how your reaction and movie change. What differences do you perceive in your movie? Which questions make a greater difference or are most useful?

NONVERBAL STRATEGIES

Nonverbal strategies can be employed in solution-focused interviewing to help the client reach his or her goal. These include using a whiteboard or flip chart, making drawings, and applying topographic interventions.

Using a Whiteboard or Flip Chart

The professional and the client use a whiteboard, a flip chart, or a sheet of paper to outline in drawing and writing the solution-focused steps of goal formulation, exceptions, and scaling questions. It is recommended that the professional let the client do as much of the drawing and writing as possible in order to stimulate an active attitude on his or her part. As soon as the goal has been formulated, one can draw a circle on the board or paper and write the goal down in it. Next to the circle, one may draw a scale and indicate where on the scale the client currently is if 10 is the goal and 0 is the worst moment he or she has ever experienced. The professional can then ask solution-focused scaling questions: "How did you manage to be at that number? What would 1 point higher look like and what is needed for you to get there? And what else?" Around the circled goal formulation, one may draw a second circle in which the professional (or, better yet, the client him- or herself) writes down all the means on the whiteboard or flip chart that can bring the client closer to the goal, that is, the exceptions that have helped in the past and all the other possibilities that might help as well. When all the means have been noted in the second circle, the professional asks with which of these possibilities the client wants to get started and how others can help make that possibility a success. One or more of these means can be assigned as homework suggestions.

Making Drawings

The professional asks the client to make two drawings: one of the current problem and one of the preferred future that the client would like to realize. Then the client is asked to draw a road or a bridge from the first drawing to the second drawing. This exercise reveals how the client views the road or the bridge, what part of the road he or she has already traversed, and what part he or she has yet to travel. The steps that the client can take to reach the goal can also be sketched in a few additional drawings. In this way, one can make a solution-focused comic strip of, say, six drawings. The order in which the six drawings are made is important here. The first drawing is the current situation and incorporates the problem. Then the last drawing—the drawing in which the goal has been reached—is made. The drawings in between pertain to the steps the client can take to arrive at the situation in the last drawing.

If there are multiple clients, they can discuss the drawings together and compare them with each other's. The professional can then ask how the clients can reach their goal and in what way each client can assist the others in the process.

If the technique of externalizing the problem is used, the client may also draw the problem. What form, what colors, does the problem take? What does it look like? Does it scowl? Subsequently, the client can conceive a battle plan with which to conquer the problem. Others who may be of help, including the professional, may play along. The client may draw this plan on the same or a separate sheet of paper.

Using Topographic Interventions

Topographic interventions are interventions for which the professional acts as a director giving instructions as to where the client (or clients) should sit. Topographic interventions require that the professional not consider clients' or his own positioning in the room to be a matter of coincidence and insignificance but reflect on whether the physical space that everyone occupies is conducive to the conduct of the sessions.

Erickson, the psychiatrist mentioned in Chapter 1, often used topographic interventions to work with different combinations of client groups over the course of a single session. During a family session, for example, he asked the child to leave the room and had the mother take the child's place, explaining that when she is in her child's seat, she can think about him more keenly and put herself more in his place.

The professional, as well as the clients, mustn't be too attached to his or her own spot. When the professional acts in a supportive way, he or she can move his or her chair closer to the client. The reverse is important as well: By moving his or her chair back, the professional indicates that he or she does not want to be involved in a certain part of the session (see the discussion of interventions for clients who argue). If there are two professionals, for instance, in group therapy, different configurations are possible as well.

The professional can also change the seating plan during the session or go into a different room. Selekman wrote: "Sometimes we go into a completely different room when beginning this part of the assessment session. I say: Now we can talk about solutions and change—where you want to be when we have a successful outcome here" (1997, p. 57). Not every professional is in the fortunate position of having a "problem room" and a "solution room" at his or her disposal—nor is this necessary, needless to say.

A variation was provided by Metcalf (1998). In group therapy she uses a combination of topographic interventions and projection in time called the three-chairs technique. The first chair represents life 5 years ago, the second chair stands for the present, and the third chair signifies life in 5 years' time. The intervals can be decreased or increased. The group members are all invited to take a seat in the three chairs and talk about themselves as if the time indicated by the chair is now. The other group members may ask the following questions:

- "Are you happy?"
- "What was your greatest fear?"
- "In which chair did you feel less fear or more happiness?"
- "How did you manage to solve your problems in the past?"
- "What advice would have helped you then?"

CASE 14

During a relationship therapy session, husband and wife initially sit beside each other, facing the therapist. The mood is grim; they barely look at one another. The session proceeds entirely via the therapist. After awhile, when the therapist inquires about a mutual goal and exceptions and asks scaling questions, the clients are asked to sit at a 90-degree angle from each other. The therapist explains the reason for the change: The remainder of the session will be about collaborating to formulate a goal and ways to reach it. Somewhat surprised, the clients do as the therapist asks. This makes it easier for the clients to look at each other and design their joint goal. In addition, thanks to this topographic intervention, the therapist ceases to be the pivot of the session.

USING ROLE-PLAY (THE PRETEND TASK AND THE SURPRISE TASK)

Most clients assume that they have to wait until the problem has been solved before they can begin to behave differently. Rather than waiting for the problem to disappear of its own accord, pretending that the problem has been solved offers the client the opportunity to feel stronger and to experience the feeling of gaining some control of the problem. Therefore, the professional may invite the client to pretend that things are going better. This can happen during the session: The client or clients (e.g., a couple or a family) can pretend that the problem has been solved, that things are going better, or that the goal has already been reached in a role-play. In doing so, they are invited to pay particular attention to the differences with the current situation. The pretend task may also be offered as a homework suggestion. The task entails pretending for a certain period of time (an hour, a day) between sessions that part of the miracle has happened or that the client has already assigned a higher rating to the situation. If there is more than one client, everyone can guess when the others chose to carry out the pretend task. During the next session they can talk about what they noticed about each other. The pretend task is a behavioral task and therefore only suited to clients who are customers and who are motivated to change something about their own behavior.

A variation on this is the surprise task, which is also appropriate for customers only. One client is asked to do something (subtly) different to surprise the other in between sessions with the professional. The other person can try to work out what the surprise is and talk about it during the next session. He or she will be more inclined to pay attention to what the surprise might be, which leads to a more positive view (and often leads the other person to guess that the surprise entailed a entirely different set of desired behaviors). When the goal for adolescents is to surprise their parents, the surprise task may involve doing something positively startling.

The purpose of both tasks is to bring about exceptions in the clients' interactions. This can be a way of highlighting positive behavior and can lead problematic behavior to fade into the background. When this positive behavior is noticed, it gives clients something to build on.

INTERVENTIONS FOR CLIENTS IN CRISIS

Sometimes a client wants to make an appointment right away because he or she is experiencing a crisis. When dealing with crises, professionals often have a tendency to take the reins from the client and start working in a problem-focused manner. They have a notion that one cannot work in a solution-focused way until much later. However, even if the client is in crisis, one can productively intervene in a solution-focused way from the very start (Bakker & Bannink, 2008). After all, most people in crisis quickly stabilize if they are invited to direct their attention to what they want to be different (goal formulation) and to make use of their past successes and their competencies. In crisis situations, these are often (temporarily) hidden from view. Not all clients in crisis will accept the invitation to talk about their goals and how they want things to be, as they are often very intent on describing their problems. In that case, it may be wise to focus the conversation on competencies, that is, how the client copes and what strategies he or she deploys to keep his or her head above water. Some solution-focused questions for clients in crisis are:

- "What are your best hopes? What difference would that make?"
- "How can I help you?"
- "What have you already attempted and which of those things helped (even if only a little)?"
- "What would you like to be different?"
- "Suppose a miracle occurs while you're asleep tonight . . ." (the miracle question).
- "Suppose you were feeling calmer and everything became clearer to you. What would be different then?"
- "Suppose you were feeling calmer and everything became clearer to you. What is the first thing you would do?"
- "How do you keep your head above water?"
- "How did you manage to come here and ask for help?"
- "What are you doing to take care of yourself under these circumstances?"
- "Who (and what) do you think would help the most at this moment?"
- "How do you manage to . . . , given everything you've been through?"
- "What has helped you pull through up to now?"
- "What, in your opinion, is the most useful thing that I as a professional can do?"
- "Could things be worse than they are now?"
- "How come things aren't worse?"
- "What is the most important thing for you to remember in order for you to handle this situation?"
- "On a scale of 10 to 0, where 10 means that you're dealing optimally with the situation, and 0 means that you can't deal with it at all, how well are you dealing with all of this?"
- "How is it that you are already at that number?"
- "What would a higher number on the scale look like?"
- "How would you be able to tell that you were 1 point higher?"
- "How would you be able to go up 1 point?"
- "How motivated are you to go up 1 point?"
- "How much confidence do you have that you will succeed in going up 1 point?"
- "What difference would it make for you if you went up 1 point?"

INTERVENTIONS FOR CLIENTS WHO ANSWER THAT THEY DO NOT KNOW

Clients sometimes say that they don't know the answer to a question. This often leads to feelings of irritation, discouragement, or insecurity on the professional's part. It may be an indication that the client is not a customer yet and is therefore not prepared to reflect on these questions. It helps, then, to ask open questions, that is, questions that begin with the words "what," "how," and "when." If the professional asks closed questions, the risk that the client will respond with "I don't know" is much greater, especially with visitors and complainants. In such cases, it is not unusual for the professional to have to conclude at the end of the session that he or she has worked harder than the client.

Compare the following two questions about exceptions:

- "Has there been a moment recently when the problem was absent or was less of a problem?"
- "When has there been a moment recently when the problem was absent or was less of a problem?"

The first (closed) question invites the client to answer yes or no, after which the professional has to come up with something else. The second (open) question implies that there *have been* exceptions and invites the client to think and talk about them.

Some interventions and questions that the solution-focused professional can use when the client responds with "I don't know" are:

- You may ask yourself whether it's important to your client that he or she knows the answer to the question.
- You can simply wait. In most cases, your client will offer another response within 6 seconds. Mentally count t six, remain calmly seated, and look at the client expectantly.
- You can respond with "That's a difficult question, isn't it?" and wait for a reaction.
- You might reply: "Take a guess."
- You might say, "It's a difficult question," then continue with: "Suppose you did know" or "Suppose you pretended that you knew."
- "What would your life look like if you did know?"
- "What difference would it make if you did know?"
- "What would be better in your life if you did know?"

- You can say, "Suppose you did know. What would you say?" and wait for a response. The client will understand that you expect a real answer and that you respect him or her enough to grant him or her the time to formulate a good response. In Chapter 1 I wrote about hypothetical questions and my supposition that they primarily draw on the right cerebral hemisphere, by virtue of which the client often does know the answer to that question.
- "Of course you don't know yet, but what do you think?"
- "Suppose there's someone who knows you as well as you know yourself. What would that person say?"
- "If I were to ask your partner (child, colleague), what would he or she say?" (interactional matrix)
- "What would your partner (your best friend, an important person in the client's life) say about how you did that?"
- "Suppose your partner (your best friend, an important person in the client's life) were sitting right here. What would he or she say? Would he or she be surprised? Who would be the least surprised?"

EXERCISE 22

Choose a partner. One of you opens the conversation with: "I'm too embarrassed to tell you why I've come to you. I don't dare tell you." The other replies, "Suppose there is a solution," followed by "What difference would it make in your life?" or "What would your life look like then?" or "How would you be able to tell that there is a solution?" Other questions are possible, too.

When you do this exercise, you will discover that it isn't necessary for you to know anything about the problem or the secret to help your client achieve the future he or she hopes for. In due course, one can examine whether talking about the problem or disclosing the secret is at all necessary or useful.

INTERVENTIONS FOR CLIENTS WHO DO NOT WANT TO OR ARE UNABLE TO TALK ABOUT THEIR PROBLEMS

Sometimes a client will not or cannot talk about his or her problem. The reason may be that it involves a secret or that he or she is too embarrassed. I once had a client in treatment who refused to say anything about the incest with her father; if she did, she would no longer be able to deny that it had actually happened. For that same reason, she didn't want to write about it either. Under such circumstances, most professionals are at a loss as to how the session can continue.

In cases such as these, one does well to put the client at ease and to respect that the client isn't ready (yet) and may never be ready. In solution-focused interviewing one doesn't need to know what the problem is and what its origins are.

INTERVENTIONS FOR CLIENTS WHO ARGUE

Clients may keep getting into arguments or may not be able to stop arguing. Most clients see only one side of the coin: how the argument began and how it progressed. The other side (i.e., how one managed to put a stop to the argument) is routinely overlooked. If clients become more keenly aware, through the professional's questions, of their power to end an argument themselves and the fact that they need not persist in their usual patterns, the times when they are able to stop by themselves become the exceptions to the problem upon which they can build.

What follows are some tips for professionals when clients argue.

- You might say: "This is valuable time; it would be best if you did your arguing at home."
- You can move your chair back, thus indicating that you do not want to be involved in the conversation for awhile (a topographic inter- vention).
- You can leave the room, make yourself a cup of coffee, and return when your clients are done arguing.

Some solution-focused responses to and questions for clients who argue are:

- "Thank you for showing me how you argue. I've seen enough; as far as I'm concerned you can stop now."
- "Take all the time you need . . . I can see how important this is for you." (Usually, clients soon desist.)
- "In what way will arguing (here) help you reach your shared goal?"
- "How do you usually manage to end an argument? Which of those things can you apply right now?"

INTERVENTIONS TO INCREASE MUTUAL TRUST

Mutual trust among clients does not here refer to the clients' confidence in their ability to reach their collective goal. That kind of trust was discussed in Chapter 2. Nor will I elaborate here on the clients' faith in the professional, except to say that, in my view, the question whether one can put one's trust in the professional can only be answered by clients who have worked with him or her. Under consideration here is mutual trust in relationships. Many clients identify increasing mutual trust as the goal of the therapy. It is important to keep in mind, however, that this is a means rather than a goal. "What difference would it make for you both if you were to trust each other again? How would your life together be different?"—these questions bring the mutual preferred future into view.

Lewicki and Wiethoff described the concept of trust, trust development, and trust repair. They argued that mutual trust is the glue that holds relationships together. They provided the following definition of trust: "an individual's belief in, and willingness to act on the basis of, the words, actions, and decisions of another" (Lewicki & Wiethoff, 2000, p. 87). According to them, sharing a collective goal is one of the ways to build or rebuild mutual trust.

Susskind and Cruikshank (1987) claimed that it is unrealistic to demand mutual trust from clients. Trust must be earned. The most important consideration for each client in trusting the other is reciprocity: Why should I stand by agreements if the other person doesn't? The professional must therefore assume that the sessions commence without mutual trust and that mutual trust can only develop if the clients behave in accordance with the prerequisite of reciprocity.

Kelman (2005) described the difficulty of building mutual trust in relationships, which enemies such as the Israelis and the Palestinians encounter: How can you work on the peace process in the complete absence of mutual trust and how can you build mutual trust if you haven't even started the peace process? Among other things, he described the answer as lying in small steps toward the collective goal ("successive approximation of commitment and reassurance," p. 644). Solution-focused scaling questions, which represent an invitation to work toward successive approximation of a desired outcome, can be very useful in this respect.

Some solution-focused questions about mutual trust and about how to increase trust are:

- "What has the other person said that gave you the sense that he or she wants to find a solution to the problem?"
- "What has given you the sense that the other person understands you, even if only to a very small degree?"
- "Suppose there were more mutual trust between you. What would change or be different in your relationship?"
- "How can (more) mutual trust help you reach your shared goal?"

- "If a 10 means that mutual trust is optimal and a 0 that there is no mutual trust at all, what rating would you give? How do you manage to be at that number?"
- "What would 1 point higher on the scale look like?"
- "What would have changed in your relationship then?"
- "What would help to go up 1 point? How can you contribute to that?"
- If the client thinks the other person should change: "What would you yourself be doing differently then?"
- "At what rating would both of you like to end up? What number would you find (sufficiently) acceptable?"
- "How would you be able to tell that you were at that number? How else? And how else?"
- "When in the past did you trust each other? How did you do that?"
- "Which of those things could you now do again to get closer to your goal?"

CASE 15

During a mediation concerning a custody arrangement, mutual trust between the former spouses has completely disappeared. The clients find it important that trust be sufficiently restored for the sake of the children. The mediator asks both of them how they might be able to regain that mutual trust. The man says that he would consider it a sign of trust if the woman gave him her cell phone number. At this point, he is a complainant; he thinks the other person should change. Given their history, however, the woman is not prepared to do so. The mediator asks: "Suppose she did give you the number. What would you do differently then?" The man says he would then mail a birthday card to his daughter. At that moment, the man realizes that he could of course mail a card right now, regardless of whether he has the woman's cell phone number, and he decides to do so. This produces a small positive change in the communication between him and the children. The woman is appreciative of this, which in turn produces a small positive change between the two parents as well.

INTERVENTIONS TO IMPROVE MUTUAL COMMUNICATION

It is often the clients' wish to improve mutual communication—not only to solve the existing problem but also to be able to work things out together, without the help of a third party, should a new problem arise. Here too clients often identify the improvement of mutual communication as a goal, although it actually constitutes another means of reaching the preferred future. The professional does well to keep this distinction firmly in mind, as the sessions might fail if this means proves unattainable. If the collective goal (e.g., a solid cooperative relationship) has been formulated clearly, there will be multiple roads to Rome, the improvement of mutual communication being one.

Some solution-focused questions about mutual communication and about how communication can be improved are:

- "If you both rate the quality of your communication at this moment, where 10 = excellent and 0 = very poor, what rating would you give?"
- "How do you manage to be at that number?"
- "What would 1 point higher on the scale look like?"
- "Suppose you communicated well (again). What would have changed in your relationship?"
- "How can (better) mutual communication help you reach your preferred future?"
- "What would you be doing differently then?"
- "How would the other person be able to tell that you're up 1 point?"
- "How would you be able to reach a higher rating?"
- "What can the other person do to help you move up 1 point?"
- "What can you do to help the other person move up 1 point?"
- "At what rating would you both like to end up? What number would you consider satisfactory?"
- "How would you be able to tell that you were at that number? How else? And how else?"
- "When did you communicate well in the past? How did you do that?"
- "Which of those things could you try again to get closer to your goal?"

SUMMARY

- The possibilities of externalizing the problem were discussed in this chapter.
- The use of projection into the future (letter from the future, advice from and reflection by one's older and wiser self, reflection on one's situation 1 year in the future, the 5-year plan, and attending one's own funeral) and use of the interactional matrix were described.
- Nonverbal techniques (using a whiteboard or flip chart, making

drawings, applying topographic interventions) and the use of role-play (with the pretend task and the surprise task) were explained.

- Solution-focused questions for clients in crisis, clients who answer that they don't know the answer to a question, clients who will not or cannot talk about their problem, and clients who argue were outlined.
- Solution-focused questions for increasing the clients' mutual trust and improving the clients' mutual communication were discussed.

CHAPTER 8

Working With Other Professionals

> If you have an apple and I have an apple and we exchange
> apples then you and I will still each have one apple. But if
> you have an idea and I have an idea and we exchange these
> ideas, then each of us will have two ideas.
>
> —George Bernard Shaw

PUTTING TOGETHER A GOOD TEAM

For his book on success, de Bono interviewed Chris Bonington, a famous mountaineer and journalist. Bonington said his successes wouldn't have been possible without his talent for picking a good team: "Successful management is where people at the end of the day say: yes, that was a good thing" (de Bono, 1984, p. 11).

> The first thing in picking a team is to decide what it is you're trying to do. You then decide how you're going to do it. And from these two things you decide both how many people you need, what kind of people, and what skills you require. Having decided all this, you then sit down and try to fit the right person into the job. This might sound terribly obvious, but it's amazing how many expeditions (and I suspect how many other functions) don't allow that very simple kind of line. (p. 158)

In other words, formulating a goal and devising ways to reach it are of the utmost importance in putting together a team.

De Bono (1984) viewed choosing colleagues, like solving a problem or conflict, as a design exercise. In their work, colleagues must have a clear idea of what is expected of them. How do they fit into the larger whole? Gaining a clear sense of this is valuable, as having advance knowledge of a well-defined goal has an enormously motivating effect as one strives toward it. After that, success is self-maintaining. And although it is by no means always possible for professionals to choose the people they work with, it is usually possible to agreeably collaborate with others in a solution-focused way.

WORKING WITH PROBLEM-FOCUSED PROFESSIONALS

If one works with other professionals, it is very likely that they are still thinking and acting in a problem-focused way. Therefore, they place greater emphasis on problems (and are more prone to finding problems). A few points for collaborations suggested by Berg and Steiner (2003) are:

- Make sure you keep your clients' goals in mind and that their goals are always your guide. It is easy to get distracted. The session may get bogged down in a lengthy discussion of problems or complaints about another person or other people. In a meeting, always ask what the goal of the meeting is so that you can work in a solution-focused way.
- Establish a positive framework. Making the (hidden) positive motivation of everyone involved explicit may put the clients and their advisors at ease and allow them to work in a goal-oriented manner.
- Compliment other professionals and always explicitly express your appreciation of the progress being made and the favorable collaboration.
- During the meeting, regularly point out the successes and strong points of all the attendees and summarize them. Be generous. Use tentative language. It increases the chances of your being listened to and may elicit better cooperation from others. Examples are: "It sounds as if what you actually want is . . . " and "Could it be that . . .?"

WORKING WITH REFERRERS

Referrers are people from other agencies who have an interest in the outcome of the sessions because they work with the same client or because they have referred the client to the professional. Examples of referrers are the family doctor, a medical specialist, a teacher, a probation office, and the court. Referrers often have clear-cut ideas about what is necessary and what should be done, and they often work within a problem-focused framework. The interventions that one can use when working with colleagues apply here as well. Find out what the referrer wants and what his or her goal is. What has he or she done that has been of help to the client or clients? Show respect and offer acknowledgment and appreciation. The professional can establish an excellent solution-focused collaboration with the referrer, too.

Chevalier (1995) discussed collaborations with referrers. She saw the referrer as a "second client." Her advice was to go along with the referrers' views, compliment them on their involvement, and ask them about the times when the cooperative relationship between the referrer and the client has been better (exceptions). One may ask what the referrer has done to improve the relationship and whether he or she is prepared to lend further help. According to Chevalier, one may therefore also give referrers homework suggestions. These depend on the referrer's motivation: Is he or she a visitor, complainant, or customer? If the referrer is a customer, one might suggest that he or she continue doing what works (if there were things that were helping) or observe what works (if nothing has helped yet or if the referrer is a complainant).

It may be useful to directly involve the referrers in the sessions. Some solution-focused questions for referrers are:

- "What is the smallest change you can accept from the client at this time?"
- "When was the last time that he or she was doing a bit better or acted a bit more as you would like?"
- "What was he or she doing differently then?"
- "What do you think helped him do that?"
- "Can you indicate on a scale of 10 to 0 to what extent you're willing to do some of the things that were helpful then?"

Other solution-focused questions for the referrer can be found in Appendix H.

WORKING WITH COLLEAGUES

Colleagues' frames of reference have usually been established and developed over a long period of time. There is little point in challenging or fighting these referential frameworks. Instead of criticizing them, it is better to adopt the stance of not knowing, which involves respectful questions like:

"You must have a good reason to hold this opinion or make this statement. Please tell me more."

In this context, I refer to Bateson (1979), who described how ideas develop from two or more different descriptions of the same process. The reward, the idea, emerges from the differences between the descriptions. By way of illustration, he used the metaphor of depth perception. The right eye sees the surroundings in one way, and the left eye sees the surroundings in another way. The difference between what the two eyes see leads to the bonus of depth perception. It isn't that the right eye is right and the left eye wrong, or vice versa; rather, having different ideas, or different views, may lead to an added bonus, such as a new idea or discovery.

It may be helpful to pay attention to what your colleague wants to achieve in his or her interaction with you (goal formulation). Paying compliments and showing respect are important, too. If colleagues are interested in the solution-focused method, that is, if they are customers as far as learning about the solution-focused model is concerned, you can tell them how solution-focused interviewing is conducted and how this can help clients.

The solution-focused professional is always advised to use "Yes, and" instead of "Yes, but" (see Chapter 2). Repeat exercise 12 to experience the difference between conversations with others in which "Yes, but" and "Yes, and" are used.

In most cases the professional works alone. Sometimes not one but two professionals are present during the session, as in group therapy or co-mediation. The two professionals can work in tandem if they know each other well and have experience collaborating, in which case they can deftly complement each other. It is recommended that professionals unambiguously indicate what their methodology is, not just to their clients and referrers, but also to each other. If two solution-focused professionals work together, the sessions can be conducted in a solution-focused manner from beginning to end. On the other hand, if a solution-focused professional and a problem-focused professional collaborate, the problem-focused professional can start with the introductions, explain the structure of the session, and take stock of and analyze the problem. The solution-focused professional can then take over to ask questions about goal formulation, after which they may proceed to examine what the clients would like to have achieved by the end of the session or sessions. In this way, the problem-focused professional can acquaint him- or herself with the solution-focused professional's modus operandi and note how solution-focused sessions differ from problem-focused sessions.

SOLUTION-FOCUSED CLIENT DISCUSSIONS, SUPERVISION, AND PEER CONSULTATION

Working effectively in a solution-focused way is also possible during client discussions, supervision, and peer consultation. A colleague who wants to present a case to the team or submit a case for peer consultation can first be asked what the goal is: What needs to be achieved by the end of the discussion for him or her to be able to say that presenting the case has been useful and valuable? In my experience, it often turns out that the actual content of the case need not be discussed, which can save a lot of time. Moreover, not every professional who presents a case is a customer; sometimes he or she is a complainant who mainly wants appreciation for all his or her efforts and some acknowledgment of any feelings of irritation, discouragement, or insecurity. A question like "How do you manage to put up with this client?" is more fitting then. After all, only a professional who is a customer will be prepared to listen to what he or she might do differently in the sessions with clients. Only then does it become meaningful for colleagues to offer advice.

It is interesting how the language used by the person presenting the case determines the reaction of the team members. When words like "extremely difficult," "complicated," and "irremediable" are used to introduce a case, the other team members often lean back and do not feel very motivated. Or the other team members may immediately dispense all manner of advice when the colleague who presents the case is a complainant. It is better to use solution-focused words like "challenging" and "interesting" in order to rouse colleagues' curiosity and willingness to act.

Differences of insight may persist: Solution-focused sessions are simply very different from problem-focused sessions. Problem-focused professionals sometimes argue that the connection between the problem and its solution does not receive enough attention. Another objection that may be raised is that the clients' perceptions are given too much attention, at the expense of expert problem analyses and interventions by the problem-focused professional. It rarely makes sense to fight these often deep-rooted views, nor is it always necessary. It is more valuable to conduct outcome research about the different forms of interviewing.

One can open a supervisory meeting in a solution-focused way by asking the supervisee about the goal of the supervision:

- "What would you like to have achieved by the end of this supervision so that you can say that it has been useful to you?"
- "How would you notice that you didn't need any further supervision?"
- "What would you be doing differently then, or what would I see you do differently then (in concrete, positive, and realistic behavioral terms)?"
- "If I were to make a recording of how you work right now and a recording of how you'll work at the end of this supervision, what differences would I see, and how would I know which is the recording taken after the supervision?"
- "How would your colleagues be able to tell that you've reached your goal?"
- "How would they feel about that?"
- "What difference would that make for your colleagues and your clients?"
- "What would your colleagues do differently once you've reached your goal?"

Following these questions about goal formulation, one may inquire about exceptions ("When have you already caught a glimpse of where you want to end up?") and ask scaling questions ("If 10 means that you have reached your goal in full, and 0 means that you haven't done anything to reach your goal, where are you now?") with their customary follow-up questions. In solution-focused supervision, one frequently inquires about the supervisee's areas of competence and offers compliments and positive character interpretations. One may also ask the four basic solution-focused questions from Chapter 3.

During supervision it is worthwhile to discuss topics other than the clients about whom the supervisee has questions or with whom the sessions have come to a standstill. Otherwise, the supervisee often ends up feeling inadequate, because all the attention is directed at impasses and failures. Problem-focused supervision often causes insecurity on the supervisee's part, which surely cannot be the intention of supervision. Talking about successful sessions and about how the supervisee managed to make them happen often generates more self-confidence and a more pleasant atmosphere: "How did you succeed in making this treatment a success? What helped?"

It has been my experience that a great number of the clients who are discussed during supervision and who are viewed as being "stuck" are clients with whom the professional thinks he or she has a customer relationship (or whose level of motivation and relationship type the professional simply hasn't considered), but with whom there is, rather, a visitor or complainant relationship. If one asks those clients questions and gives them homework suggestions that befit a customer relationship, the sessions will stagnate. In that case, a good question for the supervisee is: "Suppose this client weren't a customer but a visitor or complainant. What would you do or have done differently?"

In many training programs, students only learn about modification procedures that are appropriate for customers, who are usually a minority in professionals' caseloads. It is high time that training programs pay more attention to clients' motivation for behavior change and to how professionals can match said motivation, which I believe could prevent impasses, failures, and burnout. A number of solution-focused peer consultation models are described in Chapter 11.

CONDUCTING SOLUTION-FOCUSED MEETINGS

Team and company meetings are often dominated by complaints or problems. In consequence, meetings—which are often long lasting—are not usually deemed enjoyable activities by most professionals. They yield little benefit because they focus on the past; on the question of who is to blame; and on hypotheses, analyses, and questions related to the problem. The atmosphere is often negative and the participants' willingness to act is limited.

Problem-focused meetings can be turned into solution-focused meetings (see Table 8.1 for the differences). The atmosphere improves if the goal of the meeting is defined, if attention is paid to people's and the team's strengths, and if previous successes are discussed. Suggestions from coworkers are appreciated and put to use. A greater willingness to act emerges, which can be further enhanced by questions about what might be the first concrete step that all those involved can take in order to get closer to the collective goal.

CONSENSUS BUILDING

In order to build a consensus, a number of participants with divergent interests must convene to discuss a topic prior to the final decision-making point in order to develop an action plan together. The benefit of gathering stake-

	TABLE 8.1	
	Differences Between the Problem-Focused Meeting Model and the Solution-Focused Meeting Model	
Problem-focused meeting model	**Solution-focused meeting model**
Focus is on problems.	Focus is on the (collective) goal.
The problem is analyzed and a hypothesis formulated.	Positive traits and resources of all attendees and the team as a whole are explored.
The emphasis is on exploring the history of the problem or looking for the person or people to blame.	The emphasis is on attendees' and the team's previous successes.
Questions about the past are raised.	Suggestions from attendees and the team are put to use.
No predictions are made, and no action is taken.	The attendees' and the team's first step is formulated, and taking action is emphasized.

holders to draft a proposal is that it often leads to greater connectedness with and a greater sense of responsibility for the eventual outcome. A broad coalition offers a better basis for the realization of proposals.

In solution-focused consensus building, all attendees are asked to think about the preferred future. This first involves mapping the desired collective goal (goal formulation) and then working backward to the here and now. Chapter 1 touched upon Erickson's approach of asking students to read the last page of a book and speculate about what preceded. Covey wrote in this respect:

> To begin with the end in mind means to start with a clear understanding of your destination. It means to know where you're going so that you better understand where you are now and so that the steps you take are always in the right direction. (1989, p. 98)

Some solution-focused questions for consensus building are:

- "Can all of you give a description of what the situation will look like a year from now" or another relevant period of time "when everything goes well or gets better?"
- "What has been done to make that happen?"
- "Who has helped in reaching this point?"

- "What exactly did those people do?"
- "What have you yourself done to reach this point?"
- "How did you come up with that fine idea?"
- "And what else did you do?"
- "What did you worry about a year ago?" (considering present circumstances)
- "What has helped ease your worries?"

The answers are summarized and, on the basis of the suggestions made, one determines what one wishes for the situation to look like a year from now. One then goes on to discuss the proposed plan and decides what the first step toward achieving that goal will be. If there are too many people involved or if the problem is a wide-ranging and complex one, one may also apply a variation of consensus building, that is, a minimum plan.

Some solution-focused questions for a minimum plan in consensus building are:

- "What happens if you do nothing?"
- "What are you able to do to help?"
- "What would happen if you did that?"
- "What will be the next step? Who will execute it, with whom, and when?"

Coleman and Deutsch (2000) discussed how in the Mohawk tradition it is the chief's responsibility to think seven generations ahead. It is based on the notion that decisions that were made seven generations ago still influence people living today and that decisions made today will influence the seven generations that follow. Although this kind of long-term thinking is rare, exceptions do exist. One such exception is focused social imaging, whereby participants in social conflicts are asked to withdraw from the present for awhile and step into the future:

> They are asked to put themselves into a future approximately twenty to thirty years from the present, in which their concerns have been effectively dealt with. As the participants begin to develop some sense of the social arrangements and institutions in this idealized future, discussion ensues. Together, they begin to create a vision for a community that has the institutions and relationships necessary to effectively address their shared concerns. (Coleman & Deutsch, 2000, p. 447)

Subsequently, the participants are asked to go slowly back in time and to formulate steps to make such institutions and relationships a reality.

WORKING TOGETHER IN GROUPS AND ORGANIZATIONS

Selekman (1997) identified six elements that can increase the success of group collaborations:

- Create a climate of respect, tolerance, and trust. Everyone has a voice and is treated respectfully. Everyone is treated as an equal and gets time to ventilate his or her story and, if necessary, concerns.
- Allow communication to proceed in a flexible and spontaneous manner. Too much structure is often counterproductive. Problem-focused conversations can be turned into solution-focused conversations. This generates mutual trust and appreciation, causing group members to feel encouraged to develop ideas and think of solutions.
- Provide a context in which different points of view can complement each other ("Yes, and"). New ways of looking at problems may thus emerge and new "problem-free" stories can be developed. This reassures group members about the situation.
- Provide a context in which one can experiment with different points of view and uncertainty is viewed as an opportunity for further exploration.
- Consensus is unnecessary for and irrelevant to the creation or discovery of new possibilities. Because there is no emphasis on reaching consensus, one may discover that there are many ways of looking at a situation, one being no more correct than another (see Bateson, 1979).
- There are no restrictive boundaries as to who does what. One often doesn't need to appoint people to execute tasks or responsibilities. If group members notice that their knowledge and expertise are respected, they're prepared to take more risks by undertaking additional action.

Bunker mentioned investigating the future ("the future search") as a method of collaboration for large groups of people:

> Then there are activities that ask people to dream about their preferred future in the face of the reality they now confront. Finally,

there is work to agree on the best ideas for future direction, and action planning to begin to make it happen. Although the overall plan is rational, the activities themselves are interesting, fun, and challenging. The interactions that occur among people create energy and motivation for change. (2000, p. 550)

Metcalf stated that in solution-focused brief therapy groups, the focus is directed at times when the problem of the individual or group is not a problem:

The beauty of such groups emerges when members observe how others are able to discover such problem-free times, motivating them to try and find such discoveries within themselves. When group members participate in this collaborative process, the strategies grow geometrically. The result? Group conversations become even more efficient in promoting discussion of problem-free times and clients become more action oriented. (1998, p. 7)

It is worth noting that the phrase "problem-free times" is negatively phrased and hence still problem focused. A positive formulation whereby clients indicate what they would like to see instead of the problem would be more solution focused.

A solution-focused approach can also be helpful in realizing an organization's goal. When problem descriptions and problem analyses make way for solution-focused conversations among the management of an organization, hope and motivation among the staff may increase and positive changes may occur in the organization (Stam & Bannink, 2008).

According to Cauffman, the solution-focused manager's adage is: "Together Each Achieves More" (2003, p. 207). The combination of the first letter of each word in the sentence represents every organization's greatest asset: TEAM. He offered some advice for the solution-focused manager to elicit and boost coworkers' cooperation.

- Always be on the lookout for the resources that your coworkers possess and ask your coworkers about the solutions that they themselves have already found. Showing an interest in the modest successes that occur over the course of the collaboration is at least as important as the end result. Accept failures as inherent components of progress.

- Take an interest in the moments when the problems occur less or not at all. Create an atmosphere in which change becomes possible and desirable, and do not fruitlessly fight problems.
  Pay compliments, approve of everything that is in any way approvable, and congratulate your coworkers as often as possible.
  Practice judo rather than boxing. Bend like a reed and always bounce back.
- Be empathetic and put yourself in the other person's place.
  Do not be afraid to show empathy.
- Adapt to your coworkers' verbal and nonverbal styles.
- Make sure that your coworkers' need for stability and continuity is always respected. Always try to further develop your working relationships.
- Allow your coworkers to choose tasks for themselves (if feasible, from a range of possibilities); do not impose them.
  Never forget that, as manager, you are an expert in managing processes, while your coworkers are experts regarding the content of the work.
- It falls to your coworkers to carry out their tasks well, while you, as manager, guide them in this and create the preconditions necessary for them to do this.

In her book *Counseling Toward Solutions*, Metcalf quoted Ben Furman, a solution-focused psychiatrist and trainer who in business meetings does not ask the miracle question but asks the dream team question: How will your team function in the future when it works together like a dream team? (1998). He proceeds to inquire about goal formulation and what the benefits of reaching the goal will be, in part to increase motivation. He encourages clients to view the path toward the goal as a stepwise process and asks them what actions are needed tomorrow, next week, and next month. He also looks at the resources within and outside the company and asks staff members to look for exceptions. Instead of using the term "exceptions," he refers to "times when progress toward the stated goal took place" during another project. Questions one can ask are:

- "Who contributed to that?"
- "What about recent progress? Who or what made a difference?"
- "How did you do that?"

During a follow-up meeting one can assess what progress has been made and who deserves credit for it. More information about this can be found at www.reteaming.com. Questions for training management and staff can be found in Chapter 10.

SUMMARY

- To put together a team, the goal of the enterprise must first be clear.
- It is recommended that professionals indicate what their methodology is, not just to their clients and referrers, but also to each other. A successful solution-focused collaboration can be realized with problem-focused colleagues and referrers, as well as in groups and organizations.
- One can also engage in successful solution-focused work when collaborating with colleagues, as well as during client discussions, supervisory and peer consultation meetings, and team or company meetings.
- Solution-focused tips for managers were provided in this chapter.

CHAPTER 9

Impasse and Failure

Anyone who has never made a mistake has
never tried anything new.
—Albert Einstein

SEVEN WAYS OF BRINGING ABOUT FAILURE

Not all sessions go as planned. Sometimes stagnation occurs, causing the professional and the client to lose hope that the client's goal can be reached.

There are seven ways of bringing about failure. De Shazer (1991) stressed the importance of a sound goal formulation to a successful outcome. The goal—the presence of desired behavior and the desired future situation, rather than the absence of undesired behavior and the undesired situation of the present or past—must be expressed in concrete, positive terms. "Some failures can be seen as related to a difficulty in shifting from a 'problem/complaint-focused language game' into a 'solution-focused language game'" (p. 159).

In the problem-focused medical model, the decrease or absence of the problem (the undesired situation) is presented as the goal, but that doesn't necessarily mean that the desired situation has been reached.

Too often the client is willing to accept the absence of the complaint as "goal enough," but the absence can never be proved and, therefore, success or failure cannot be known by either therapist or client.

Unless clearly established through negotiations beforehand, even the presence of significant changes is not enough to prove the absence of the complaint. . . .

. . . This is, of course, another point at which the conversations between therapist-client can break down, when a digressive or stability narrative develops rather than a progressive narrative. The fault here is situated neither on the therapist's side nor on the client's side: both are in it together. Most frequently, failures that develop in this way mean that the therapist has been unable to help the client see exceptions as differences that can be made to make a difference. (de Shazer, 1991, p. 159)

On the subject of finding exceptions, Wittgenstein said that they are often so close in front of us that we fail to spot them: "The aspects of things that are most important for us are hidden because of their simplicity and familiarity (one is unable to notice something—because it is always before one's eyes)" (1953/1968, p. 129). If the client doesn't even notice the exceptions or dismisses them as trivial, they remain hidden. The client doesn't recognize them as differences that make a difference, which may bring about stagnation or failure.

Duncan et al. (1997, 2004) claimed to have learned from their clients that there are four ways of ensuring the failure of a treatment, and I have encountered two additional ways as well.

The first way that Duncan et al. (1997) identified is anticipating failure. If the professional assumes that a treatment will not produce any result, it is likely that it in fact won't. Rosenhan (1973) demonstrated, by means of an experiment in which he and a number of colleagues (among them Seligman, the founder of positive psychology) had themselves admitted to a psychiatric hospital as pseudopatients, that what one expects is what one subsequently believes to be seeing. If one expects to see someone who is psychotic, that is indeed what one sees, the research showed. It required a lot of effort on the part of Rosenhan and his colleagues to get discharged from the hospital, even though they had been saying from the time of admission that they were feeling fine and that their (fictitious) hallucinations had disappeared. Those who treated and nursed them continued to see signs of illness in much normal behavior. That is how it works with failures as well. If one expects failure, one sees failure. Grave diagnostic labels and fat case files tend to have the same effect. Mention of a serious personality disorder, for instance, often has a negative effect on the professional's hope and expectation that the problem can be solved successfully. Therefore, thick files from the hospital or the court had better remain closed, because their problem-focused contents are not usually relevant to reaching the client's goal and may deprive professionals of any hope for a successful outcome.

The second way in which a treatment might fail, according to Duncan et al. (1997), concerns a discrepancy between the professional's theory and the client's. Holding fast to one's own theory may lead to too much simplification and may limit the possibilities for bringing about change. Someone who brings a hammer thinks everything should be nailed down; collaboration with another person may fail if the latter doesn't care for hammers or thinks no nails should be used.

The third way Duncan et al. mentioned is continuing with an approach that doesn't help. If problems do not improve, one had better try another tactic (if something doesn't work, do something else). Chronicity of a problem is often caused not by the client's attributes but by the ineffective way in which the client and (sometimes) the professional try to solve the problem (Watzlawick et al., 1974).

The fourth way in which Duncan et al. believed a treatment may fail has to do with a failure to take the client's motivation into account. As far as they are concerned, unmotivated clients do not exist. However, the client's goal may differ from the professional's. If the latter sticks to his or her own goal and doesn't examine what the client wants to achieve, or if the professional fails to give the client's goal precedence over his or her own, failure is inevitable. The chance of success increases if the professional is prepared to adopt the client's frame of reference and theory of change and if he or she is willing to go along with the client's worldview. It is also vital that one cling less to one's own theory and devote more attention to the cooperative relationship with the client (I refer here to the classification of visitor, complainant, and customer relationships).

Chapter 1 argued that resistance is not a useful concept and that a solid cooperative relationship with the client is hampered if the professional thinks in terms of resistance. Validate the client, recognize his or her concerns, make sure that the client does not suffer a loss of face, and believe in the client and his or her possibilities.

To these five ways of bringing about failure described by de Shazer and Duncan et al., I believe we can add two more. A treatment may also fail if the client's goal is unrealistic or unattainable. Is one dealing with a limitation or a problem? In the case of a limitation, the goal is to deal with that limitation the best one can. In the case of a problem, the goal is what the client wants to see instead of the problem.

CASE 16

A client in solution-focused psychotherapy is asked the miracle question. He describes an unrealistic situation in which both of his parents, who died a few years before, are still alive (which, incidentally, is a means, not a goal). Only then would he no longer feel lonely and listless; he would be joyful and feel happy again. The solution-focused therapist acknowledges the client's sorrow and asks a hypothetical question: "Suppose your parents were still alive. What would be different in your life?" The client says he would have a place where he would feel safe and someone who cared about him. The therapist goes on to ask: "What difference would it make for you to have a safe place and the sense that someone cares about you?" Then: "What might you be able to do to attain a sense of that safety and the sense that someone cares about you?" The client realizes that he can try to mend his relationship with his only sister. In the wake of a serious argument, he has seen little of her. After he calls her, the relationship slowly begins to improve.

Even if a client puts forward an unrealistic goal, the solution-focused professional can examine with him or her what this would mean for him or her and what possibilities there are.

If no collective goal is formulated when there are two (or more) clients and the sessions are nevertheless continued, there is risk of failure as well. This is the seventh and final way in which failure might be ensured. The same applies if one only talks about means ("roads to Rome") and the goal (Rome) has not been clearly delineated first. The risk that the professional and the clients become stuck in the unattainability of a means is considerable then.

CASE 17

A client states as her treatment goal that she wants to become more assertive, especially with her husband. This is not a goal, however, but a means. The goal only comes into view if the therapist asks: "What would your life look like if you were as assertive as you would like to be? What difference would that make for you and your husband? What would you be doing differently? How would your husband react to that? How would other people notice that you were more assertive and that you had reached your goal?" However, the therapist accepts "becoming more assertive" as the goal, and assertiveness training is begun. After some time, it turns out that the client has not made any progress; she still dares to do very little, especially at home. The client and the therapist lose hope for change. Their motivation dwindles, too. The therapist is irritated: Didn't they extensively practice all this in role-plays? The therapy probably would have gone differently and more positively if the therapist had had the client come up with a sound goal at the very start of the sessions.

Some solution-focused questions for the professional, outlined by Walter and Peller (1992), for dissolving an impasse are:

- Who is a customer? Are you working with someone who is willing to change?
- Are you working on your client's goal? Make sure that the client wants to reach the goal more than you do and speaks more than you do so that you can sit back.
- Are you dealing with not just a complaint or wish (to bring about a different feeling or a change in another person) but with an actual goal, the attainment of which lies within the client's control (a soundly and positively formulated goal)?
- Do you want too much too soon? Look for smaller changes, use scaling questions regarding the goal or the exceptions, or counsel the client not to move too fast.
- Is the client not doing his or her homework? Only provide feedback for the client to reflect on, or assign an observational task rather than a behavioral task. Your client may not yet or may no longer be a customer.
- When you've taken all these steps, is there anything else you should do differently? For instance, does your client often say, "Yes, but"? Your team or a consultant may help you take some distance and see what you can do differently in the relationship with your client.

Some solution-focused questions suggested by Berg and Steiner (2003) that the professional can use to dissolve an impasse are:

- If you were to ask your client what you've done that has helped him or her, even if only a little bit, what would he or she respond?
- What does the client consider a sign of a successful outcome?
- Is that outcome realistic?
- What do you, your program, and your funding institution consider signs of success?

- If your view differs from the others', what needs to be done so that you can work toward the same goal?
- On a scale of 0 to 10, where would your client say he or she is right now?
- What needs to happen to bring him or her 1 point closer to 10?

The progress made by the professional and the client can be measured by scaling questions, which can be asked of both the client and the important people in his or her life. Sometimes the goal changes over time, and it may turn out that more is possible than was first assumed. You can find more options for reflection on the session by both the professional and the client in Chapter 11.

CASE 18

During a mediation concerning a labor dispute, employee and employer talk about the fact that they hadn't thought their relationship could get any better once they had reached 5 (where 10 means an optimal collaborative relationship, and 0 refers to the situation when the employee went on sick leave). When things started going considerably better, both became hopeful that more improvement was possible and on a new scale the 5 looked more like a 3 or 4. Both felt that a new scale was desirable and they described what the new 10 would look like. Then they thought about what the new 5 would look like and how they could reach that number. They even considered a future position for the employee as the company's co-manager.

INTERVENTIONS FOR CLIENTS WHO KEEP TALKING IN A PROBLEM-FOCUSED WAY

If the client continues to talk in a problem-focused way, the professional considers whether the client is a customer or a complainant. In addition to all the other questions for complainants, he or she may also fall back on the following questions:

- "How do you think that talking about your problem will help you reach your goal?"
- "You must have a good reason to talk this much about your problem . . . Please tell me."
- "Suppose you said everything you want to say about your problem.
- What would change for you (or in your relationship) then?"

- "Suppose you had this problem not with so-and-so but with your child or your best friend, for example. What would you think about the situation then? How would you react ? What's the difference between how you would react and how you are reacting now?"

It is important that the professional not do the same as his or her predecessors if what they did didn't help. One may ask the client: "What was pleasant or annoying about previous treatments? What was useful and what wasn't? What should I not do and what should I definitely do, based on your experience with previous professionals?" If the professional's manner and way of working correspond to the client's ideas about how change takes place and he or she acts in accordance with those ideas, there will always be cooperation. Chapter 11 includes solution-focused questions that the professional can ask him- or herself to reflect on the session and his or her own performance.

Duncan (2005) has suggested seven tips for clients:

- If you do not like the therapist, find a different one.
- If you think your therapist doesn't like you and doesn't understand or appreciate your ideas, find a different one.
- If you disagree with the therapist's goals or find that they are not your goals, find a different therapist.
- If you disagree with your therapist's ideas or suggestions or if you do not get what you ask for and your feedback does not make your therapist change his or her approach, find a different therapist.
- If you believe that your therapist views your problem or situation as hopeless or impossible to solve or thinks that it will be years before anything changes, find a different one.
- If you do not notice anything positive within three to six sessions, you may want to bring it to your therapist's attention. If no progress is made, find a different therapist.
- If the therapist or your doctor recommends psychiatric medication when you haven't asked for it or are doubtful about its necessity, find a different one. If anyone tells you that you have a chemical imbalance, ask what that means exactly. If you think that medication is the right choice for you, give it a try.

SUMMARY

- Impasse or failure may occur if the goal hasn't been formulated in positive, concrete, and realistic terms or if the client fails to recognize exceptions as such.
- Seven ways of bringing about failure were described in this chapter.
- This chapter included solution-focused questions that the professional can ask him- or herself in order to dissolve an impasse. Also supplied were interventions and solution-focused questions in case the client keeps talking in a problem-focused way.
- The professional can reflect on the session by asking him- or herself solution-focused questions and by asking the client for feedback.
- Seven tips were offered that can help the client determine whether a therapist is right for him or her or whether it would be best to look for a different therapist.

CHAPTER 10

·················

1001 Solution-Focused Questions

The wise man is not the man who provides the right answers,
but the one who asks the right questions.
—Claude Lévi-Strauss

Solution-focused questions form a large part of the solution-focused professional's tool kit. The questions invite the client to think about transformation and help him or her make desired changes in his or her life.

Students often tell me that they feel it is imperative that they know a great many solution-focused questions, which is why I have included in this chapter a list of 1001 solution-focused questions that I have gathered over the years. They are simply examples of questions that one might ask; I do not mean for these questions to be prescriptive or mandatory. Moreover, one can come up with many more questions than I have collected in this book. And it should be noted that the questions in this chapter may also be asked in different situations and in a different order than indicated here.

An enjoyable way to learn and refresh one's knowledge of solution-focused questions is doing a brainstorming exercise. When I do this exercise with my students, we all take turns coming up with solution-focused questions, and we count how many questions we think of together. It can also be used as an evaluation tool for a course or training program; at the end, the students will be able to come up with a great deal more questions than at the beginning. Experience shows that it becomes easier to hold on to the solution-focused thread as one's familiarity with these questions increases. I would therefore like to thank all the students I have come to know for their contributions to the list of questions through their participation in this exercise.

In Chapter 3 I discussed the importance of using open questions to invite the client to reflect as much as possible and to provide answers that go beyond a mere yes or no. *How*, *what*, and *when* questions are examples of open questions. The next chapter includes solution-focused questions that the professional may ask him- or herself in order to reflect on his or her work.

The questions are divided into two categories: solution-focused questions for general use and solution-focused questions for use in specific situations or with specific clients. These categories are not mutually exclusive: Questions in one category can often be used in situations in the other, too. For instance, questions about goal formulation for general use can also be used in specific situations, for example, when one is dealing with children or relationships. The division into categories will hopefully make it easier to find the right questions. This list is by no means exhaustive; if you have any additions, they are most welcome.

In the category of solution-focused questions for general use you will find:

- Questions about goal formulation
- Questions about exceptions
- Questions about competencies
- Scaling questions
- Questions with which to conclude and evaluate the session

In the category of solution-focused questions for use in specific situations or with specific clients you will find:

- Questions for clients in a visitor relationship
- Questions for clients in a complainant relationship
- Questions for referrers
- Questions for clients who have experienced traumatic events
- Questions for increasing hope
- Questions for clients in a crisis situation
- Questions for externalizing the problem or conflict
- Questions for children
- Questions for groups (couples, families)

- Questions for clients in cognitive therapy
- Questions about medication
- Questions about relapse
- Questions for coaching managers, teams, and organizations
- Questions for clients in a conflict

SOLUTION-FOCUSED QUESTIONS FOR GENERAL USE

Questions About Goal Formulation

1. "What brings you here?"
2. "How is that a problem for you?"
3. "How do you think that is a problem for the other person or people?"
4. "What is the least that you would like to achieve?"
5. "In an ideal world, what would you like to achieve at best?"
6. "What would you like to be different as a result of these sessions?"
7. "What would go better if the problem were solved?"
8. "What would be a good outcome for you?"
9. "What are your best hopes? What difference would that make?"
10. "What will be different in your life when you have reached your goal?"
11. "How would that change make a difference for you?"
12. "How can I be of service to you?"
13. "What is the purpose of your visit?"
14. "How will you know that you have reached your goal?"
15. "How would important people in your life (partner, friends, colleagues) be able to tell that you had reached your goal?"
16. "How would the referrer be able to tell that you had reached your goal?"
17. "How would I be able to tell that you had reached your goal?"
18. "What else would you like to achieve?"
19. "What else will be different when you have reached your goal?"
20. "What would make this session worthwhile for you?"
21. "If your problem were solved, what would be different?"
22. "You say you would like to have less . . . What would you like to see more of?"
23. "What do you want to see instead of the problem?"
24. "What do you wish to have achieved by the end of this session so that you can say that it has been meaningful and useful?"

25. "What do you wish to have achieved by the end of the sessions so that you can say that it has been meaningful and useful?"
26. "What will take the place of the problem?" (positive rather than negative goal formulation)
27. "What would your preferred future be?"
28. "Suppose you reached the preferred future. What and who would have made that possible?"
29. "What have you done to make that possible?"
30. The miracle question: "Suppose you're asleep tonight and a miracle happens. The miracle is that the problems that bring you here have been solved (to a sufficient degree). You are unaware of this, however, because you are asleep. How would you first notice tomorrow morning that a miracle has happened? How else? And how else?"
31. In the case of an unrealistic miracle: "That would be a tremendous miracle indeed. If you were to make the miracle smaller and more attainable, what might it look like?"
32. "After you, who would be the first person to notice that the miracle has occurred?"
33. "What would the other person (e.g., your significant other) say if he or she had to explain how you would be different tomorrow morning?"
34. "What would the day after the miracle look like?"
35. "Suppose you could choose one scene, a picture of the moment when the miracle occurred. What would that picture look like?"
36. "What would it be like if your problem no longer existed?"
37. "How could you make it easier to accomplish that?"
38. "How would your partner or another important person in your life notice that the miracle had occurred? How would he or she react? And how would you, in turn, react?"
39. "What would your partner or another important person in your life be doing differently as a result of the miracle?"
40. "If I were to ask your partner or another important person in your life what you would be doing differently then, what would he or she say?"
41. "What part of the miracle is easiest to start with?"
42. "What are you not doing now that you would be doing then?"
43. "Are you ready for a small thought experiment?" Proceed to ask the miracle question.
44. "I can see that this is a problem for you. How would you like things to be different?"

45. "What would you be doing differently if you knew what you had to do?"
46. "Suppose you did know. What would you say?"
47. "What would change if you did know?"
48. "What would already be different if you did know?"
49. "Who might know?"
50. "Suppose I were to ask your partner or another important person in your life the same question. What would he or she say?"
51. "What would your partner or another important person in your life say is your goal?"
52. "What would I say is your goal?"
53. "What would God (or Allah) or a deceased person say is your goal?"
54. "What would an ideal day look like for you?"
55. "What would I see you doing differently then?"
56. "What would you like to see go well or smoothly again as a result of these sessions?"
57. "What is the best that could happen?"
58. "If you were to have a dream about how you would like your life to look in the future, what would you dream?"
59. "If you were to have a dream about a solution to your problem, what would you dream?"
60. "What would change if you didn't have any financial constraints, for instance, because you had won the lottery?"
61. "How would you organize your life if the doctor told you that you had another 10 or 15 years—without major health problems—to live?"
62. "Suppose you only had 24 hours to live. What would you regret not having done?"
63. "Suppose you go to a funeral 3 years from now and the funeral turns out to be your own. What would you like the important people in your life (family, friends, colleagues) to say about you? What difference would you like to have made in their lives?"
64. "What needs to happen for you to go home satisfied after this session?"
65. "Pretend you are living 1 year, 5 years, or 10 years in the future. Looking back, what would you say your goal was when you came here?"
66. "How will you be able to tell that you don't need to come back again? What will be different then?"
67. "When will you consider these sessions a success?"

68. "How can we know when to stop meeting like this?"
69. "In what area would you like to see the most improvement?"
70. "Suppose I were to make a recording of the present and one of a time in the future when you have reached your goal. What difference would I see that would allow me to say, 'This is the recording of the present and that is the recording of the future'?"
71. "Suppose I were a fly on the wall in your home when the miracle had happened and your goal had been reached. What would I see you doing differently then? What else would be different?"
72. "And how would others react to that?"
73. "Suppose you did have a goal. What might it be?"
74. "Suppose you did know why you do certain things. How would that bring you closer to your goal?"
75. "What would be your dream solution?"
76. "How is that different from the way things are now?"
77. "What would I see you do differently then?"
78. "Suppose there were a solution. What difference would that make for you? What would be different?"
79. "Suppose you made a full recovery. What would have been of help to you or what would you have done to recover?"
80. "Suppose I ran into you 6 months from now, once your problems were solved, and I asked you what steps you had taken to successfully conclude the therapy. What would you say?"
81. "What will you do when you have solved your problem (to a sufficient degree)?"
82. "When will you do that?"
83. "What are you going to do about that?"
84. "What have you done this week to obtain a better life?"
85. "What is needed to make a very small piece of the miracle happen?"
86. If the client talks about the absence of a problem or complaint: "How would you feel when the problem was gone?"
87. "How would you most like to see yourself?"
88. "When are you at your best? What does that look like?"
89. "How can you do more of what is making things go well?"
90. "Suppose a friend of yours had the same problem. What would you think his or her goal was?"
91. "Suppose your friend had the same problem. What solutions would he or she find?"
92. "Suppose your friend had the same problem. What would you advise him or her to do?"

93. "If you were to think of something that someone else who is in the same situation as you might benefit from, what would it be?"
94. "What would be a sign that you are on the right track to reaching the preferred future?"
95. "What would you consider the first sign that you are on the right track?"
96. "What would you consider a sign that things are starting to go a tiny bit better?"
97. "Suppose this session produces a plan. What would you consider a start to your being on the right track? And what else?"
98. "What do you enjoy about those times?"
99. "How will you be using your time differently then? What difference would that make?"
100. "When you feel better, what do others notice about you that makes it clear to them that you're feeling better?"
101. "How would your partner or another important person in your life be able to tell that you are on the right track, headed toward your goal?"
102. "What will you be doing differently when this is no longer a problem for you?"
103. "What do you need to know by the end of this session that you don't know right now that would allow you to say that it was good that you came?"
104. "How can these sessions make a difference for you?"
105. "If you were to look into a crystal ball, what improvements would you see in a week, a month, or a year, and what would you see if the problem had been solved or your goal had been reached?"
106. "What and who could help you keep your goal in view?"
107. "Suppose *you* could change. What would be different in your life then?"
108. "Suppose you were able to change something or someone. What change would you make and what would be different about your life then?"
109. "How can insight, the processing of a traumatic event, or skills training help you reach your goal?"

Questions About Exceptions

110. "What has changed since you made an appointment for this session?"

111. "What is already going better since you made the appointment for this session?"
112. "What is better already?"
113. "What is already working in the right direction?"
114. "What have you already tried, and which of those things helped, even if only a little bit?"
115. "How could you make that happen more often?"
116. "Of the things you did, what helped the most?"
117. "What do you need so that that will happen more often in the future?"
118. "What else has helped so far?"
119. "At what times do you already see parts of the miracle or the desired outcome?"
120. "What is different about those times?"
121. "How do you manage that? And how else?"
122. "What could you already do differently right now?"
123. "When have you caught already a small glimpse of the miracle or the desired outcome?"
124. "What are you doing differently then?"
125. "What did you do differently in the past?"
126. "What other successes have you had in the past?"
127. "How did you notice those changes?"
128. "What do you think you did to make that happen?"
129. "What would the important people in your life say is different then?"
130. "What would the important people in your life say you do differently then?"
131. "Suppose another person were present. What else would he or she say about that?"
132. "What is he or she doing differently then? How do you react to that?"
133. "When did that small miracle last happen?"
134. "What was different about that moment?"
135. "What do you think that other person would say is the likelihood of this happening again?"
136. "What do you think he or she would say you could do to increase the likelihood that it will happen again?"
137. "If you were to do that, what do you think that other person would do differently then?"
138. "If he or she were to do that, how would things be different for you in your relationship?"

139. "In what situations do you feel better already?"
140. "How is that new for you?"
141. "When was the last time you had a good day?"
142. "When did you manage to behave in a way that was consistent with how you would like to be?"
143. "When is the problem absent or less of a problem? What are you doing differently then? What is different then?"
144. "Think back to a moment in the past week (month, year) when the problem was completely absent or was less of a problem. What was that moment?"
145. "When is the problem not a problem? What are you doing differently then? What is different then?"
146. "When is the problem not a problem for other people? What are they doing differently then? What is different then?"
147. "Suppose you *could* think of an exception. What might it be?"
148. "What happens when the problem becomes less of a problem or when things are going a little better?"
149. "What were you doing differently then that made things go better?"
150. "What were other people doing differently then that made things go better?"
151. "Who needs to do what to make that happen again?"
152. "Suppose a miracle occurs and the miracle is that you are able to find an exception. What might that exception be?"

Questions About Competencies

153. "Could you tell me about your assets and good qualities?"
154. "How do you manage to . . . ?"
155. "How did you previously manage to . . . ?"
156. "How did you know you were able to . . . ?"
157. "How did you know you could carry out that experiment?"
158. "How did you know what was needed?"
159. "How do you think you did that?"
160. "How have you tackled the problem up to now, and what has helped?"
161. "How did you find the courage to . . . ?"
162. "What gave you the strength to . . . ?"
163. "How did you bring yourself to do that?"
164. "Where do you find the courage to change when you want to?"
165. "How can you make sure that you will reach your goal?"
166. "How will you do that, exactly?"

167. "How could you bring about more small miracles?"
168. "How does that good feeling help you for the rest of the day or week?"
169. "How can you make it easier for you to perform the desired behavior?"
170. "What do you think *you* did to make that happen?"
171. "How did you decide to do that?"
172. "How did you succeed in doing that?"
173. "You have a lot of great ideas. How do you come up with them?"
174. "How do you know that this problem can be solved?"
175. "How did you come up with the great idea to do it that way?"
176. "How do you manage to stop that undesired behavior?"
177. "How do you manage to be resolute enough to . . . ?"
178. "Is that how you do it? Can you tell me more about that?"
179. "What good intention did you have when you . . . ?"
180. "How did you find out that these are ways that work for you?"
181. "How did you discover that you . . . ?"
182. "When did you learn that this is a good way for you?"
183. "What gave you the sense that it was the right time to . . . ?"
184. "What makes you want to make an effort here?"
185. "What drives you to put some work into it now?"
186. "What makes you so resolute in your opinion?"
187. "What is the most important thing you need to be reminded of doing in order to maximize the chance that that happens again?"
188. "What is the second most important thing to remember?"
189. "How can I help you? What role do you see me playing in this?"
190. "How did you manage to come today, despite the fact that you're doing badly or worse?"
191. "How did you manage to motivate yourself to come here today?"
192. "How do you manage to stay on the right track?"
193. "How do you manage to get back on the right track?"
194. "What ideas do you already have for reaching your goal?"
195. "When was your last success? How did that go, and who did what? What was your role in achieving this success?"
196. "Suppose you were to compliment yourself on your effort. What would you say?"
197. "What qualities and skills does this success show you that you have?"
198. "When did you become aware that you had those qualities?"
199. "When did other people become aware that you have those qualities?"

200. "In what situations are those qualities most noticeable?"
201. "How could you avail yourself of those traits and skills even more than you're doing now?"
202. "How would others notice that you're making greater use of those qualities?"
203. "What is already going well and doesn't need to change?"
204. "How can you do more of what is already going well?"
205. "Can you tell me where your interests lie?"
206. "What would your partner or another important person in your life reply if asked what your interests are?"
207. "If you had a month-long vacation, what would you do?"
208. "How do you most enjoy spending your time?"
209. "What are you good at? What exactly does that involve?"
210. "What do the important people in your life (partner, child, friend, parent) like about you?"
211. "What do you like about yourself?"
212. "What do you do better than others?"
213. "What is easy for you that others probably find difficult?"
214. "What was easy for you when you were a child?"
215. "What are your hobbies?"
216. "What activities do you find relaxing?"
217. "What activities that you used to do would you like to pick up again?"
218. "What have been the most significant experiences of your life (e.g., traveling, studying, winning a competition)?"
219. "Have you ever conquered a bad habit (e.g., smoking, nail-biting)? How did you manage that?"
220. "If so-and-so (e.g., a deceased person) could see how you live your life now, what would he or she be proud of you for?"
221. "If it were possible for that person to see how you live your life now, what would he or she say about you?"
222. "How would he or she say you've accomplished that?"
223. "Who helped you with that?"
224. "How did you see your parents deal with similar situations?"
225. "How did others react when your parents dealt with those situations in that way?"
226. "What have you achieved that you're proud of?"
227. "What effect did that have on you?"
228. "What effect did it have on others?"

229. "What effect would it have on you if you were given the opportunity to do that more often?"
230. "What have you achieved that the important people in your life are proud of you for?"
231. "What would you like to do in your life that would give you a sense of pride?"
232. "Suppose you were able to do that. What difference would that make for you?"
233. "In what situations have you received compliments from others?"
234. "What difference would it make for you if you did agree with my compliment?"
235. "What qualities do others value in you?"
236. "We all have something unique to offer. What is it that you offer?"
237. "In what situations do you compliment yourself?"
238. "What is or was your best subject in school?"
239. "What positive things would your teacher say about you?"
240. "What is your specialty at work?"
241. "In what area do others consult you?"
242. "Who inspires you in your work?"
243. "According to them, what is important for you to remember in your work?"
244. "Which people encourage you to do this work?"
245. "What did they notice about you that makes them encourage you?"
246. "Which of your abilities and qualities are most valued by the people with whom you come into contact at work?"
247. "Who in your network knows that you have these qualities and abilities?"
248. "What is the most important quality you should remember that you have when you are under pressure?"
249. "What good traits would your partner or another important person in your life say you have that will help you reach your goal?"
250. "How does your faith help you?"
251. "How do you manage to keep your head above water?"
252. "What were some successful moments for you this past week?"
253. "What have been some successful moments in your life?"
254. "What have been the high points of your life?"
255. "What tells you that it's a good idea to go on engaging in the desired or undesired behavior?"
256. "What are your good qualities?"

257. "What do important people in your life consider to be your good qualities?"
258. "Where do those qualities come from?"
259. "Which qualities can you make use of to address your current problem?"
260. "How can you utilize those qualities to address your current problem?"
261. "How can you continue or expand on this success?"
262. "What have you learned about your problem, and how does that help?"
263. "What have you learned from solving problems in the past that you can apply right now?"
264. "How did you find that out?"
265. "What advice do you get from others?"
266. "What do we need to discuss for this session to be useful?"
267. "You must have a good reason to . . . Please tell me more."
268. "Not everyone would have been able to say or do that. So you are the kind of person who . . . ? Please tell me more." (positive character interpretation)
269. If a client asks for advice: "Suppose you got advice from me. How would that help you?"
270. "What compliment could your partner or another important person in your life give you about that?"
271. "Suppose your partner or another important person in your life had been present in that situation. What would he or she say you did well?"
272. "Whom could we invite to these sessions to put you on the path toward your goal?"
273. "In your opinion, what else needs to happen for things to go better?"
274. "What have you considered on occasion but not yet attempted?"
275. "How can you make it happen that . . . ?"
276. "What in this conversation has made you discover that?"
277. "Suppose we had sessions about mourning, insight, or processing trauma. How would that help you reach your goal or bring you closer to it?"
278. "How do you hope I can help you with this problem?"
279. "What is the best way for me to work with you?"
280. "What did the previous therapist do and which of those things helped?"

281. "What should I avoid, and what should I definitely do?"
282. "What do you do to control the urge to engage in an undesired behavior?"
283. "What else do you do to ease the problem?"
284. "How did you get through such difficult circumstances without giving up hope?"
285. "How does change usually take place in your life?"

Scaling Questions

286. "What is better since the previous session?"
287. "What else is better?"
288. "What's going better?"
289. "What is different or is going differently?" (with pessimistic clients)
290. "On a scale of 10 to 0, where 10 means that the problem that brings you here has been (sufficiently) solved or your goal has been reached, and 0 is the worst moment you've experienced, where are you now?"
291. "What does that number stand for?"
292. "How is it that you are already at that number?"
293. "How did you manage to remain at that number?"
294. "What would one step higher look like?"
295. "What would 1 point higher on the scale look like?"
296. "How do you already manage to be halfway there?"
297. "How would you notice that you'd gone up 1 point?"
298. "What would 1 point higher on the scale look like? What would you be doing differently then?"
299. "What difference would that make for you and the important people in your life?"
300. "What do you see as a next step?"
301. "In your opinion, what would be a very small step forward?"
302. "What does that small step look like exactly? What would you be doing differently then?"
303. "How would others see that you've taken a small step?"
304. "What would be the very smallest step that you could take?"
305. "How great is the chance that that will work out?"
306. "How much confidence do you have that you will succeed in doing that again?"
307. "Suppose I'm a fly on the wall. What do I see you doing differently when you are up 1 point?"

308. "Suppose I make a recording of the situation in which you are up 1 point. What do I see you doing differently?"
309. If the client reports a lower rating: "How did you previously manage to get from that number to a higher number?"
310. "How do you manage to remain at that number or to stay stable?"
311. "What is needed for you to maintain that number?"
312. "How would you be able to move up 1 point on the scale?"
313. "What is needed for you to be able to move up 1 point?"
314. "What will be different when you move up 1 point?"
315. "What is needed for you to pretend that you are up 1 point?"
316. "How do others with the same problem manage to move up 1 point?"
317. "At what number do you need to end up to be content?"
318. "At what number do you need to be so that you do not have to come back here anymore?"
319. "Were you able to imagine you would get this far?"
320. "What is the highest number at which you've ever been?"
321. "Suppose I were to talk to people who knew you when you were at that number. How would they describe you?"
322. "Suppose I were to talk to people you knew when you were at a somewhat lower number. How would they describe you?"
323. "How has going from a . . . to a . . . helped you?"
324. "Suppose the positive moments were to last longer. What difference would that make for you?"
325. "Suppose the positive moments were to last longer. What conclusions would you draw from that?"
326. "On a scale of 10 to 0, what are the chances that you will find a solution?"
327. "On a scale of 10 to 0, where 10 = very confident and 0 = no confidence at all, how much confidence do you have that the problem that brings you here can be resolved?"
328. "What is happening that gives you the sense that this problem can be resolved?"
329. "On a scale of 10 to 0, how much confidence do you have that you can keep doing . . . ?"
330. "What makes you think that that can be achieved?"
331. "On a scale of 10 to 0, where 10 means 'I am willing to give it my all' and 0 means 'I have no motivation at all,' how motivated are you to solve the problem that brings you here or to reach your goal?"

332. "On a scale of 10 to 0, how motivated are you to keep doing . . . ?"
333. "On a scale of 10 to 0, where 10 = 'I have every hope' and 0 = 'I have no hope at all,' how hopeful are you that the problem that brings you here can be resolved?"
334. "How come you (already/still) have that much confidence, motivation, or hope?"
335. "How do you manage to have so much confidence, motivation, or hope?"
336. "What would one number higher look like? What would that take?"
337. "How would you notice that you were one number higher? And how would others notice?"
338. "If you were to rate how much better you're doing since our previous session, where 10 = optimal improvement and 0 = no improvement whatsoever, what rating would you give yourself?"
339. "How come you're not at a lower number? How do you do that?"
340. "How has moving from a . . . to a . . . given you hope?"
341. "What would it take for you to drop as quickly as possible from the number where you currently are to a 1 or even a 0?" (relapse prevention)

Questions With Which to Conclude and Evaluate the Session

342. "What question would you like to hear that I haven't yet asked?"
343. "Is there anything else I should know?" (closed question at the conclusion of the session)
344. "Anything else? And what else?" (closed question at the conclusion of the session)
345. "Is it necessary or would it be useful for you to come back?" If so: "When would you like to come back?"
346. "What might be the next sign of progress or your next step?"
347. "What would indicate to you that it would be a good idea for you to make another appointment?"
348. "What improvement would you like to tell me about next time?"
349. "What would you wish to achieve at the next session to feel that that session had been useful?"
350. "What will you be doing differently after this session?"
351. "Who in your life will be the first to notice that? How?"
352. "How will you celebrate when you've reached your goal?"
353. "Who will you invite to celebrate?"
354. "What will you say in the speech that you give at the celebration?"

355. "What symbol will you choose for your victory?"
356. "What homework suggestion would you like to receive when you leave?"
357. "Suppose you did want a suggestion. What might it be?"
358. "Suppose you wanted to give yourself a homework suggestion. What might it be?"
359. "Has anything been neglected or gone unaddressed that merits attention now or next time?"
360. "What feedback would you like to give me about today's session?"
361. "What has been most useful to you today? What has been of help?"
362. "What have you gained from this session?"
363. "What had you hoped to gain from this session that you haven't? How can we remedy that?"
364. "Before we end the session, can you tell me which questions have helped you and what questions you would have liked me to ask?"
365. "What is the best or most valuable thing you've noticed about yourself today?"
366. "What can you take from this session to reflect or work on in the coming period?"
367. "What can you take from this session that can help you . . . in the coming week?"
368. "What can you take from this session that will enable you to tell me that things are going better next time?"
369. "What difference has this session made for you?"
370. "Would you be willing to carry out a task in the upcoming period? Which task appeals to you?"
371. "On a scale of 10 to 0, to what extent did you feel heard, understood, and respected during this session?"
372. "On a scale of 10 to 0, to what extent did you talk about and work on things that are important to you during this session?"
373. "On a scale of 10 to 0, how good a fit is my approach for you?"
374. "On a scale of 10 to 0, how good was today's session for you?"
375. "What in these sessions has helped and what hasn't?"
376. "Which solutions were most practicable for you?"
377. "When you leave here and you're on the right path, what will you be doing differently and how will you be thinking differently?"
378. "Suppose you could talk about what has helped you most at a training course for professionals. What would you tell the students?"

379. "Suppose we could start the sessions anew. What could I or we do differently or better?"

380. "Suppose I came across a client with the same problems as you. What advice would you give me?"

381. "In the future, may I consult you as an expert on how you solved the problem if I treat other clients with the same problem?"

382. "Would you be willing to join a team of experts in order to help other clients solve their problems?"

SOLUTION-FOCUSED QUESTIONS FOR USE IN SPECIFIC SITUATIONS OR WITH SPECIFIC CLIENTS

This second group of questions offers solution-focused questions for specific situations. All questions about goal formulation, exceptions, and competencies; the scaling questions; and the questions for concluding and evaluating sessions can also be asked in addition to those listed here. If any of the questions in the first group can be used in a special way in a specific situation or with a specific type of client, they are included here as well.

Questions for Clients in a Visitor Relationship

383. "Whose idea was it for you to come here?"

384. "What are your thoughts about why you're here today?"

385. "What do you understand about the situation?"

386. "You must have a good reason to think that. Please tell me more."

387. "What makes the referrer think you should come here?"

388. "In your opinion, how is that a problem for him or her?"

389. "How could it also be a problem for you?"

390. "Do you agree that the concerns that the referrer has about you are valid?"

391. "What does the referrer think you should do here?"

392. "What does the referrer think you should do differently?"

393. "What, at a minimum, would the referrer say you have to do differently?"

394. "According to the referrer, what is the reason you have this problem?"

395. "What would it take for you not to have to come back?"

396. "What do you need to do to convince the referrer that you don't have to come back here?"

397. "Is that something you might want to do?"

398. "What, at a minimum, would you say you could or should do differently?"

399. "How would you be able to motivate yourself to do that?"
400. "What, at a minimum, are you prepared to do to appease the referrer?"
401. "What is the most that you are prepared to do to appease the referrer?"
402. "Knowing yourself, which of those things would you be able to do?"
403. "How do you know you can do that?"
404. "When was the last time you did that?"
405. "What was different in your life then?"
406. "How did you manage to do that then?"
407. "What would the referrer say he or she noticed about you then?"
408. "If you were to decide to do that again, what would be the first small step you could take?"
409. "On a scale of 10 to 0, where 10 = very confident and 0 = not confident at all, how much confidence do you have that you can do that (again)?"
410. "What would the referrer say the odds are that you would do that (again)?"
411. "If you decided to do that, how would things change between you and the referrer?"
412. "How would the referrer say that would help him or her?"
413. "Suppose you decided to do that. What other differences would that make in your life?"
414. "What would happen in your life that isn't happening now?"
415. "Suppose you had to pretend that the miracle had happened. What would be the first small step that you would take?"
416. "How will you know that you've done enough?"
417. "Who will be the first to notice those changes?"
418. "When that other person notices those changes, what will he or she do differently then?"
419. "And when the other person does that, what will that be like for you?"
420. "How would you know that coming here today was a good idea after all?"
421. "In what way would your life change if you were in charge?"
422. "Suppose you did have a goal. What might it be?"
423. "How do you hope I can help you with this problem?"
424. "What is happening that gives you the sense that this problem can be resolved?"
425. "What would happen if these sessions didn't continue?"

426. "What should and shouldn't I do, based on your experience with previous professionals?"
427. "Is there anything else that you're curious about that we could look at together?"
428. "What do you think will happen here that makes you think, 'That, never'?"
429. "In addition to all the reasons you have for not wanting that, do you perhaps also have any thoughts as to why you *might* want it, how it *could* work or solve something?"
430. "What would we have to put on the agenda for you to be able to say: 'This has been meaningful to me'?"
431. "You say: 'These things are not in my hands.' What can you exert influence over?"
432. "What happens if you do nothing?"

Questions for Clients in a Complainant Relationship

433. "How do you cope?"
434. "How come you're not doing worse?"
435. "How do you survive that?"
436. "I can't change the other person or the rest of the world. How *can* I help you?"
437. "What would you like to keep as it is?"
438. "What would you like to keep as it is because it's going well (enough)?"
439. "What should definitely not change?"
440. "What have you been holding onto that it might be time for you to let go of?"
441. "How is this a problem for you?"
442. "What gives you the idea that this problem can be resolved?"
443. "When is the problem absent or less noticeable?"
444. "When is the problem not a problem, or when has it not been a problem for a short period of time?"
445. "How might your problem be useful to you?"
446. "What would you like to achieve at a minimum?"
447. "Suppose your partner (other family members, your colleague) were to change in the way you want. What would that mean to you?"
448. "Suppose the other person changes in the way you want. What would you do differently then?"
449. "Suppose the other person changes in the way you want. What would you consider doing differently then?"

450. "What would be different between you and the other person if the other person were to change in the way you wish for?"
451. "What would be different and what would you be doing differently?"
452. "How might that help you?"
453. "Suppose the other person were to do the things you would like him or her to do. How would he or she say you treat him differently?"
454. "Suppose I had a magic wand and could make so-and-so do everything you wish he or she would do. What difference would that make for you and what would you do differently then?"
455. "And suppose you did want to change something about yourself. What might it be?"
456. "What is the smallest thing you might change about yourself?"
457. "If you can continue to do that, how will that bring you closer to your preferred future?"
458. "In what area would you like to see the most improvement?"
459. "What have you considered but not yet tried?"
460. "Suppose your partner (family member, colleague) won't change in the way you wish for. What will you do then?"
461. "Suppose your partner (family member, colleague) won't change in the way you wish for. What can you yourself do to improve the situation regardless?"
462. "Suppose your life stays the way it is. What will change for you then?"
463. "What do you hope to achieve with all the attempts you've already made?"
464. "What can I do to help you?"
465. After asking a scaling question: "How do you manage to remain stable at that number?"
466. "How do you manage to . . . with everything you've been through?"
467. "What has seen you through until now?
468. "Could things be worse than they are? How come they aren't?"
469. "What have you done to ensure that things didn't get worse but stayed the same?"
470. "Suppose you did want to change something about yourself. What might it be?"
471. "Suppose the two of you did have a common goal. What might it be?"
472. "Suppose the other person respected your need to . . . What would be different between the two of you?"

473. "How do you rate your chances of finding a solution on a scale of 10 to 0, where 10 means a very good chance and 0 means no chance?

474. "You have talked a lot about how you don't want things to be. What *would* you like?"

475. "What would you like instead of the problem?"

476. If the client says he or she doesn't know: "Suppose there's someone who knows you as well as you know yourself. What would that person say?"

Questions for Referrers

477. "What would be the best possible outcome of a collaboration among you as referrer, the client or clients, and me (our institution)?"

478. "What are the client's strengths and what aspects of his or her performance are satisfactory and should be maintained?"

479. "What are the limitations that we need to take into account?"

480. "What resources does the client have?"

481. "What is the first thing that would indicate to the client that a treatment is meaningful and useful?"

482. "When has this happened? Can you give an example?"

483. "What is the smallest change you can accept from the client at this time?"

484. "When was the last time that he or she was doing a bit better or acted a bit more as you would like?"

485. "What was he or she doing differently then?"

486. "What do you think helped him or her do that?"

487. "Can you indicate on a scale of 10 to 0 to what extent you're willing to do some of the things that were helpful then again?"

Questions for Clients Who Have Experienced Traumatic Events

488. "How can I help you?"

489. "How have you managed to survive?"

490. "What else has helped you survive?"

491. "How have you helped others survive?"

492. "What helps you deal with what you've experienced?"

493. "Is this the worst thing you've ever experienced? On a scale of 10 to 0, where 10 = the worst and 0 = not bad at all, indicate how bad it was."

494. "What else have you been through that was difficult and what helped you then?"

495. "Which of the things that helped you then could be useful to you again now?"

496. "Do you know anyone else who has been through the same ordeal? What has helped that person deal with it?"

497. "What does it mean for you to have survived these traumatic events?"

498. "If a miracle were to happen in the middle of the night, and you overcame the consequences of the traumatic events well enough that you didn't have to come here anymore and were (relatively) satisfied with your life, what would be different then?"

499. "What will you be doing differently when these traumatic events are less of a problem in your daily life?"

500. "How will you use your time differently?"

501. "What will you think about and what will you do instead of thinking about the past?"

502. "How will you know that you're doing that and how will you know that you'll be able to keep doing it?"

503. "When have there been times when this occurred, even if only by a little degree?"

504. "What is different at those moments? How do you manage to make those moments happen?"

505. "What would others say is different then and how would they say you manage that?"

506. "What difference will those healing changes make in your life when they have lasted for a longer period of time (days, weeks, months, years)? What difference will it make in your relationships with the important people in your life?"

507. "What difference will the changes that you've accomplished make for future generations of your family?"

508. "How will you be able to tell that you're handling it a little better or that it's a little easier for you?"

509. "What would be the smallest sign that things are going better? What difference would that make for you?"

510. "What would be the next small sign? And the one after that?"

511. "How could you regain hope that life can get easier in the future?"

512. "How much hope do you have that you can regain a better life in the future?"

513. "What do you think your next step could be? When you've taken that step, what difference will that make for you?"

514. "What did the traumatic event not change and how did you manage that?"
515. "What things in your life together do you wish to maintain, despite what has happened?"
516. "What would you like your life to look like a month from now, with the same people and with the same circumstances still in place, but when your behavior is less influenced by the traumatic event?"
517. "Considering that goal, how would you react, feel, or think about yourself if you saw yourself as a victim a month from now?"
518. "Considering that goal, how would you react, feel, or think about yourself if you saw yourself as a survivor a month from now?"
519. "Is thinking of yourself as a victim or as a survivor most helpful to you in reaching your goal?"
520. "Under what circumstances have you successfully made use of this behavior, this feeling, or these thoughts?"
521. "How did you succeed in doing it that way?"
522. "How would others who know you well say you succeeded?"
523. "Imagine you're a wise old man or woman looking back on your life. What advice would the wise old you give the present-day you to help you get though the current phase of your life?"
524. "According to the wise old you, what should you be thinking about?"
525. "According to the wise old you, what would be most helpful to you as you heal?"
526. "What would the wise old you say to comfort you?"
527. "And what advice does the wise old you have about how the treatment could be most useful and could help the most?"
528. "What helps you keep traumatic images (intrusions) and memories under control?"
529. "How do you manage to gain control of your memories?" (externalizing)
530. "On a scale of 10 to 0, where 10 = you are handling what's happened very well and 0 = you can't handle what's happened at all, where are you now?"
531. "What would you have done differently had you known about the trauma that the other person has experienced?"
532. "What difference could that have made in your relationship?"
533. "What can you do in your relationship now to compensate for what you couldn't do then?"
534. "With whom did you used to feel safe as a child?"

535. "How did you manage to feel safe with that person and what difference did that make for you?"
536. "Which experience of safety or comfort from the past could you make use of now?"
537. "What symbol for that safety or comfort could you use to help with this?"
538. "How do you now manage to sometimes feel safe and to have control of your life?"
539. "How can you comfort yourself now? How do you do that?"
540. "Who can comfort you now, even if only a little bit?"
541. In cases of, for example, dissociation or self-mutilation: "You must have a good reason to . . . Please tell me more."
542. "How does this help you?"
543. "How do you manage to come out of the dissociation into the here and now, or how do you manage to stop hurting yourself? How do you do that? What else helps in this respect?"
544. "What ritual would you be able to perform when you have reached your goal?"
545. "What ritual would you be able to perform when you've taken the first small step?"
546. "How will you celebrate your victory?"
547. "If you were to make a mental picture of a situation in the future that you are still avoiding now or that still causes you to experience fear, what would that picture look like?"

Questions for Increasing Hope

548. "What has kept your hope alive during the time that this has been a problem?"
549. "What are your best hopes?"
550. "Suppose you had more hope. How would your life or your relationship change?"
551. "How would (more) hope help you reach your goal?"
552. "What is the smallest difference that would give you more hope?"
553. "How will you notice that you are starting to have more hope?"
554. "How will you be able to tell that you have enough hope?"
555. "When *did* you feel hopeful and how did you manage that?"
556. "When you think of hope, what does it conjure up for you?"
557. "If you had a painting on your wall that reminded you of hope every morning, what would that painting look like?"

558. "What smell, color, song, or sound makes you think of hope?"
559. "If you were to choose a symbol for hope that you could carry around with you, what would it be?"
560. "What rating do you give yourself on a scale of 10 to 0, where 10 = lots of hope and 0 = no hope?"
561. "How do you manage to be at that number?"
562. "What would 1 point higher look like? What would you be doing or how would you be thinking differently?"
563. "How might you be able to go up 1 point?"
564. "Can you tell me about a period in your life when you had a lot of hope or more hope?"
565. "If you were to examine your problem, what information would give you more or less hope?"
566. "What would someone who did have (more) hope think and do in your situation?"
567. "What or who can give you more hope or take your hope away?"
568. "What would you have to do to really lose all hope?"
569. "What can you do to give yourself more hope at a time when you have no hope?"
570. "If you wanted to have more hope by the next session, what would you do or like me to do before we see each other again?"
571. "What in our conversation has given you more hope, even if only a little?"
572. "What indicates that you are on the right track to solving this problem?"
573. "Suppose the positive moments were to last longer. What difference would that make for you?"
574. "How has going from a . . . to a . . . given you hope?"

Questions for Clients in a Crisis Situation

575. "How did you manage to come here?"
576. "How did you manage to get out of bed this morning?"
577. "What have you already attempted in this situation and what helped, even if only a little?"
578. "What would you like to be different when this is over?" (goal formulation)
579. "How do you manage? How do you keep going?"
580. "How do you get from one moment to the next?"
581. "How have you been able to hold on long enough to come here?"

582. "When was the last time you ate something, and how did you manage to do that? How did that help you?"
583. "When was the last time you slept, and how did you manage to do that? How did that help you?"
584. "When do you not have these (e.g., suicidal) thoughts?"
585. "When the miracle occurs, what will take the place of your pain and your thoughts of killing yourself?"
586. "How have you managed to withstand . . . for so long?"
587. "What are you doing to take care of yourself even just a little bit in this situation?"
588. "Who and what do you think would help the most at this moment?"
589. "How do you manage to . . . , given everything you've been through?"
590. "How did you manage for so long not to have to seek professional assistance?"
591. "How did you manage to stop the undesired behavior?"
592. "How did you manage to pick up the phone and call the crisis hotline?"
593. "How would hospitalization or medication be able to help you now?"
594. "How did you manage to mobilize others to help you?"
595. "What has helped you pull through up to now?"
596. "What helped you pull through before (in a comparable situation)?"
597. "Which of those things helped the most?"
598. "Who helps or has helped you the most? And who else?"
599. "How did you know that . . . would help?"
600. "What is so helpful about that person?"
601. "What did you do to get that person to help you?"
602. "What would it take for that person to help you again?"
603. "If you were to get that help again, what difference would it make for you now?"
604. "If 10 = rest and order and 0 = chaos and being at your wits' end, where are you now?"
605. "And what else helped?"
606. "Compared to other bad days, what did you do differently this morning that helped you get up and come here?"
607. "What do you think the most useful thing that I can do at this moment is?"
608. "Could things be worse than they are? How come they aren't?"
609. "How would you notice that you had overcome the crisis?"

610. "What is the most important thing for you to remember to continue to cope with this situation?"
611. "What has helped you the most up to now and which of those things can you put to use at present?"
612. "What is the most important thing you need to remember when things go badly?"
613. "What do people around you say you do well, even under difficult circumstances?"
614. "Suppose you look back 1 year, 5 years, or 10 years from now. What will you see that has helped you emerge from this crisis?"
615. "Suppose a miracle happens tonight, and the miracle is that you can cope with this difficult situation, but you are unaware that the miracle has happened because you are asleep. How would you first notice tomorrow morning that the miracle has taken place?"
616. "Suppose that 1 year, 5 years, or 10 years from now you look back together with a friend. What do both of you say you have done in the preceding year or years that has helped you come out of this so well?"

Questions for Externalizing the Problem or Conflict

617. "What name do you give to your problem (X)?"
618. "How would you draw or represent X?"
619. "When does X not trouble you or trouble you less? What is different at those times? How do you manage that?"
620. "When does X not trouble others or trouble them less? What is different at those times? How do they manage that?"
621. "When has X not been a problem for you?"
622. "When has X not been a problem for those around you?"
623. "How much do you think X suits you?"
624. "What do you do when X has the upper hand or has control of you?"
625. "What difference does it make for you when X has the upper hand?"
626. "How does X manage to control you?"
627. "How do you then manage to regain control?"
628. "How would you notice that you had more control of X? And how else?"
629. "What is the first small step you could take to gain more control of X?"
630. "What difference would it make for you to take that first small step successfully?"

631. "How does X help you?"
632. "How do you manage to have control of X?"
633. "What are you doing when you have the upper hand and have more control of X?"
634. "Where do you now rate yourself on the control scale?"
635. "What was last week's (or last session's) rating?"
636. If the rating is higher than the previous rating: "How did you manage to reach a higher number?"
637. If the rating is the same as the previous rating: "How did you manage to maintain the same number?"
638. If the rating is lower than the previous rating: "What did you do before to get ahead? What did you do in a comparable situation in the past that was successful?"
639. "What have important people in your life noticed about you this past week? How did that influence their behavior toward you?"
640. "How have you recently been able to deceive X?"
641. "What do you (and others) do when you're planning to attack X?"
642. "What weapons do you use to attack X? Which weapons help the most?"
643. "What do you know about the way in which others who are also troubled by X attack X and take control of X?"
644. "How will you celebrate your victory over X?"
645. "Who will you invite to celebrate your victory over X?"
646. "In your speech, what will you say about how you managed to conquer X?"

Questions for Children

647. "What is your best subject in school?"
648. "What are you good at?"
649. "Whose company do you enjoy? What do they like about you?"
650. "Is there a grown-up you trust?"
651. "Whom can you talk to and who listens to you?"
652. "With whom do you feel connected?"
653. "How did you become friends with your best friend?"
654. "What other friends do you have and how did you succeed in becoming friends with them?"
655. "What do your friends and other people like about you?"
656. "How might you be able to use the qualities that allow you to build friendships to find someone who can support and help you?"

657. "How old are you? You must be . . . years old."
658. "If you were in charge, how would you want your life to change?"
659. "Suppose a wizard visited your house tonight and, with his wand, magically made the things that are troubling you go away. What would be different tomorrow morning and what would you be doing differently?"
660. "You must have a good reason to . . . Please tell me more."
661. "What would you say your parents (teachers, siblings) are doing now that is helpful?"
662. "What would you like your parents or teachers to do that they aren't doing now to help you with . . . ?"
663. "What difference would that make between you?"
664. "Would you tell me more about what you did instead of engaging in the problematic behavior?"
665. "How do you do that? Would you show me?"
666. "When did you realize that you had to start doing something else?"
667. "Are you a person who . . . ? How do you do that? Where did you learn that?"
668. "Suppose I were to talk to your parents (or teacher). What would they say is going better?"
669. "Suppose I were to talk to your parents or teacher. How would they say you managed that?"
670. "What would your best friend say you would like to be different?"
671. "What would your best friend say is going better and how would he or she say you managed that?"
672. "How could your best friend be able to help you?"
673. "Do you think it would be a good idea to bring your friend along sometime so that we can explore together how he or she can help you?"
674. "What would your best friend say you're like when you get along well together?"
675. "What would your parents say you're good at, even if you're too shy to talk about that here?"
676. "What does your mother (father, teacher) like about you? What makes him or her proud?"
677. "What would your teacher say if I asked him or her what you're good at in school?"
678. "How can you surprise your parents?"
679. "Suppose you were to pretend, at home or in school, that a miracle

had happened and that the problems were all gone. What would you be doing differently?"

680. "If you could make three wishes, what would you wish for?"
681. "What would you do differently if your wishes came true?"
682. "Suppose you could design a nice day at home. What would everyone at home have to do for it to be a good day for you?"
683. "Suppose I could magically transport the two of us 1 year or 2 years into the future. What would we see when we look at you when you're doing fine?"
684. "What animal most resembles you when you're doing well? What does that animal do then?"
685. "What animal most resembles you when you're not doing well? What does that animal do then?"
686. "What animal would you rather be than the animal you are right now?"
687. "How can you change from the animal that you are right now into the other?"
688. "When are times when you've already begun to change from the one animal into the other? How do you do that?"
689. "How would your parents or teacher see that you've begun to change into the other animal?"
690. "What difference would that make between you?"
691. "Suppose you were to make a drawing of how you would like to be. What would you draw?" The child may then actually make the drawing.
692. "And if you made a drawing of the current problem, what differences would I see between the two drawings?"
693. "Suppose you were to make a drawing of how you would like things to look at home. What would that drawing look like?"
694. "You say you don't need to be here. How come you don't need to be here?"
695. "Whose idea was it for you to come? What do you think he or she would like to be different as a result of our session here?"
696. "How do you feel about that? How do you see it?"
697. "You undoubtedly have a good reason to say that I can't help you. Please tell me more."
698. "What happened during sessions with previous therapists, and what could they have done differently so that the sessions *would* have been useful?"

699. "How would you be able to surprise your parents or teachers?"
700. "What would your parents or teachers say they would have to see to know that you no longer have to come here?"
701. "Suppose you decided to do those things. What would be different between you and them?"
702. "Would you tell me what you're doing well that makes you say that you don't need help and don't need to be here?"
703. "What are you good at at home? And at school? What sports and activities are you good at?"
704. "What do you do that makes you think things aren't so bad after all?"

Questions for Groups (Couples, Families)

705. "What is your common goal?"
706. "How is that a problem for each of you?"
707. "What do the two of you want to see instead of the problem?"
708. "How would the two of you like your relationship to be different?"
709. "What kind of relationship would you like to have?"
710. "What difference would that make for each of you?"
711. "What would you do differently in the relationship that you hope to have?"
712. "How would that help the other person?"
713. "What would the other person do differently in the relationship that you hope to have?"
714. "How would that help you?"
715. "What would be the first small step you could take to improve the relationship?"
716. "What would be the first small step the other person could take to improve the relationship?"
717. "What would your ideal relationship look like?"
718. "If the ideal relationship is a 10 and a 0 is the worst relationship you can imagine, where are you together?"
719. "If 10 = pure cooperation, and 0 = pure conflict, where are you together?"
720. "How come things aren't worse?"
721. "Who has contributed to things not being worse than they currently are?"
722. "Who was the first to think that you should seek help, and what gave him or her that idea?"

723. "Suppose you did have a common goal. What might that goal look like?"
724. "Where do you want to be together in 5 or 10 years? What do you want things to look like then?"
725. "What would your children like your relationship to look like in the future?"
726. "What would your children say is needed for that to happen?"
727. "What would your children say the first step could be?"
728. "How would your children notice that you'd reached your preferred future (to a sufficient degree)?"
729. "How might your children be able to help you reach your preferred future?"
730. "How will you celebrate with your children when you attain your goal?"
731. "What have you done together to make things go better this week?"
732. "What are you good at together?"
733. "What qualities do you value in the other person?"
734. "What positive expectations did you have about the relationship that have been realized?"
735. "How can you catch each other doing something for which you could pay each other a compliment?"
736. "What else do you both think needs to happen?"
737. "How will your lives change if that happens more often in the coming weeks?"
738. "What do you know about the other person that gives you hope for improvement?"
739. "What does the other person know about you that gives him or her hope for improvement?"
740. "How is the other person's problem a problem for you?"
741. "How do you explain that problem to yourself or to the other person? How can that help you?"
742. "Suppose the other person were able to tell me what has happened or what has caused this problem. How might that help him or her?"
743. "What will indicate to you that things are going a little better for the other person, knowing him or her as you do?"
744. "What difference will it make between you and the other person when things are going somewhat better?"
745. "What difference will it make for the other person's relationships

with the people around him or her when things are going somewhat better?"

746. "How can you end your relationship in as positive a way as possible
for you both?"

747. "How can you end your relationship in as positive a way as possible
for the children?"

748. "What would the ideal termination of your relationship look like?"

749. "On a scale of 10 to 0, how would you rate the current situation?"

750. "At what number would you like to end up so that you will both be
satisfied with the end of the relationship?"

751. "How might you make this a win-win situation for you both?"

752. "How have you ended relationships in a positive way in the past, and
which of those strategies can you apply again?"

753. "How will your life be different when you've been able to end this
relationship in a positive way?"

754. "What price are you willing to pay to make things as hard as possible
on the other person?"

755. "How much energy do you want to expend on that, and how much
energy does that leave you for other—probably more enjoyable—
things in life?"

756. "How long do you want to keep on paying that price?"

757. "How can you surprise your partner (child, parent)?"

758. "Suppose you were to do something subtle to surprise the other
person. What might it be?"

759. "What will you do when you see the other person do that for you?"

760. "Suppose you woke up in 'Parent Land' tomorrow morning, where
all parents are highly valued and all children are always on their
best behavior. What would you see those parents doing for
themselves and their children that makes them so happy?"

761. "And if you were to take two of the things you learned from those
parents back with you to try at home with your own children, what
would those two things be?"

762. "How have you as parents solved comparable problems in the past?"

763. "How does the other person (your family) explain the improvement?"

764. "What tells you that your child is capable of engaging in the desired
behavior?"

765. "How did you notice that your child responded well to this?"

766. "In the coming weeks, what will all of you do so that things will go (even) better at home?"
767. "When do you want members of your family to help you?"
768. "How do members of your family know that you would like them to help you?"
769. "When do you want your partner to help you?"
770. "How does your partner know that you would like him or her to help you?"
771. "How does your progress help your partner or family?"
772. "Who has been the most helpful so far?"
773. "What does your partner (family) know about you that gives him or her confidence that you will succeed in . . . ?"
774. "What will your partner (family) do differently when he or she is no longer worried about you?"
775. "Suppose your child did all the things you would like him or her to do. How would he or she say you treat him or her differently?"
776. "What will you do differently together when this is no longer a problem for all of you?"

Questions for Clients in Cognitive Therapy

777. "What is already going well and doesn't need to change?"
778. "What do you want to see instead of the problem behavior?"
779. "What do you want to see instead of the dysfunctional cognitions?"
780. "What desired behavior is already present sometimes?"
781. "What desired behavior do you want to engage in more in the future?"
782. "How can you motivate yourself to engage in that behavior more often?"
783. "How can others motivate you to engage in that behavior more often?"
784. "How can I motivate you to engage in that behavior more often?"
785. "When does the desired behavior (or cognition or emotion) manifest itself? How do you manage that?"
786. "What are the consequences (advantages and disadvantages) of the desired behavior (or cognition or emotion)?"
787. "How does the desired behavior (or cognition or emotion) help you reach your goal?"
788. "How can pretending help you reach your goal?"

789. "What functional cognitions or schemata do you already have sometimes?"
790. "What functional cognitions or schemata do you want to have more of in the future?"
791. "When do the desired cognitions or schemata already occur? How do you manage that?"
792. "What are the consequences (advantages and disadvantages) of the desired cognitions or schemata?"
793. "How do these cognitions or schemata help you reach the goal?"
794. "What positive basic assumptions would you like to have (instead of negative ones)?"
795. "What positive basic assumptions do you already have?"
796. "How do those assumptions help you?"
797. "Suppose you had more positive assumptions. What difference would that make for you?"
798. "What would you do differently then?"
799. "How would others notice that you have more positive assumptions?"
800. "Suppose I were to make a film of your situation in the future, when you have more positive basic assumptions. What would I see that would tell me that it's a film of the future?"
801. "How credible are those positive assumptions now?"
802. "How credible would you like those assumptions to be in the future?"
803. "How would you notice that those positive thoughts have become (sufficiently) credible?"
804. "How would others notice that those positive thoughts have become (sufficiently) credible?"
805. "When do you already have some of those positive assumptions for a short period of time?"
806. "When have the negative assumptions been absent or less of a problem?"
807. "How do you manage that? What is different then?"
808. "What small experiment could help you get one step closer to your goal?"
809. "What experiments have you done before that have helped you?"
810. "What experiments have you considered but not yet carried out?"
811. "What is needed for you to carry out those experiments?"
812. "Who or what can help you make the experiment a success?"
813. "Where will you find the courage to start this experiment?"

814. "Suppose you engage in the desired behavior. What would that mean for you?"
815. "What helpful thoughts take the place of unhelpful thoughts?"
816. "What does that mean for you? What else could it mean?"
817. "Suppose you were given a diagnosis. How would that help you get closer to your goal?"
818. "Suppose you had insight into the origin of your problem. How would that bring you closer to your goal?"

Questions About Medication

819. "Has anyone ever suggested to you that medication might help you reach your goal?"
820. "What are your thoughts about the usefulness of this medication for you (or the other person)?"
821. "How do you think this medication could work for you (or the other person)?"
822. "Have you (or has the other person) ever used medication before, and how did it help?"
823. "Suppose this medication were effective. What changes would you see that would allow you to say that the medication works well for you (or the other person)?"
824. "Suppose this medication were effective and you were doing well. What would your life look like? What would you be doing differently then? What difference would that make for you?"
825. "What do you think you could do to make sure that the medication works for you (or the other person)?"
826. "You must have a good reason to take a critical view of the use of medication. Please tell me more."
827. "What do you already know about the effects of this medication?"
828. "How can you maximize the chance that the medication will be effective?"
829. "What do you already know about the possible side effects of this medication?"
830. "How does knowing about possible side effects help you?"
831. "What reassurance do you need in order to consider a trial with this medication?"
832. "Who can reassure you on this score?"
833. "What possible side effects would you be willing to live with?"

834. "Suppose you were to consider an experiment with this medication. What experiment could it be?"

835. "What would be the maximum dosage you would be willing to take as an experiment?"

836. "What is needed for you to persevere in using this medication?"

837. "How would you notice that you no longer need this medication?"

838. "How would others notice that you no longer need this medication?"

839. "How can you maintain control of your life, even if you use this medication?"

840. "What medication have you considered but not yet tried?"

841. "What is needed so that you *would* do that as an experiment?"

842. "What do you think such an experiment would have to entail to maximize your chance of success? Who or what can best help you with that?"

843. "Pretend that we are living 1 year, 5 years, or 10 years in the future and you are feeling good. Looking back on the present, what would you say helped you take medication?"

844. "Suppose a good friend had the same problem and was considering medication. What would your advice be?"

845. "Suppose your child had a problem that might be helped by medication. What would you do as a parent?"

Questions About Relapse

846. "What can you do to ensure that things start going badly for you again as quickly as possible?"

847. "What would you advise someone who would like to have this problem to do?"

848. "What can you do to prevent a relapse?"

849. "How do you prevent yourself from being at a lower number on the scale?"

850. "How did you manage to prevent relapse before?"

851. "How do you manage to get back on the right track?"

852. "How did you manage to get back on the right track before?"

853. "What did the right track look like?"

854. "How did you notice you were on the right track again?"

855. "How did you find the courage then to get back on the right track and not throw in the towel?"

856. "How would you be able to do the same thing again in the future?"

857. "How do you know that you will have the strength and courage to get back on the right track?"
858. "What other qualities do you have that you can use to help yourself do that?"
859. "What have you done before to get back on the right track?"
860. "Who and what helped you do that then?"
861. "Who and what could be of help in the future, should that be necessary?"
862. "How would you like to be helped, should that prove necessary?"
863. "What needs to happen to ensure that you maintain positive results?"
864. "What can you yourself do to ensure that you maintain positive results?"
865. "On a scale of 10 to 0, where 10 = great confidence and 0 = no confidence at all, how much confidence do you have at this moment?"
866. "On a scale of 10 to 0, where 10 = very motivated and 0 = not motivated at all, how motivated are you to maintain your current success?"
867. "What can you remember and use from these sessions if a time comes when things are not going as well as they are now?"
868. "How will you pull through, even if you're at a very low number?"
869. "How do you manage to handle adversity?"
870. "Where did you learn that?"
871. "You must be a very resolute person, a fighter. Please tell me more."
872. "In what other situations have you been that resolute?"
873. "What do others need to do to help you relapse as quickly as possible?"
874. "What do others need to do to help you get back on track as quickly as possible?"

Questions for Coaching Managers, Teams, and Organizations

875. "How will your team function in the future when it works together as a dream team?"
876. "What would a greatly improved work environment look like?"
877. "What would your dream solution look like?"
878. "Where does your organization want to be 1 year, 5 years, or 10 years from now?" (goal formulation)
879. "What does that look like in concrete, positive, and realistic behavioral terms?"

880. "What would the outcome of this discussion have to be so that you can walk out the door thinking it was good for you to have this discussion?" (goal formulation)
881. "What do you personally want to achieve?"
882. "Which of those things would you most like to see realized in the coming year?"
883. "Which of those things is the most important for you to realize in the coming year?"
884. "What would indicate to you that you are headed in the right direction?"
885. "How will you know that your organization's goal has been reached?"
886. "What small steps do you think you need to take to get there?"
887. "When have you successfully collaborated with another person in the past, and how did you manage that?"
888. "What is happening in your team or your organization that you would like to keep the way it is?"
889. "What have been good times in your organization?"
890. "Who does what to make those good times happen?"
891. "What is going well in your organization, despite the current problems?"
892. "What are your organization's strong points and how are they achieved?"
893. "What are your coworkers' strong points?" How do they manage to . . . ?"
894. "What compliments can you pay your coworkers?"
895. "What compliments have you already paid your coworkers?"
896. "What compliments can they pay each other?"
897. "What compliments do they already pay or have they already paid each other?"
898. "How can you see to it that you pay your coworkers more compliments?"
899. "How can you see to it that your coworkers pay each other more compliments?"
900. "How would the collaboration in your organization change if that were to happen?"
901. "How can your organization's strong points best be deployed to reach the goal?"
902. "What successes has the organization achieved in the past?"

903. "What are the best memories that you have of your organization?"
904. "What do you not want to lose in your organization?"
905. "What should definitely remain the same in your organization?"
906. "What did you do differently as an organization when a previous project ran aground?"
907. "What aspects of that deadlocked project still work well?"
908. "How do your coworkers succeed in resolving situations that aren't working in the right direction?"
909. "What would indicate to the organization that a small improvement had occurred?"
910. "What would you be doing differently then? What would the members of your team be doing differently then? What would the organization do differently then?"
911. "What difference would that make for your coworkers and the organization?"
912. All scaling questions regarding the organization's goal
913. "On a scale of 10 to 0 of how hopeful you are that you will reach your goal, where would you say you are today? What is already working in the right direction?"
914. "How do you handle difficulties or setbacks that your team or company experiences? What works best?"
915. "Who in your team or company deals well with difficulties or setbacks or is untroubled by them? What do they do differently?"
916. "What could you or your team have done differently to prevent this from happening or to ensure that it was easier to deal with?"
917. "How can that help you face difficulties in the future?"
918. "What might be an indication that this meeting was useful?"
919. "What would have to be different so that you would no longer have to meet with me about this problem?"
920. "How did you manage . . . for that long?"
921. "When does the mutual collaboration work well or better?"
922. "How did you succeed in finding a solution that quickly?"
923. "How will your director or management notice that you have made this project a success?"
924. "What concrete signs will tell you that . . . is a success?"
925. "What will be the first small sign that improvement is on the way?"
926. "What would help your coworkers to better meet their commitments?"
927. "What solutions have your coworkers already found by themselves? How did they manage that?"

928. "What are qualities that your coworkers value in you as an executive?"
929. "What do you think makes them value that in you?"
930. "What are the qualities that your manager values in you?"
931. "What makes him or her value those qualities?"
932. "What are qualities that your colleagues value in you?"
933. "What makes them value those qualities?"
934. "What has been a high point in your career? Can you tell me something about that?"
935. "How are successes in your organization usually celebrated?"
936. "What would it be like for you if there were more opportunities to experience such high points?"
937. "Which person from your work life do you especially value?"
938. "What have you learned from that person?"
939. "How does that lesson manifest itself in your daily life and at work?"
940. "What is your favorite way of showing your coworkers that you value what they do?"
941. "How would it affect your coworkers (your team) if you showed your appreciation in this way more often?"

Questions for Clients in Conflict

942. "What *do* you already agree on?"
943. "What *does* work in your communication? How did you do that before the conflict arose?"
944. "How have you resolved conflicts before together?"
945. "What did you learn from that and which of those lessons could you use again now?"
946. "What positive contribution does the other person make to your relationship? What do you think the other person wants to achieve by doing that?"
947. "What could he or she do differently in the future to encourage you to adopt a different attitude?"
948. "Would you be willing to try that approach now to see whether it works?"
949. "Is there anything you would like to apologize for?"
950. "What would you like to give the other person credit for?"
951. "What would you like the other person to give you credit for?"
952. "In what ways would your relationship improve if you didn't do those negative things anymore?"

953. "How can the gap between you and the other person be made smaller so that you can bridge it?"

954. "What is needed for you to stop trying to convince the other person that you're right?"

955. "What would you most like to hear from the other person at this moment?"

956. "What would you like to be different as a result of mediation?"

957. "What would be the first signs that things are going better between you?"

958. "What has the other person said to convince you that he or she wants to find a resolution to this conflict?"

959. "What would he or she say that both of you need to do to get along better?"

960. "Suppose you *were* able to find a way to resolve the conflict. To what extent would you be willing to dedicate yourselves to it?"

961. "Suppose you were unable to find a way to resolve the conflict. What problems would that produce? And how would you want to deal with that?"

962. "What have you noticed that gives you the sense that the other person understands you, even if only a tiny bit?"

963. "Suppose you did have a common goal. What might it be?"

964. "What small sign have you already detected that gives you the sense that this conflict can be resolved?"

965. "I understand what is important to you both. What solution would meet both your wishes?"

966. "Suppose the other person were to respect your need to . . . What would be different between the two of you?"

967. "What are you not talking about that still needs to be discussed?"

968. "If 10 indicates that you completely trust the other person, and 0 that you don't trust the other person at all, what rating would you give? How do you manage to be at that number? What would 1 point higher look like?"

969. If the client believes that the other person should change: "And what would you yourself do differently then?"

970. "Suppose you had this conflict not with so-and-so but with someone else. What would your thoughts about the situation be if the other person weren't so-and-so but, for instance, your child or your best friend? What difference would that make? What solutions would

you then be able to come up with to resolve the conflict and what would your approach be?"

971. "Suppose you *were* able to agree on what the dispute is about in the mediation. How would you describe the dispute?"

972. "Suppose you were to sign a settlement agreement that only includes commitments you can both agree on. What might such a contract look like?"

973. "What will happen if this mediation fails?"

974. "When has the conflict been absent or less of a problem and what has been different then?"

975. "At what times does the conflict cease to be a problem? How do you put a halt to it and what are you doing differently at that moment?"

976. "How were you able to end a previous conflict together?"

977. "How do you treat each other differently at times when there is no conflict?"

978. "How do you resolve conflicts in other situations?"

979. "In what way will arguing help you reach your (collective) goal?"

980. "In what way do you usually manage to end an argument? Which of those strategies can you apply now?"

981. "How did you work together before the current conflict arose?"

982. "What do you want to achieve with the conflict for . . . (the organization, the children)?"

983. "What do you need from the other person to establish or reestablish a good relationship?"

984. "What can you offer the other person to establish or reestablish a good relationship?"

985. "What do you need from the other person so that you can split up amicably?"

986. "What can you offer the other person so that you can split up amicably?"

987. "Suppose the other person were to offer you what you need to establish or reestablish a good relationship. What would you do differently then?"

988. "Suppose the other person were to offer you what you need to split up amicably. What would you do differently then?"

989. "How much energy do you want to expend on the conflict? How much energy does that leave for other—more enjoyable—things in your life?"

990. "What is needed for you to give up or to learn to accept this conflict and move on with your life?"
991. "What are you still not able to forgive the other person for? What price are you willing to pay for not forgiving him or her? How long do you want to keep paying that price?"
992. "How can this conflict improve your life?"
993. "What is funny or even ridiculous about your conflict? How does that help you?"
994. "If this were your last conversation with the other person, what would you want to say?"
995. "Suppose the other person apologized. What would change in your relationship? What difference would that make?"
996. "Suppose the other person apologized. What would you start doing differently?"
997. "How do you think the other person would react to that?"
998. "What would it mean to you if the other person reacted differently to that? And how would you, in turn, respond to that?"
999. "Suppose the other person doesn't apologize. How can you go on regardless?"
1000. "How can apologizing help you reach your common goal?"
1001. "What do you eventually want to achieve by demanding an apology?" (goal formulation)

....

CHAPTER 11

Reflecting on the Session

Seeing yourself as you want to be
is the key to personal growth.
—Anonymous

REFLECTION ON THE SESSION

The professional can reflect on sessions in the case of a successful treatment and in the case of stagnation or failure of the treatment. "What did work in these sessions and what would I do again next time in a comparable situation? What did not work in the sessions and what would I do differently next time in a comparable situation?" In principle, the professional does well in any case to reflect for awhile on each session he or she conducts. Reflection may also take place in the company of colleagues, in the form of peer consultation or supervision.

The solution-focused professional always asks him- or herself a number of solution-focused questions at the end of a session. These questions may also be asked in the presence of colleagues. The questions help the professional reflect on his or her contribution to the session. They also help develop his or her solution-focused skills. The questions from the interactional matrix can also be helpful in this respect.

SOLUTION-FOCUSED QUESTIONS FOR THE PROFESSIONAL

Some solution-focused questions for the professional to ask him- or herself about his or her professional performance are:

- Suppose I were to conduct this session again. What would I do differently or better next time?

- What would the client say I could do differently or better?
- What difference would that make for the client?
- What difference would that make for me?
- Suppose I conduct sessions in the future with a client who has a comparable problem. Which interventions would I use again and which wouldn't I?
- How satisfied do I think the client is with my performance (on a scale of 10 to 0)?
- What would he or she say about how I've managed to get to that number?
- What would it look like for him or her if I were 1 point higher on the scale?
- What difference would that make for the treatment?
- What would the client say if I asked him or her how I could move up 1 point?
- How satisfied am I myself with my performance (on a scale of 10 to 0)?
- How did I manage to get to that number?
- What would 1 point higher on the scale look like?
- What difference would that make for the treatment?
- How could I move up 1 point?
- What would that take?
- What positive aspects of this treatment stand out?
- What useful information have I received from the client?
- Which of his or her competencies and features can I compliment the client on?
- What does the client want to achieve in meeting with me?
- What competencies can this client utilize to solve the problem that brings him or her here?
- What kind of resources does the client need from his or her environment? Which resources are already available?
- What information about or impression of this client do I have that may help in determining his or her goal?
- What do I see in this client (these partners, this family, this team) that tells me that he or she can reach his or her goal?
- What aspects of my professional performance do I definitely want to maintain?

In addition to scaling questions about reaching the goal, and about hope for change, motivation, and confidence, some solution-focused questions for the professional to ask about his or her performance are:

- What aspects of my personal life do I definitely want to maintain?
- When I experience problems on a personal or professional level, what works best in helping me solve them?
- What resources do I have at my disposal in my personal or professional life?
- What competencies and qualities do I have?
- How can I utilize them to find solutions to potential problems?
- Where would I like to be in 1 year, 5 years, or 10 years?
- What would the miracle look like for me?
- What would indicate to me that I am on the right track?
- What would indicate to others that I am on the right track?
- What would be the first small step I could take on that path?
- What difference would that make to me? And to others?
- How would things change between me and the important people in my life?

Berg and Steiner (2003) have suggested the following solution-focused questions for the professional if there has been no progress:

- If I were to ask the client how my contribution has helped, even if only a little bit, what would he or she respond?
- What does the client consider to be a sign of a successful outcome?
- How realistic is that outcome?
- What do I myself consider to be a sign of success?
- If the client's and my views differ, what needs to be done so that we can work on the same goal?
- On a scale of 0 to 10, where would the client say he or she is right now?
- What needs to happen to bring the client 1 point closer to 10?

At the end of each solution-focused session, the professional may request that clients offer feedback (see Chapter 3). If not only the professional but also the client provides feedback, there will be greater equality in the cooperative relationship. Client feedback is a good source of information for the professional. Usually, the client can indicate in precise terms what the professional should continue to do and what he or she could do differently. It is a shame when professionals do not solicit their clients' feedback, because it can help them to further develop professionally. Chapter 2 described the SRS, the Session Rating Scale, devised by Duncan et al. (2004). Their research has shown that sessions are more effective when the professional gets direct feedback from the client about how he or she experienced the session and the cooperative relationship.

Wampold and Bhati (2004) argued that the persona of the therapist is of much greater significance to the success of a treatment than the treatment itself, and that evidence-based research concentrates on less consequential matters (i.e., the treatment itself). Their research indicated that the therapeutic relationship is 7 times as important as the treatment itself. Aspecific variables such as offering hope and the professional's belief in his or her own method appear to be more significant to a successful outcome than the methodology that the professional employs.

A follow-up session a few months after the treatment has ended may provide information not only about the client's current situation but also about what has worked and what is going better. Moreover, clients generally experience this form of aftercare as solicitous and pleasant. A follow-up conversation may of course take place via phone or e-mail as well. In my opinion, such follow-up sessions could be conducted more frequently than has been customary. One might also ask clients for feedback more often.

SOLUTION-FOCUSED PEER CONSULTATION MODELS

Another form of reflection involves peer consultation. One can work effectively in a solution-focused way during peer consultation, too. In peer consultation, it is customary to present problem cases or "stuck" cases; the emphasis is on what isn't going well and what should be different. With a solution-focused approach, one looks, rather, at what *is* going well: When was a treatment successful and who did what to make that success happen?

EXERCISE 24

At the end of the next 10 or 20 sessions, ask the questions suggested by Berg and Steiner for cases in which there is no progress, regardless of whether you deem the sessions successful or not. You may also invite your client to give feedback or to give feedback more often: "What was important to you in this session? What helped? What would you like to be done differently?" Allow yourself to be surprised by the client's ideas and your own ideas about what does and doesn't work in your interviewing.

The underlying idea is that participants learn just as much from their own and each other's successes as they do from failures. What follows are a number of solution-focused peer consultation models.

Little-Time-and-Many-Cases-Model: The Hardest Case

In this model, the most difficult case is presented and a limited amount of time (5 minutes maximum) is allotted to each case. Peer consultation may occur in pairs or in groups, with everyone taking a turn.

The goal is to go through a large number of cases in a short amount of time. This model takes up little time and calls for a lot of input. The focus is on how the professional can move up 1 point on the scale. Background information about the case is unnecessary; what matters is what the person presenting the case is able or willing to do to move up 1 point on the scale. What would he or she do (differently or more often) to achieve a 1-point improvement? Or what would this person do differently or more often if he or she had more confidence that the client would reach the goal or if he or she had more hope? The objective is for the presenter to recognize small improvements. The model is to the point, relaxed, fun, and effective in its search for solutions. Questions that are asked include:

- "How would you rate the last session, if 10 means that the therapy is going well and 0 means there has been no improvement. Is the client making progress?"
- "What makes you give it that rating (and not a lower one)?"
- "If the next session were rated 1 point higher, what would be different then and how would you notice that? What would you do differently?"
- "What ideas does everyone else have?"

These questions may be repeated for everyone's second most difficult case.

Do-More-of-It Model: The Best Session

This form of peer consultation is best undertaken in pairs. In this peer consultation model, positive experiences are discussed (15 minutes per participant). The nub is: "How did you manage to make it such a good session?" The focus is on repeatable interventions and on exceptions. The conversations pertain to positive experiences that the professional's partner can magnify by asking for details about them.

This model, as well as the previous one, is conducive to fostering a good atmosphere. Questions that are asked include:

- "What was your best session recently?"
- "What made it such a good session?"
- "How did you do that?"
- "What does that say about you?"
- "How would you be able to do that more often (or again)?"

Cognitive Model: The Stagnating Case

This model is used in the event of an impasse and focuses on the ideas and convictions of the professional that are impeding the progress of the therapy. Which of his or her cognitions are perpetuating the impasse? The central point is that the motivation that the professional attributes to the client carries over into the cooperative relationship. It is important to examine whether a different interpretation of the behavior and the motives of the client might break the impasse. Positive relabeling and reinterpretation take place. What may constitute another credible explanation for the client's behavior? In that case, what would the professional do differently during the session and how might it run more smoothly then? This model appeals to the professional's self-reflectiveness.

- What exactly do you and the client do during the session?
- How much motivation would you say that the client has, if you were to vent your frustrations to a colleague (if you really poured out your heart)?
- How does your interpretation always cause you to react in the same manner?
- How might you look at it differently? What more positive motivation might the client have?
- If you were to act in accordance with a different interpretation, what would you do differently then?
- What difference would that make? How would the next session go better then?

Team-Behind-the-Mirror Model: The Reflecting Team

The members of the team sit in a circle, and the presenter's case is discussed according to protocol. Roughly 20 minutes are allotted to each case. In addition to the presenter, there is a discussion leader, who is seated outside the circle and, acting as a director, does not participate. The others form the helping team that addresses the problem that has been presented. This collegial input often has a positive effect on how the team functions, as participants are able to familiarize themselves with each other's expertise. The maximum size of the group is eight people. The model has clear steps and is somewhat rigid. However, the presenters often derive much benefit from the clarifying questions as well as the affirmations, which they may receive with a thank you. The steps are as follows:

1. *Preparation.* Everyone thinks of a case to introduce. The first group member is asked to present his or her case.
2. *Presentation.* The first presenter briefly describes his or her case and specifies what he or she would like help with. The others listen without interrupting.
3. *Clarification.* The group members take turns asking one clarifying question and one follow-up question (*what, where, when, who,* and *how* questions; preferably no *why* questions). Everyone remains silent until it's his or her turn.
4. *Affirmation.* Taking turns, each group member discusses what about the professional he or she is most impressed by in the described situation. The professional remains silent (except to say thank you).
5. *Reflection.* Anything that seems relevant can be shared: technical guidance, advice, contemplation, metaphors, poetry, associations, and so forth. Sometimes someone offers a reflection prompted by an earlier reflection. Each group member says something or skips his or her turn.
6. *Conclusion.* The presenter talks about what most appealed to him or her in the discussion, what seemed applicable, and what he or he is planning to do.

This model can also be used in the client's presence.

Brief-and-Recent-Success Model
In this short-form model, all participants briefly describe a recent success. This succinct model may also be used as a warm-up for other variations of peer review models.

Success-Maximizing Model
In this long form, one success (or more) is probed in greater depth. The following steps are taken:

1. All participants briefly mention a success. A few successes are chosen for further discussion, depending on how much time is available.
2. For each successful case, the participants ask each other questions, and together they examine what the success entails exactly, what helpful interventions have been applied, and what the success signifies for the professional and the client.
3. The participants take turns complimenting the professional who presented the case on what he or she did well as well as other things about the presenter that they respect and value.
6. Each participant briefly relates what he or she has learned from discussing the successful case and how he or she might put that knowledge to use.
7. All participants indicate what about the meeting they found useful and beneficial and which of those things they might implement.
8. The meeting is concluded and another one is scheduled.

Competence Model
In a team or a peer consultation group, participants pair up to explore each other's competencies. This occurs as follows:

1. Everyone thinks back to a recent session success.
2. One member of the pair interviews his or her colleague to find out what worked. The colleague subsequently interviews the other person to find out what worked for him or her (15 minutes combined).
3. Participants share their colleagues' success factors with at least two colleagues (10 minutes).

In this model, participants hear four success stories in quick succession: their own story, the story of the colleague they interviewed, and the stories of two other colleagues. This model allows for some physical activity, as participants mingle with their colleagues to recount their partners' success factors.

Finally, a participant may volunteer to present a case. The others one may ask the four basic solution-focused questions:

1. "What are your best hopes?"
2. "What difference would that make?"
3. "What is already working?"
4. "What would be the next sign of progress? What would be your next step?"

Asking these four questions often makes discussing the case itself unnecessary.

REFLECTION ON THE SESSION BY THE CLIENT

It has been said that competency enhances efficacy. That is why so much training and so many courses are offered. But research shows that there is barely any relationship between professionals' level of experience and their effectiveness (Clement, 1994). It is even possible that the more training a professional has, the less effective he or she is! Hiatt and Hargrave (1995) found that therapists who demonstrated low effectiveness had worked more years than therapists who demonstrated high effectiveness. They also found that ineffective therapists were unaware that they were ineffective. In fact, these therapists considered themselves just as effective as the genuinely effective therapists in the study! It seems important, therefore, for the professional's competence to be assessed not just by the professional him- or herself but by his or her clients as well. To that end, Miller et al. started asking their clients for brief feedback after each meeting. They have argued that the use of client feedback invites clients to become equal partners in the sessions: "Giving clients the perspective of the driver's seat instead of the back of the bus may also enable consumers to gain confidence that a positive outcome is just down the road." They further stated: "We advocate routine and systematic assessment of the client's perceptions of progress and fit, so that the clinician can empirically tailor the therapy to the client's individual needs and characteristics" (S. D. Miller et al., 1997, p. 15).

S. D. Miller et al. (1997) developed the SRS, the Session Rating Scale. At the end of each meeting, the client provides the professional with feedback on three areas that research has shown determine how effective cooperative relationships are in bringing about change—the relationship, goals and topics, and approach or method—and the session itself. The client is given a piece of paper with four 10-centimeter-long lines, each representing one of the areas that determine effectiveness. For relationship, for example, 0 means "I did not feel heard, understood, and respected," and 10 means "I felt heard, understood, and respected." The client places an x on the line to indicate the extent to which he or she felt heard, understood, and respected during the session. After the client has completed all the scales, the scores for all four scales are then summed. Higher scores (above 30, the maximum score being 40) reveal a better cooperative relationship and a greater likelihood of change; lower scores indicate that the relationship requires extra attention. In that case, the professional should ask: "What can I do differently during the next meeting to earn a higher rating?" The SRS is first and foremost intended to be a tool promoting conversation between the client and the professional. Duncan stated:

> Clients whose therapists had access to progress information, like the SRS, were less likely to get worse with treatment and were twice as likely to achieve a clinically significant change. These are amazing, if not revolutionary, results—nothing else in the history of psychotherapy has been shown to increase effectiveness this much! (2005, p. 183)

The SRS can be found in Appendix E and at http://heartandsoulof change.com/measures. There is also an SRS for children and adolescents, and the SRS is now available in many languages. Registering on the Web site gives users access to all the scales, permission to use them, and information on how to use them.

SUMMARY

- Reflection by the professional on his or her own performance results in better sessions and helps him or her develop solution-focused skills.
- The professional may ask solution-focused questions about his or her professional performance at the end of each session and in cases where the no progress is made during the session.
- Reflection by the client at the end of each meeting by means of, for example, the Session Rating Scale significantly contributes to the effectiveness of the therapy.
- There are many solution-focused peer consultation models. They focus predominantly on the professional's successes and competencies.

CHAPTER 12

Solution-Focused Interviewing
from Start to Finish

People have all they need to solve their problems.
—John Walter

Kevin is a 52-year-old high school math teacher. He presents with complaints of insomnia, heart palpitations, panic attacks, diminished concentration, unexpected crying fits (even in class), and elevated blood pressure. The family doctor has referred him to a clinical psychologist. He has been home on sick leave for over 2 months and the mere thought of going back to school causes him unpleasant physical reactions: He becomes nauseous and begins to shake. Since he's been at home, the situation has deteriorated rather than improved: He is having more crying fits and the physical symptoms have worsened. He has started drinking a fair amount of alcohol in recent months. He is not taking any medication.

THE FIRST SESSION

The first session begins with introductions; the professional works to foster a positive atmosphere by connecting with the client through discussion of his interests, relationships, and hobbies. The therapist compliments Kevin on his decision to seek help. The therapist provides some information about the solution-focused method, which appeals to Kevin. The opening question is: "What brings you here?" Kevin briefly relates his troubles and adds that he views a colleague's suicide the previous year as the cause of his complaints. He says it was a great shock and that the school administration did not arrange for counseling. He has felt alone in processing this and is angry about that. On the home front, meanwhile, his ailing father, who needs a lot of care, was living with him and the house was being remodeled, which demanded a lot of him. In addition, he mentions that another colleague is having psychological problems, too, and often fails to come to work for that reason, causing Kevin to have to work more hours. He is afraid that this colleague will commit suicide, too; she has, on occasion, made statements to that effect. The rapport and sense of camaraderie among the teachers at school have deteriorated, and arguments have arisen about this teacher's well-being and the allocation of her hours.

The therapist then asks the question regarding goal formulation: "What do you wish to have achieved by the end of the therapy to be able to say that it has been meaningful and useful?" Kevin replies he would like to be teaching again, get along well with his colleagues, and feel relaxed at school. This means that he would be able chat with his colleagues in the teachers' lounge again and have time for a cup of coffee before classes commence, that the tension and stress surrounding the teachers' teaching schedules would be alleviated, and that the teachers would once again support each other if someone is unable to come in because of illness. He wants to joke with the students again, to laugh, and to be able to casually lean back every now and then during class. He wants to reduce his alcohol consumption to a normal amount. In response to a scaling question, where 10 is his goal and 0 the worst moment he has ever experienced, he says he is currently at 2. The therapist then asks a competence question: "How do you manage to be at 2? How come you're not at 1 or even 0?" The client says he is at 2 because he receives a lot of support from his wife and children and sometimes he has days when he is doing a little better. The therapist inquires about these exceptions. The therapist also asks Kevin what number he would like to reach in order to end the therapy. Kevin says that a 7 or 8 is sufficient. The therapist compliments him on having sought help and on expressing his complaints and his goal so clearly. With this client, there is a customer relationship: He sees himself as part of the problem and part of the solution, and he is motivated to change his behavior. The professional asks Kevin whether he would like to come back, and if so, when.

THE SECOND SESSION

At the second session, which takes place two weeks later, Kevin is asked a scaling question: "On a scale of 10 to 0, where 10 represents the moment when you feel completely fine again and are back at work (the goal) and 0 represents the moment when you felt the worst, how would you rate your current state?" His answer is that he is now at 4. He indicates that he is at 4 because his mood has improved somewhat, he is more active (for example, he attended a concert with his wife), he is sleeping better, and he feels more comfortable with other people. He is reading a little again, is able to concentrate a bit better, feels calmer, and is able to enjoy things a bit more. His wife would give him a 4, too, he thinks, for she also notices that he is doing a little better and that he is more cheerful. In response to the competence question about how he managed to get from 2 to 4 that quickly, he says that formulating his goal during the first session has helped him focus his attention on what he wants and where he wants to end up, and that he "simply started doing things." He doesn't want to think about school just yet; he declines any contact with his colleagues. He did receive a bouquet of flowers with a card from the students, however. That also helped him get to 4.

After complimenting him on his rapid progress, the therapist asks the following scaling question: "What would a 5 look like? What would tell you that you were at a 5?" He replies that he would then have some contact with colleagues (he immediately adds that he really isn't ready for that yet) and that the physical symptoms would have subsided. When asked to state what would take the place of the "subsided physical symptoms" in positive terms, he answers that he would feel fitter then. He would get up earlier and maybe go for a run.

The homework suggestion that he receives is to go on with what works (a behavioral task), to reflect on what else he associates with a 5, perhaps also to ask others how they envisage a 5, and to observe when he gets a glimpse of a 5 and what he is doing differently or what is different at those times (an observation task). He wants to return in three weeks.

THE THIRD SESSION

The opening question of the third session is: "What is better?" Kevin indicates that the physical symptoms have further diminished, that he sent an e-mail to one of his colleagues to apologize for his part in an argument (that possibility had briefly come up during the previous session), and that he received a positive response from the colleague. His alcohol consumption has drastically decreased. He has also called the school principal and told her that he wants to be included in the class schedule again, starting with half the usual number of teaching hours. On a progress scale, he is now at a 6.5. The therapist again gives compliments and positive character interpretations: "You must be really resolute. Please tell me more."

To a scaling question about his confidence regarding the success of his return to school, he responds that he is at 7 or even 8. After all, he feels more rested, is happy with his colleague's kind response, and feels like going back. He has also decided to distance himself from the colleague with psychological problems. After the therapist compliments Kevin on everything he has already achieved and his great confidence that his return to school will be a success, the session is concluded. The homework he receives include the suggestion to continue with what works and the pretend task: "Choose a few days to pretend that you are 1 point higher on the scale than you actually are and note what difference it makes in your life and relationships so that you can tell me about it the next time."

THE FOLLOW-UP SESSION

At Kevin's request, a follow-up session takes place 3 months later. Again the opening question is: "What is better?" Kevin replies that things are going just fine. He's started school and enjoys being back. His colleagues and students welcomed him heartily, which moved him greatly. His physical complaints have largely disappeared and he reports that he's feeling stronger, that he's taking pleasure in everything again, and that he no longer frets as much about things like his colleague's suicide. He feels rested and he's been jogging. He really enjoyed the pretend task. On the progress scale, he now gives himself a rating of 8.5. His mood is positive and stable. The therapist asks some additional questions from the interactional matrix: "What rating do you think your wife would give you now?" He thinks she would give him an 8. The school principal and his students would give him an 8 as well, he believes, because everyone can see that he is considerably more cheerful and that he can laugh and joke again.

At Kevin's request, relapse prevention is discussed. The therapist asks: "What would you have to do to go back to a 4 or even a 2?" He says that he would have to get into arguments with colleagues again, work a lot of overtime at school, and place high demands on himself and his students. With a laugh, he says he'll be sure to guard against it coming to that (and he comfortably leans back as he says this). After the therapist has extensively complimented and congratulated him on the dynamic way in which he has managed to get his life back on track, the therapy is terminated. Kevin says he is happy with the result. Finally, the therapist asks: "How will you celebrate having reached your goal?" Kevin thinks for a minute and then decides to go to a nice restaurant with his wife for a festive meal. On this special occasion, it's fine to have a drink again, he thinks.

CHAPTER 13

Solution-Focused Brief Therapy as a Form of Cognitive Behavioral Therapy

An alternative approach is simply to build on your stability.
—W. Timothy Gallwey

There are differences and similarities between solution-focused brief therapy and forms of problem-focused therapy such as psychodynamic therapy, client-centered therapy, problem-solving therapy, cognitive behavioral therapy, and interpersonal therapy. The differences between solution-focused brief therapy and other therapies involve, among other things, phasing and the stance taken by the therapist.

The phases of problem-focused therapy usually are:

1. The client describes the problem, and data are gathered in a problem anamnesis.
2. The therapist analyzes the problem.
3. The therapist devises and suggests interventions (modification procedures).
4. The client carries out the intervention.
5. Treatment is evaluated and contact between the therapist and client may continue.

The phases of solution-focused brief therapy were discussed in Chapters 1, 3, and 4.

De Shazer (1991) wrote that if the professional accepts the client's description of the problem when he or she begins treatment, by the same logic the professional should also accept the client's declaration that he or she has sufficiently improved as a reason to end the treatment. This gave rise to the idea that the client's goal and his or her solutions are more important than the problems the client discusses. In this way, the distinction between problem and solution became clear and solution-focused brief therapy came into existence.

Solution-focused interviewing is sometimes referred to as "Carl Rogers with a twist," because the empathetic attitude of the professional (derived from Rogers's client-centered therapy) is combined with the client's behavior change.

Cepeda and Davenport (2006) drew a comparison between client-centered therapy, which they referred to as "person-centered therapy," and solution-focused brief therapy. They proposed an integration of the two forms of therapy, although there are significant differences in terms of the therapist's role and the timing of the components of the therapy. In their opinion, solution-focused interviewing can be useful at a later stage of client-centered therapy (part II), when the client has had the opportunity for self-actualization and growth in the first part of the therapy and has become the person he or she would like to be. Only then would the client be motivated to work on his or her goal (i.e., becoming his or her ideal self). In the case they described, part I lasted 20 sessions, and part II, during which solution-focused interviewing was used, followed. They argued that, from the client-centered point of view, long-lasting and generalizable improvement can only be gained when the client has the courage to confront *all* aspects of the self. As solution-focused brief therapy alone may offer too little to that end, they proposed an integration:

> [Solution-focused] techniques may offer the clients tangible evidence that they are indeed on the road to becoming the person of their dreams, their ideal self. Employing [solution-focused] techniques within the [person-centered] therapy framework should increase awareness and acceptance of the self to achieve long-lasting change and congruence. (Cepeda and Davenport, 2006, p. 13)

This chapter describes how solution-focused brief therapy can be viewed as a form of cognitive behavioral therapy (CBT). To that end, a comparison is made between problem-focused CBT and solution-focused brief therapy.

It turns out that they apply the same theoretical learning principles and that they follow the same behavioral therapeutic process. Therefore, solution-focused brief therapy may be considered a kind of CBT. CBT and solution-focused cognitive behavioral therapy can be seen as two sides of the same behavioral therapeutic coin (Bannink, 2005, 2006c).

CBT AND SOLUTION-FOCUSED BRIEF THERAPY: SIMILARITIES

CBT and solution-focused brief therapy have a number of similarities. Hawton, Salkovskis, Kirk, and Clark (1995) and Orlemans et al. (1995) defined behavioral therapy as the application of methods and findings from experimental psychology. Specifically, it concerns the application of experimentally verified learning principles: Pavlov's classical conditioning and Skinner's operant conditioning. Both CBT and solution-focused brief therapy draw upon these learning principles. Solution-focused therapists apply these principles directly during the sessions with the client by selectively paying attention to conversations about goals and solutions and by withholding attention (as much as possible) from conversations about problems and complaints.

CBT and solution-focused brief therapy also have the same goal: to help clients make desired changes in their lives (Hawton et al., 1995).

CBT and solution-focused brief therapy can be mapped on largely identical flow diagrams of the behavioral therapeutic process as described by Orlemans et al. (1995). C. W. Korrelboom and ten Broeke (2004) deviated slightly from this process with a division of the therapy into three phases (diagnostics, interventions, and conclusion), yet the similarities with the behavioral therapeutic process discussed by Orlemans et al. are greater than the differences. CBT and solution-focused brief therapy are concerned with changing both cognitions (i.e., the way one views and thinks about the problem) and behavior (i.e., the acting out of the problem). The focus is not on emotions in either form of therapy, although the impact of emotions is acknowledged and validated. Although the term "functional analysis" is not generally used in solution-focused literature, the solution-focused therapist always conducts functional analyses with the client. These are not functional analyses of problem behavior but rather analyses of exceptions, of times when the desired behavior (or desired functional cognitions) already occurs (de Shazer, 1985). In addition, CBT and solution-focused brief therapy both make frequent use of suggested homework and evaluation of the treatment provided.

Problem-focused behavioral therapeutic process	Solution-focused behavioral therapeutic process
TABLE 13.1 Comparison of the Problem-Focused and the Solution-Focused Behavioral Therapeutic Processes	
Introductions	Introductions
Problem analysis ◄——————┐	(Problem discussion) Goal analysis ◄——————┐
Baseline measurements	Baseline measurements of desired behavior
Functional analysis	Functional analysis of desired behavior
Plan and goal formulation	Modification procedures (already present)
Modification procedures	
Execution	Execution
Evaluation	Evaluation (each session)
Decrease problem behavior——►No ↓ Yes——►Stop/continue/change	Increase desired behavior ————►No ↓ Yes——►Stop/continue/change

SOLUTION-FOCUSED COGNITIVE BEHAVIORAL THERAPY

What follows is the "translation" of CBT into solution-focused brief therapy (called solution-focused cognitive behavioral therapy, or SFCBT), with an overview of the differences at each stage. The stages of the flow diagram of the behavioral therapeutic process described by Orlemans et al. (1995) are used as a guiding principle (see Table 13.1). The names of the stages are derived from the solution-focused behavioral therapeutic process.

Stage 1: Introductions
Building the cooperative relationship
During this stage, each (behavioral) therapist works on building a positive cooperative relationship, or rapport. He or she does so by listening to the client with empathy and by asking questions. The solution-focused therapist inquires explicitly about things the client is good at and about successful moments in his or her life. The solution-focused therapist pays the client compliments and asks competence questions: "How did you manage to . . . ?

How did you come up with the great idea to . . . ?" Competence questions invite the client to compliment him- or herself and thus build self-confidence. This immediately sets the tone: SFCBT looks at what is going well already and where the client is successful.

If the client wants to talk about his or her problem or complaint, the solution-focused therapist listens attentively and acknowledges the client's suffering. As quickly as possible, he or she asks what the client wants to see instead of the problem. There is no further exploration of the problem. In solution-focused brief therapy, the past is only used to uncover the client's previous successes and to use them, if possible, in solving current problems.

Assessing the motivation for behavior change
In SFCBT, the client's motivation for behavior change is assessed as early as the first session. During the session and in assigning homework, the solution-focused therapist matches the client's given motivation as closely as possible.

Stage 2: Goal Formulation (Choice of Desired Behavior)
In SFCBT, the client's goal is formulated during the first session. In CBT, goal formulation takes place *after* the problem choice and the analysis. The goal of solution-focused brief therapy is not the reduction of the complaint or problem (forestalling negative outcome goal) but an increase in the client's desired behavior (approach goal). To that end, one doesn't need to know much about the problem behavior. Desired behavior also comprises desired functional cognitions; after all, cognitions can be considered a form of internal behavior.

A solution-focused question about goal formulation is: "What do you want instead of the problem (or problem behavior) in concrete, positive, and realistic terms?" From that moment onward, the treatment concerns itself as much as possible with desired behavior. If the client formulates an unrealistic goal, the therapist may acknowledge the unattainability of the goal and examine with the client which part of the goal *is* achievable. SFCBT often uses scaling questions: On a scale of 10 to 0, the client can indicate where he or she stands and how close he or she has come to the goal. In scaling questions, the unrealistic goal may also be equated with 10 and the client can examine what number he or she might conceivably reach. It is rare for a client to want to end up at 10.

SFCBT is a diagnosis-transcending treatment method. One may choose to commence treatment immediately and if necessary pay attention to diagnostics at a later stage. Severe psychiatric disorders or a suspicion thereof justify the decision to conduct a thorough diagnosis, since the tracing of the underlying organic pathology, for instance, has direct therapeutic consequences.

Outpatients in primary or second-line health care are suitable for a solution-focused approach. During the first or follow-up sessions it will become clear whether an advanced diagnosis will be necessary, for example if there is a deterioration in the client's condition or if the treatment fails to give positive results. Analogous to "stepped care," one could think of this as "stepped diagnosis" (Bakker, Bannink, & Macdonald, 2010).

SFCBT inquires about desired behavior in the past, present, and future (by means of questions about goal formulation or about exceptions). In CBT, the therapist invites the client to share the story of his or her problem and they use the session to explore and analyze the problem. The therapist thus positively reinforces problem talk during the sessions. In SFCBT the therapist moves on to the question about goal formulation as quickly as possible. There is positive reinforcement during the session of goal and solution talk and negative punishment for problem talk through the withholding of attention (leading to extinction of the problem talk). Negative punishment also takes the form of questions about what the client would like to see instead of the problem. In SFCBT the client does receive acknowledgment of the impact the problem has on his or her life (see Chapter 3).

In SFCBT, problem development becomes competence development. Qualities and characteristics that promote resilience can be inventoried. In the process, one reflects on how the client has learned and applied functional cognitions and functional behavior.

Stage 3: Baseline Measurements

The baseline measurements in CBT consist of registrations of situations in which undesired cognitions or undesired behaviors occur. Dysfunctional cognitions are traced (and later challenged, in order to teach the client to develop and apply more functional cognitions). In SFCBT the registrations are concerned with situations in which the desired cognitions or desired behavior already occur or have occurred (exceptions). "When did or do those moments occur, what were or are you doing differently then, and what are the consequences of that behavior?" Together with the client, the therapist examines when there are or were functional cognitions in certain difficult situations and the client is invited to apply those functional cognitions more often. One may suggest an observation task as homework. The client is then asked to pay attention to when he or she already has functional cognitions so that he or she can tell the therapist about it during the next session. It is up to the client to decide whether to write down his or her observations. Topographic analyses are descriptions of situations in which the desired behavior manifests itself.

Stage 4: Functional Analysis
In SFCBT, functional analyses are always about desired behavior rather than undesired (problem) behavior. The professional conducts the analysis by finding exceptions in the past or present or by asking about goal formulation and the miracle (the future).

Questions about situations when the problem has been absent or less of a problem
Stimulus Sd = When has the problem been absent or less of a problem?
Response = What exactly have you done (differently) then?
Consequences = What were or are the consequences of that behavior?

The client is asked about behavior and cognitions (operant responses) and emotions.

Questions about situations when the desired behavior or cognition has been observed
S = When have you observed the desired situation, even if just a little?
R = What exactly have you done (differently) then?
C = What have been the consequences of that behavior?

Questions about the future
S = The miracle has happened (or the goal has been reached) and the problem that brought you here has been solved (to a sufficient degree).
R = What are you doing (differently) then or what will you do differently then? What does that look like in concrete and positive terms?
C = What will the consequences be?

Burger (1994) pointed out that one can make functional analyses of desired behavior:

> Incidentally, one could easily have the procedure commence with desired behavior (which is perhaps not yet or too infrequently displayed). Only the manner in which therapeutic measures are linked to the Cs would then have to be inverted in the sense that inhibiting Cs are undercut and stimulating Cs are enhanced. (p. 30)

Stage 5: Modification Procedures

In CBT the therapist is the expert who tells the client what he or she needs to do to alleviate his or her problem. SFCBT views the client as someone who is capable of solving his or her problem him- or herself and who already possesses knowledge of the necessary modification procedures and the ability to use them. By asking about exceptions ("How did you previously manage to . . . ? How do you currently manage, even if only a little, to . . . ? What do you know about what others do to solve the same problem?"), the solution-focused therapist inquires about the client's competencies. Compilation of an inventory of coping strategies in the early stages (holistic theory and competence development, baseline measurements) puts the modification procedures at the ready. In principle, solution-focused brief therapy doesn't add anything new, unlike problem-focused therapy, in which the acquisition of skills is customary. Solution-focused brief therapy assumes that one can always find exceptions that the client can repeat or do more often. Theoretically speaking, "learning" is therefore not a solution-focused term; rather it is more accurate to speak of "becoming better at" a specific skill. In this way, one offers recognition of what is already there: the road the client has already traveled. Should the client take an interest in which modification procedures the therapist has available, the therapist should of course feel free to tell the client about them. However, the solution-focused therapist always first invites the client to open his or her own "store" of modification procedures; the therapist only opens his or her "store" afterward. SFCBT *does not add anything new*: The client makes use of his or her previous successes and ideas to achieve the desired situation in the future. Only in the unusual case that the client can't think of any will the therapist offer suggestions him- or herself. From stage 5 onward, the behavioral therapeutic process in SFCBT is one stage ahead of CBT.

Stage 6: Execution

Doing homework is considered important in CBT. The homework usually involves congruent tasks (e.g., baseline measurements, cognitive therapy, behavioral experiments). Therapeutic impasse often occurs because clients receive these congruent homework assignments when they are not yet motivated to carry them out; in other words, the therapist is not on the same page as the client, in terms of his or her current level of motivation. This causes problems in the therapeutic relationship: The therapist experiences irritation, discouragement, and insecurity, and concepts like resistance and non-compliance crop up. The solution-focused therapist only offers homework suggestions if the client thinks it useful (see Chapter 5). Change often already takes place *during* the session, which renders homework less important. The therapist also functions as a model (providing positive reinforcement of the desired behavior through the use of solution talk instead of problem talk). Cognitive restructuring takes place when the therapist opens up multiple perspectives on the problem faced by the client, who usually has a limited and rigid explanation for the origin of the problem. Searching for multiple options for change produces a cognitive restructuring.

To the client in a visitor relationship no homework is suggested; rather, the therapist compliments the client on having come and asks whether he or she wants to return. To the client in a complainant relationship only observation tasks are suggested ("Think about what you want to keep the way it is and what doesn't need to change" or "Think about the times when the problem is absent or is less of a problem" or "Think about times when a small piece of the miracle already occurs"). Behavioral tasks (the do-more-of-what-works, do-something-different, and pretend tasks) are only suggested to clients in customer relationships. See Chapter 5 for an overview of all homework suggestions. If the client wishes, one may use congruent procedures from CBT here. Consider CBT, for instance, if the client wants to think differently about certain matters in order to get closer to his or her goal, or consider behavioral experiments that are developed in conjunction with the client. Because the client usually already carries knowledge of modification procedures (and the ability to use them) within him- or herself (e.g., because he or she has noticed that something worked), he or she will be more motivated to engage in those procedures than when the therapist prescribes a different modification procedure.

Classical learning principles are applied as well when the client is asked to practice incompatible behavior (counterconditioning) by way of the pretend task or the do-something-different task.

Stage 7: Evaluation
In CBT, the evaluation of how well the objective has been met usually occurs at the end of the treatment. Therapeutic progress is measured by the extent to which the problem has been alleviated. In SFCBT, the opening question is always: "What is better?" By asking scaling questions, one evaluates during each session how close the client has come to his or her goal and whether another appointment is necessary. Therapeutic progress is measured by increased engagement in the desired behavior. In SFCBT, the client determines whether he or she wants to return, and, if so, when, and when the

therapy can be concluded. If the client thinks that it may be useful, one may discuss relapse prevention and conduct a follow-up session.

A distinctive feature of SFCBT is that it devotes attention to the end of the treatment from the very first session on. The various questions about goal formulation make that very clear: "What would you like to have achieved by the end of this therapy?" or "What would indicate to you that you're doing well enough that you don't have to come back anymore?"

Duncan (2005) did research into the efficacy of treatment. He found that treatment is more effective if the therapist asks the client to provide brief feedback during *each* session by way of an appraisal of the session and the therapeutic relationship (see Chapter 11).

MICROANALYSIS OF THERAPEUTIC SESSIONS

Tomori and Bavelas (2007) meticulously examined a number of therapeutic sessions conducted by famous therapists such as Rogers and de Shazer. Their microanalysis showed that solution-focused therapists ask more questions than client-centered therapists. Client-centered therapists make more formulations and ask fewer questions. In addition, solution-focused therapists make more positive statements than client-centered therapists, who make more neutral or negative statements. Clients, in turn, are more inclined to make positive statements if the therapist makes positive statements, fostering a more positive atmosphere during the session.

Research has also been conducted into the differences between CBT and solution-focused brief therapy. Smock et al. came to the same conclusions (personal communication, 2009).

COMPARISON WITH TWO OTHER FORMS OF CBT

Problem-Solving Therapy

In the 1970s, the problem-solving model of D'Zurilla and Goldfried (1971) developed out of the psychoanalytic cause-effect model. Because there is sometimes confusion surrounding the terms "solution-focused brief therapy" and "problem-solving therapy," problem-solving therapy is briefly described here.

The central assumption of the problem-solving model is that there is a necessary link between the problem and the solution. The problem-solving model involves a phased process. In this model, one starts by collecting data and by describing the problem or the complaint. One studies its nature and severity and analyzes what its causes might be. A goal is formulated that is usually related to the alleviation of the problem, or that is meant to reduce the negative consequences of the problem. Interventions are then devised to reach that goal, usually by means of brainstorming. During the brainstorming session, one first generates as many options as possible; formulation of a critique of each option doesn't occur until later. After one of the options has been chosen and the intervention applied, one evaluates to what extent the problem or its consequences have lessened or disappeared.

The problem-solving model incorporates a segmentalist approach: A large problem is broken up into components and interventions are designed for each component. Afterward, all components are brought together again in the belief that the larger problem has been resolved. In reality, this rarely pans out and may even have a contrary effect. According to Cauffman:

> Like most classic management models, the problem-solving model and the segmentalist model have one element in common: the focus, fixation even, on problems and their causes. Since causes always precede the ensuing problems, these models are primarily interested in the past. (2003, p. 27)

Constructional Behavior Therapy

In 1974 Goldiamond proposed a constructional approach to problematic behavior, arguing that intervention should focus on expanding adaptive repertoires instead of eliminating maladaptive ones. In this vein, Bakker-de Pree (1987) developed constructional behavior therapy. Its main feature is a focus on the client's successful behavior (i.e., the behavior that contributes to survival and self-maintenance and results in a better personal state for the client). Restoration and extension of the successful behavior causes disordered and maladaptive behavior to become superfluous and fade away.

Although the approach is well founded on knowledge of behavior analysis and has been described thoroughly in the Netherlands, where it was developed, it has not yet been presented to the international scientific and clinical community, with the exception of several presentations at international conferences.

Unlike solution-focused brief therapy, which looks for situations in which the desired behavior occurs, constructional behavior therapy inquires into situations in which the problem behavior does not occur (all situations minus the problem behavior, or S delta). The objective of constructional behavior therapy is to look, via the S delta, for unwanted consequences or moments when the client is able to avoid the unwanted consequences of this non-problematic behavior. That is where the causes of the problem behavior are assumed to lie. In recent years, the focus of constructional behavior therapy has shifted. The goal is to strengthen the client's ability to self-regulate, prompting him or her to take control of his or her life by focusing on opportunities rather than problems. This can be done by way of mending and improving the client's adaptive functioning so that natural positive reinforcement restores his or her quality of life. Hence, the similarities between constructional behavior therapy and SFCBT have grown.

SUMMARY

- Problem-focused therapy differs from solution-focused brief therapy in its therapeutic focus and the therapist's attitude.
- There are similarities between problem-focused CBT and solution-focused brief therapy: The same theoretical learning principles are applied and the same behavioral therapeutic process is followed. Therefore, solution-focused brief therapy can be considered a form of CBT.
- There are also a number of differences between CBT and SFCBT, which are apparent from a flow diagram of the behavioral therapeutic process.
- CBT and SFCBT can be seen as two sides of the same behavioral therapeutic coin.
- In this chapter, a comparison was made between SFCBT and two other forms of behavioral therapy: problem-solving therapy and constructional behavior therapy.

Afterword

· · · · · · · · · · · · · · · · ·

What was before is left behind,
that which was not comes to be,
and every minute gives place to another.
—Ovid, *The Metamorphoses*

Panta rhei. Everything flows. In mental health care, education, management, and coaching, and in mediation, there has been an evolution from long-term to short-term forms of treatment and from curative to preventative. Brief goal-oriented interventions have the wind at their back; interventions for psychological problems and waiting lists should and can be shorter, and client emancipation is on the rise: Clients themselves are able to formulate their goals, think up solutions, and put them into effect. Professionals ought no longer reinforce the weak "whine and complain" attitude of clients but rather should make them stronger and prompt them to take action.

Problem-focused interviewing is increasingly being abandoned: "What was before is left behind." Talking about successes in the past, present, and future helps. The solution-focused professional's skill is working with the client's expertise in a goal-oriented way. Unlike in the problem-focused model, the professional is not an expert who has all the answers; he or she allows him- or herself be informed by the client, who goes on to come up with his or her own solutions. Treatment providers may cease to view psychotherapy "as a group of methods that rely as much as possible on psychologically validated knowledge to reduce emotional problematics" (K. Korrelboom, 2004, p. 227). The time is ripe for a positive objective. Instead of reducing or removing the problem, which keeps the frame of reference within which solutions are found quite limited, one may ask about goal formulation with the help of stretch goals: "What do you want to see instead of the problem?" In positive terms, most clients' response is that they desire happiness and a satisfying and productive life. Following Aristotle, de Bono (1977) asserted that men (and women) consider "happiness" the goal of existence. As de Bono pointed out, this can mean different things; each client can provide his or her own definition of happiness with respect to his or her behavior, cognitions, and emotions, and together with the solution-focused professional the client can search for the ways to get closer to his or her goal.

Clients are encouraged to work hard at realizing their goals, which leaves the professional with energy to spare at the end of the day. Because there is always cooperation with the client, the sessions take place in a positive atmosphere. Working in the solution-focused vein thus prevents complaints of burnout on the part of the professional. Solution-focused interviewing reduces costs as well, as the number of sessions is usually limited. The implications are substantial: Training in diagnostics and problem-focused treatment methods can be shortened and complemented by training in constructing a goal and solutions together with the client. This would bring much change for the better for clients and professionals alike—although Chartier's observation that "there is nothing more dangerous than an idea when it is the only one you have" (qtd. by O'Hanlon, 2000, p. 53) remains true for all methods, including the solution-focused one.

Protocols for the First Session

First Protocol
All questions are submitted to each client present.

Problem
"What brings you here? How is that a problem for you? What have you already tried and what has been useful?"

Goal Formulation
"What would you like to be different as a result of these sessions?" Here one may ask the miracle question or another question about goal formulation.

Exceptions
"When have you caught a glimpse of the miracle? How does that work, exactly? How do you manage that? How do you make that happen?" Alternatively: "When is the problem absent or less noticeable? How does that work, exactly? How do you manage that?"

Scaling
- Progress since the appointment was made: "Where are you at this time on a scale of 10 to 0? How is it that you're already at that number? How did you manage that?"
- Motivation to get to work: "10 means you're willing to give it your all, and 0 means you're not willing to put in any effort."
- Confidence that the goal can be reached: "10 means that you are very confident, and 0 means you have no confidence at all that your goal can be reached."

Feedback
- Compliments on what the client has already done that's helped and positive character interpretations
- Reason (rationale or "bridge") for the task (preferably in the client's own words)
- Task or homework suggestions: behavioral tasks for customers, observational tasks for complainants, no tasks for visitors

Concluding the Session

"Do you think that it is necessary/it would be useful for you to come back? If so, when would you like to come back?"

Second Protocol

- What are your best hopes?
- What difference would that make?
- What is already working in the right direction?
- What would be the next sign of progress? What would be your next step?

Protocol for Goal Formulation

Role Clarification
Introduction of professional, how long the session lasts, whether there will be a break to reflect before the feedback.

Problem Description
"What brings you here?"
"How is that a problem for you?"
"What have you tried and which of those things helped?"

Goal Formulation
"What would make this session worthwhile for you?" (or another question about goal formulation)

Miracle Question
Always pay attention to the difference: "What will you notice is different? What is the first thing you notice? What else? Who else will notice when the miracle happens? What will that person notice is different about you? What else? When that person notices that, what will he do differently then? What else? When that person does that, what difference does it make for you? And what will you do differently then?"

Toward Solutions
If the client is able to answer the miracle question: "If you were to pretend that the miracle had happened, what would be the first small piece of it that you would do? How might that help you?" or "What is needed to have part of the miracle happen? How might that happen? What makes you think that that's possible?"

Conclusion
- If the client gives a concrete and detailed response to the miracle question or another question about goal formulation, compliment

him or her. Then suggest: "Pick a day in the coming week and pretend the miracle has happened. Observe what difference that makes."

- If the client does not give a concrete and detailed response to the miracle question or another question about goal formulation, suggest: "Pay attention to what happens in your life that gives you the sense that this problem can be resolved." Or say: "Pay attention to what is happening in your life that you would like to keep happening because it's good (enough)."

. . . .

Protocol for Finding Exceptions

As you look for exceptions, you may inquire about the client's observations and, using the interactional matrix, about what important others might be able to perceive. One can distinguish between exceptions pertaining to the desired outcome (e.g., by means of the miracle question) and exceptions pertaining to the problem.

EXCEPTIONS PERTAINING TO THE GOAL

1. *Elicit*

   "So when the goal has been reached (or the miracle has happened), you will talk to each other about how your day has been. When do you already see glimpses of that? If your husband were here and I asked him the same question, what do you think he would say?"

2. *Amplify*

   "When was the last time you and your husband talked to each other? Tell me more about that. What was it like? What did you talk about? What did you say? And what did he say? What did you do when he said that? What did he do then? What was that like for you? What else was different about that time? If he were here, what else would he say about it?"

3. *Reinforce*

   Nonverbal: Lean forward, raise your eyebrows, make notes (do what you naturally do when someone tells you something important).

   Verbal: Show interest. "Was this new for you and him? Did it surprise you that this happened?"

   Pay compliments: "It seems that it was pretty difficult and that it required courage for you to do that, given everything that's happened in your relationship. Please tell me more."

4. *Explore how the exception came to be, ask for details, and pay compliments*

   "What do you think you did to make that happen? If your husband were here and I were to ask him that, what do you think he would say you did that helped him tell you more about his day? Where did you get the idea to do it that way? What great ideas you have! Are you someone who often comes up with the right ideas at the right time?"

5. *Project exceptions into the future*
   On a scale of 10 to 0, where 10 means a very good chance and 0 means no chance at all, how do you rate the chances of something like that happening again in the coming week (or month)? What would it take? What would help to have that happen more often in the future? Who needs to do what to make it happen again? What is the most important thing you need to keep remembering to make sure it has the best chance of happening again? What is the second most important thing to remember? What would your husband say about the chance of this happening again? What would he think you could do to increase that chance? If you decided to do that, what do you think he would do? If he were to do that, how would things be different for you (in your relationship)?

EXCEPTIONS PERTAINING TO THE PROBLEM

1. *If the client cannot describe a goal (or miracle) and only talks in problem terms.* "Can you recall a time in the past week (or month, or year) when your problem was less severe, or when the problem was absent for a short period of time?" Then continue with the five steps for exceptions pertaining to the goal (or miracle).
2. *What is better?* All subsequent sessions commence with the exploration of these exceptions. Remember to follow all five steps and to ask both individual and relational (interactional matrix) questions. After examining an exception, always ask: "What else is better?"
3. *Coping questions.* Sometimes the client is unable to find exceptions and the difficulties he faces are enormous. In that case, you may ask coping questions to find out what the client does to keep his head above water: "I'm surprised. Given everything that's happened, I don't know how you cope. How do you do that? How do you keep your head above water?"
4. *If a client describes a prolonged unpleasant situation with ever-discouraging events.* In such a case, you might say: "I understand that you have many reasons to be down. There are so many things that turned out differently than you'd hoped. I wonder how you've kept going and how you've been able to get up every morning and start a new day. Please tell me more."
5. *If the client says he or she must go on, for example, for the children's sake.* In such a case, you might say: "Is that how you do it? You think of your children and how much they need you? You must care about them a great deal. Please tell me more about what you do to take good care of them."

Protocol for Formulating Feedback

CONSIDERATIONS

- Is there a well-formulated goal? (With multiple clients: Is there a well-formulated common goal?) What is that goal?
- Has the goal been defined in positive, concrete, and realistic terms (i.e., the presence or increase of desired behavior instead of the absence or decrease of undesired behavior)?
- What exceptions are there?
- Are the exceptions repeatable (deliberate exceptions) or are they coincidental (spontaneous exceptions)?
- What type of relationship is there between the professional and the client (visitor, complainant, customer)?

FEEDBACK

- Compliments
- Rationale or bridge (reason for the task)
- Homework suggestions if the client wants to be assigned a task

Session Rating Scale (SRS)

Name _____

Date _____ (day) _____ (month) 20_____ Session no. _____

Please rate today's session by placing a cross mark on the line nearest to the description that best fits your experience.

RELATIONSHIP

I did not feel   I felt heard,
heard,understood,   understood, and
and respected.   respected.

├--┤

GOALS AND TOPICS

We did not work on   We worked on and
or talk about what I   talked about what I
wanted to work on   wanted to work on
and talk about.   and talk about.

├--┤

APPROACH OR METHOD

The professional's   The professional's
approach is not a   approach is a
good fit for me.   good fit for me.

├--┤

OVERALL

There was some-   Overall, today's
thing missing in   session was
the session today.   right for me.

├--┤

Note. From "Session Rating Scale," by the Institute for the Study of Therapeutic Change, www.talkingcure.com. Copyright 2002 by Scott D. Miller, Barry L Duncan, and Lynn Johnson. Reprinted with permission.

• • • • • • • • • • • • • • • • •

Protocol for Subsequent Sessions (EARS)

Submit all questions to each client present.

Eliciting
"What is better (since your previous visit)?"

Asking for Details (Amplifying)
"How does that work? How do you do that exactly? Is that new for you? What effect does that have on . . . ? What is different then between you and . . . ?"

Reinforcing
Give the client compliments and offer positive character interpretations.

Start Again
"And what else is going better?"

Do More of It
"What is needed for you to do that again or more often?" If absolutely nothing is better: "How do you cope? How do you get through that? How come things aren't worse? How do you do that? If you can continue to do that, would you have accomplished what you came here for?"

Scaling Progress
"Where are you now? How do you manage that? How did you make that happen? What does a higher rating look like? What would be different then? How would you be able to get there? What is needed for you to do that? Who will be the first to notice? How would that person notice? How would he react? And what would that be like for you? At what rating would you like to end up?"

Scaling Motivation and Confidence (Optional)
Feedback
- Compliments
- Reason for the assignment (bridge, rationale)
- Homework suggestions: behavioral tasks for customers, observational tasks for complainants, no tasks for visitors

Future Sessions
"Is it necessary/would it be useful for you to come back?" "If so: When would you like to come back?"

Protocol for Externalizing the Problem

Name of the problem: _____

The problem controls me/us   I/we have control of the problem

1   2   3   4   5   6   7   8   9   10

Circle your current state on the above scale.
Where are you on the scale compared to last time? If you went up on the scale, indicate below how you managed that.

_____

_____

_____

_____

If you remained at the same level as last time, indicate how you managed to stay stable.

_____

_____

_____

_____

If you ended up lower on the scale, indicate what you have done before to get ahead. What did you do in the past in a comparable situation that was successful?

_____

_____

_____

_____

What have important others in your life noticed about you this past week? How has that influenced their behavior toward you?

_____

_____

_____

_____

Solution-Focused Questions for the Referrer

1. In your opinion, what would be the best possible outcome of a collaboration among you as referrer, the client, and me or our institution?

_____

_____

_____

2. What are the client's strengths and what aspects of his performance are satisfactory and should be maintained?

_____

_____

_____

3. What are the limitations we need to take into account?

_____

_____

_____

4. In your opinion, what resources does the client have?

_____

_____

_____

5. What do you think would be the first sign that would indicate to the client that a treatment is meaningful and useful? And what would be the first sign for you?

_____

_____

_____

6. When does this already happen now? Please give an example.

_____

_____

_____

References

....

Allen, R. E., & Allen, S. D. (1997). *Winnie-the-Pooh on success: In which you, Pooh, and friends learn about the most important subject of all.* New York: Dutton.

American Psychiatric Association. (1994). *The diagnostic and statistical manual of mental disorders* (4th ed.). Washington, DC: Author.

Appelo, M. (2009). Misverstanden en mythes: Cliënten zijn veranderingsbereid [Misconceptions and myths: Clients are willing to change]. *Dth, 1*(29), 69–73.

Appelo, M., & Bos, E. (2008). De relatie tussen klachten, veerkracht en welzijn [The relationship between complaints, resilience, and well-being]. *Gedragstherapie, 41,* 241–251.

Arts, W., Hoogduin, C. A. L., Keijsers, G. P. J., Severeijnen, R., & Schaap, C. (1994). A quasi-experimental study into the effect of enhancing the quality of the patient-therapist relationship in the outpatient treatment of obsessive-compulsive neurosis. In S. Brogo & L. Sibilia (Eds.), *The patient-therapist relationship: Its many dimensions* (pp. 96–106). Rome: Consiglio Nazionale delle Ricerche.

Bakker, J. M., & Bannink, F. P. (2008). Oplossingsgerichte therapie in de psychiatrische praktijk [Solution-focused therapy in psychiatric practice]. *Tijdschrift voor Psychiatrie, 50*(1), 55–59.

Bakker, J.M., Bannink, F.P. & Macdonald, A. (2010). Solution-focused psychiatry. *The Psychiatrist, 34,* 297–300 (accepted for publication).

Bakker-de Pree, B. J. (1987). *Constructionele gedragstherapie* [Constructional behavior therapy]. Nijmegen, Netherlands: Dekker & Van der Vegt.

Bannink, F. P. (2005). De kracht van oplossingsgerichte therapie: Een vorm van gedragstherapie [The power of solution-focused therapy: A form of behavioral therapy]. *Gedragstherapie, 38*(1), 5–16.

Bannink, F. P. (2006a). *Oplossingsgerichte mediation* [Solution-focused mediation]. Amsterdam: Pearson.

Bannink. F. P. (2006b). Oplossingsgerichte mediation [Solution-focused mediation]. *Tijdschrift Conflicthantering, 7,* 143–145.

Bannink, F. P. (2006c). De geboorte van oplossingsgerichte cognitieve gedragstherapie [The birth of solution-focused cognitive behavioral therapy]. *Gedragstherapie, 39*(3), 171–183.

Bannink, F. P. (2007a). *Gelukkig zijn en geluk hebben: Zelf oplossingsgericht werken* [Being happy and being lucky: Solution-focused self-help]. Amsterdam: Harcourt.

Bannink, F. P. (2007b). Oplossingsgerichte therapie [Solution-focused brief therapy]. *Maandblad Geestelijke volksgezondheid (MGv), 62*(10), 836–848.

Bannink, F.P. (2007c). Solution focused brief therapy. *Journal of Contemporary Psychotherapy*, 37, 2, 87-94.

Bannink, F. P. (2008a). Oplossingsgerichte therapie als vorm van cognitieve gedragstherapie [Solution-focused brief therapy as a form of cognitive behavioral therapy]. *Tijdschrift VKJP, 35*(3), 18–29.

Bannink, F. P. (2008b). Posttraumatic success: Solution-focused brief therapy. *Brief Treatment and Crisis Intervention*, 7, 1–11.

Bannink, F. P. (2008c). *Solution focused conflict management in teams and in organisations.* Retrieved from: http://www.adrresources.com/docs/adr/2-4-114/SF%20Conflict%20Management%20in%20Teams%20and%20in%20Organisations%20rev.%202008.pdf

Bannink, F. P. (2008d). *Solution focused mediation.* Retrieved from http://www.mediate.com//articles/banninkF1.cfm

Bannink, F. P. (2008e). Solution focused mediation. *The Jury Expert, 23*(3). Retrieved from: http://www.astcweb.org/public/publication/documents/Bannink%20Sept%202008%20TJE1.pdf

Bannink, F. P. (2008f). Solution focused mediation: The future with a difference. *Conflict Resolution Quarterly, 25*(2), 163–183.

Bannink, F. P. (2008g). Vergelding of verzoening [Retaliation or reconciliation]. *Forum voor Conflictmanagement, 1*, 26–28.

Bannink, F. P. (2008h). *Visitor, complainant, customer: Motivating clients to change in mediation.* Retrieved from: http://www.mediate.com//articles/banninkF2.cfm

Bannink, F. P. (2009a). Building positive emotions in mediation. Retrieved from: http://www.mediate.com//articles/banninkF4.cfm

Bannink, F. P. (2009b). Editorial. *Conflict Inzicht.* Utrecht: Stili Novi.

Bannink, F. P. (2009c). *Positieve psychologie in de praktijk* [Positive psychology in practice]. Amsterdam: Hogrefe.

Bannink, F. P. (2009d). *Praxis der Losungs-fokussierten Mediation* [Solution-focused mediation in practice]. Stuttgart, Germany: Concadora Verlag.

Bannink, F. P. (2009e). Solution focused conflict management in teams and in organisations. *InterAction: The Journal of Solution Focus in Organisations, 1*(2), 11–25.

Bannink, F. P. (2009f). *Supermediators.* Retrieved from: http://www.mediate.com//articles/banninkF3.cfm

Bannink, F. P. (2009g). Visitor, complainant or customer? In J. Bertschler (Ed.), *Elder mediation: A new solution to age-old problems* (pp. 77–89). Seven Hills, OH: Northcoast Conflict Solutions.

Bannink, F. P. (2010a). *Handbook of solution-focused conflict management.* Cambridge, MA: Hogrefe Publishing.

Bannink, F.P. (2010b). Successful scaling in mediation. Retrieved from: http://www.mediate.com//articles/banninkF5.cfm

Bateson, G. (1979). *Mind and nature: A necessary unity.* Toronto: Bantam.

Beck, A. T., Weissman, A., Lester, D., & Trexles, L. (1974). The measurement of pessimism: The Hopelessness Scale. *Journal of Consulting and Clinical Psychology, 42,* 861–865.

Beck, J. S. (1995). *Cognitive therapy: Basics and beyond.* New York: Guilford.

Berg, I. K., & Dolan, Y. (2001). *Tales of solutions: A collection of hope-inspiring stories.* New York: Norton.

Berg, I. K., & Miller, S. D. (1992). *Working with the problem drinker: A solution-focused approach.* New York: Norton.

Berg, I. K., & Steiner, T. (2003). *Children's solution work.* New York: Norton.

Brewin, C. R. (2006). Understanding cognitive behaviour therapy: A retrieval competition account. *Behaviour Research and Therapy, 44,* 765–784.

Bunker, B. B. (2000). Managing conflict through large-group methods. In M. Deutsch & P. T. Coleman (Eds.), *The handbook of conflict resolution* (p. 546–567). San Francisco: Jossey-Bass.

Burger, A. W. (1994). *Functie-analyse van neurotisch gedrag* [Functional analysis of neurotic behavior]. Amsterdam: Van Rossen.

Cantwell, P., & Holmes, S. (1994). Social construction: A paradigm shift for systemic therapy and training. *Australian and New Zealand Journal of Family Therapy, 15,* 17–26.

Cauffman, L. (2003). *Oplossingsgericht management & coaching, simpel werkt het best* [Solution-focused management and coaching: Simple works best]. Utrecht, Netherlands: Lemma.

Cepeda, L. M., & Davenport, D. S. (2006). Person-centered therapy and solution-focused brief therapy: An integration of present and future awareness. *Psychotherapy: Theory, Research, Practice, Training, 43*(1), 1–12.

Chevalier, A. J. (1995). *On the client's path: A manual for the practice of solution-focused therapy.* Oakland, CA: New Harbinger.

Cladder, H. (1999). *Oplossingsgerichte korte psychotherapie* [Solution-focused brief psychotherapy]. Lisse, Netherlands: Swets & Zeitlinger.

Clement, P. W. (1994). Quantitative evaluation of 26 years of private practice. *Professional Psychology: Research and Practice, 25*(2), 173–176.

Coleman, P. T., & Deutsch, M. (2000). Some guidelines for developing a creative approach to conflict. In M. Deutsch & P. T. Coleman (Eds.), *The handbook of conflict resolution* (pp. 355–365). San Francisco: Jossey-Bass.

Covey, S. R. (1989). *The seven habits of highly effective people: Powerful lessons in personal change.* New York: Simon & Schuster.

De Bono, E. (1977). *The happiness purpose.* Harmondsworth, UK: Penguin.

De Bono, E. (1984). *Tactics: The art and science of success.* Boston: Little, Brown.

De Bono, E. (1985). *Conflicts: A better way to resolve them.* London: Penguin.

De Groot, F. (2004). Bekrachtigen, bekrachtigen, en nog eens bekrachtigen. Back to basics: Positieve bekrachtiging [Reinforcing, reinforcing, and more reinforcing. Back to basics: Positive reinforcement]. *Gedragstherapie, 37*(1), 61–66.

De Jong, P., & Berg, I. K. (1997). *Interviewing for solutions.* Pacific Grove, CA: Brooks/Cole.

De Shazer, S. (1984). The death of resistance. *Family Process, 23,* 79–93.

De Shazer, S. (1985). *Keys to solution in brief therapy.* New York: Norton.

De Shazer, S. (1988). *Clues: Investigation solutions in brief therapy.* New York: Norton.

De Shazer, S. (1991). *Putting difference to work.* New York: Norton.

De Shazer, S. (1994). *Words were originally magic.* New York: Norton.

De Shazer, S., Dolan, Y., Korman, H. Trepper, T., McCollum, E., & Berg, I. K. (2007). *More than miracles: The state of the art of solution-focused brief therapy.* New York: Routledge.

Dolan, Y. (1991). *Resolving sexual abuse: Solution-focused therapy and Ericksonian hypnosis for adult survivors.* New York: Norton.

Dolan, Y. (1998). *One small step.* Watsonville, CA: Papier-Mache.

Duncan, B. L. (2005). *What's right with you: Debunking dysfunction and changing your life.* Deerfield Beach, FL: Health Communications.

Duncan, B. L., Hubble, M. A., & Miller, S. D. (1997). *Psychotherapy with "impossible" cases: The efficient treatment of therapy veterans.* New York: Norton.

Duncan, B. L., Miller, S. D., & Sparks, A. (2004). *The heroic client: A revolutionary way to improve effectiveness through client-directed, outcome-informed therapy.* San Francisco: Jossey-Bass.

D'Zurilla, T. J. & Goldfried, M.R. (1971). Problem solving and behavior modification. *Journal of Abnormal Psychology, 78,* 107–126.

Erickson, M. H. (1980). *Collected papers of Milton H. Erickson: Vol. 1. The nature of hypnosis and suggestion* (E. L. Rossi, Ed.). New York: Irvington.

Fava, G. A., Rafanelli, C., Cazzaro, M., Conti, S., & Grandi, M. (1998). Well-being therapy: A novel psychotherapeutic approach for residual symptoms of affective disorders. *Psychological Medicine, 28,* 475–480.

Frank, J. D. (1974). Psychotherapy: The restoration of morale. *American Journal of Psychiatry, 131,* 271–274.

Frankl, V. E. (2006). *Man's search for meaning.* Boston: Beacon Press.

Fredrickson, B. (2003). The value of positive emotions. *American Scientist*, *91*, 330–335.

Frijda, N. H. (1986). *The emotions*. Cambridge: Cambridge University Press.

Furman, B., & Ahola, T. (2007). *Change through cooperation: Handbook of reteaming*. Helsinki: Helsinki Brief Therapy Institute.

Gallwey, W. T. (1997). *The inner game of tennis*. New York: Random House.

Gingerich, W. J., & Eisengart, S. (2000). Solution-focused brief therapy: A review of the outcome research. *Family Process*, *39*(4), 477–498.

Goei, S. L., & Bannink, F. P. (2005). Oplossingsgericht werken in remedial teaching, deel 1 [Solution-focused interviewing in remedial teaching, part 1]. *Remediaal, Tijdschrift voor leer- en gedragsproblemen in het vo/bve*, *5*(3), 19–26.

Goldiamond, I. (1974). Toward a constructional approach to social problems: Ethical and constitutional issues raised by applied behavior analysis. *Behaviorism*, *2*(1), 1–84.

Hawton, K., Salkovskis, P. M., Kirk, J., & Clark, D. M. (1995). *Cognitive behaviour therapy for psychiatric problems: A practical guide*. Oxford: Oxford University Press.

Haynes, J. M., Haynes, G. L., & Fong, L. S. (2004). *Mediation: Positive conflict management*. Albany: State University of New York.

Hiatt, D., & Hargrave, G. E. (1995). The characteristics of highly effective therapists in managed behavioral providers networks. *Behavioral Healthcare Tomorrow*, *4*, 19–22.

Isebaert, L. (2005). *Kurzzeittherapie: Ein praktisches Handbuch* [Brief therapy: A practical handbook]. Stuttgart, Germany: Thieme.

Kazdin, A. E. (2006). Arbitrary metrics: Implications for identifying evidence-based treatments. *American Psychologist*, *61*(1), 42–49.

Kelman, H. C. (2005). Building trust among enemies: The central challenge for international conflict resolution. *International Journal of Intercultural Relations*, *29*, 639–650.

Korrelboom, C. W., & ten Broeke, E. (2004). *Geïntegreerde cognitieve gedragstherapie* [Integrated cognitive behavioral therapy]. Bussum, Netherlands: Coutinho.

Korrelboom, K. (2004). Forum. Cognitieve gedragstherapie en "rare therapieën": Wat moeten we ermee? [Forum. Cognitive behavioral therapy and "strange therapies": What do we do with them?] *Gedragstherapie*, *37*, 225–231.

Lamarre, J., & Gregoire, A. (1999). Competence transfer in solution-focused therapy: Harnessing a natural resource. *Journal of Systemic Therapies*, *18*(1), 43–57.

Leary, T. (1957). *Interpersonal diagnosis of personality*. New York: Ronald.

Le Fevere de Ten Have, M. (2002). *Korte therapie: Handleiding bij het*

"Brugse model" voor psychotherapie met een toepassing op kinderen en jongeren [Brief therapy: Guide to the "Bruges model" for psychotherapy as applied to children and adolescents]. Leuven, Netherlands: Garant.

Lewicki, R. J., & Wiethoff, C. (2000). Trust, trust development and trust repair. In M. Deutsch & P. T. Coleman (Eds.), *The handbook of conflict resolution* (pp. 86–107). San Francisco: Jossey-Bass.

Macdonald, A. (2007). *Solution-focused therapy: Theory, research & practice.* London: Sage.

Menninger, K. (1959). The academic lecture: Hope. *American Journal of Psychiatry, 116,* 481–491.

Metcalf, L. (1995). *Counseling toward solutions: A practical solution-focused program for working with students, teachers, and parents.* San Francisco: Jossey-Bass.

Metcalf, L. (1998). *Solution focused group therapy.* New York: Free Press.

Miller, S. D., Duncan, B. L., & Hubble, M. A. (1997). *Escape from Babel: Toward a unifying language for psychotherapy practice.* New York: Norton.

Miller, S. D., Hubble, M. A., & Duncan, B. L. (Eds.). (1996). *The handbook of solution-focused brief therapy: Foundations, applications and research.* San Francisco: Jossey-Bass.

Miller, W. R. (1983). Motivational interviewing with problem drinkers. *Behavioural Psychotherapy, 11,* 147–172.

Miller, W. R., & Rollnick, S. (2002). *Motivational interviewing, Preparing people for change* (2nd ed.). New York: Guilford.

Myers, D. G. (2000). Hope and happiness. In J. E. Gillham (Ed.), *The science of optimism and hope: Research essays in honor of Martin E. P. Seligman* (pp. 323–336). Philadelphia: Templeton Foundation Press.

O'Hanlon, B. (2000). *Do one thing different: Ten simple ways to change your life.* New York: Harper.

O'Hanlon, B. (2003). *A guide to inclusive therapy: 26 methods of respectful resistance-dissolving therapy.* New York: Norton.

O'Hanlon, B., & Bertolino, B. (1998). *Even from a broken web: Brief, respectful solution-oriented therapy for sexual abuse and trauma.* New York: Wiley.

O'Hanlon, B., & Rowan, T. (2003). *Solution-oriented therapy for chronic and severe mental illness.* New York: Norton.

Orlemans, J. W. G., Eelen, P., & Hermans, D. (1995). *Inleiding tot de gedragstherapie* [Introduction to behavioral therapy]. Houten, Netherlands: Bohn Stafleu Van Loghum.

Papp, P. (1983). *The process of change.* New York: Guilford.

Prochaska, J. O., Norcross, J. C., & DiClemente, C. C. (1994). *Changing for good.* New York: Morrow.

Rijnders, P. B. M. (2004). *Overzicht, uitzicht, inzicht: Een protocol voor kort-*

durende psychotherapie [Overview, outlook, insight: A protocol for brief psychotherapy]. Houten, Netherlands: Bohn Stafleu Van Loghum.

Roeden, J. M., & Bannink, F. P. (2007a). *Handboek oplossingsgericht werken met licht verstandelijk beperkte clienten* [Handbook for solution-focused interviewing with clients with mild intellectual disabilities]. Amsterdam: Pearson.

Roeden, J. M., & Bannink, F. P. (2007b). Hoe organiseer ik een etentje? Oplossingsgerichte gedragstherapie met een verstandelijk beperkte vrouw [How do I organize a dinner? Solution-focused behavioral therapy with a woman with an intellectual disability]. *Gedragstherapie, 40*(4), 251–268.

Roeden, J. M., & Bannink, F. P. (2009). Solution focused brief therapy with persons with intellectual disabilities. *Journal of Policy and Practice in Intellectual Disabilities, 6*(4), 253–259.

Rosenhan, J. (1973). On being sane in insane places. *Science, 179,* 250–258.

Saint-Exupéry, A. de. (1979). *The wisdom of the sands* (S. Gilbert, Trans.). Chicago: University of Chicago Press.

Schippers, G. M., & de Jonge, J. (2002). Motiverende gespreksvoering [Motivational interviewing]. *Maandblad Geestelijke Volksgezondheid, 57,* 250–265.

Selekman, M. D. (1993). *Pathways to change: Brief therapy solutions with difficult adolescents.* New York: Guilford.

Selekman, M. D. (1997). *Solution-focused therapy with children: Harnessing family strengths for systemic change.* New York: Guilford.

Seligman, M. E. P. (2002). *Authentic happiness.* New York: Free Press.

Siegel, D. J. (1999). *The developing mind.* New York: Guilford.

Smeck, S., Froerer, A., & Baveles, J. Are solution-focused and cognitive-behavioral therapy the same? A microanalysis of positive and negative content. (Personal communication preceding publication of their research.)

Snyder, C. R. (2002). Hope theory: Rainbows in the mind. *Psychological Inquiry, 13,* 249–275.

Snyder, C. R., Harris, C., Anderson, J. R., Holleran, S. A., Irving, L. M., Sigmon, S. T., . . . Harney, P. (1991). The will and the ways: Development and validation of an individual-differences measure of hope. *Journal of Personality and Social Psychology, 60,* 570–585.

Stam, P., & Bannink, F.P. (2008). De oplossingsgerichte organisatie [The solution-focused organization]. *Tijdschrift VKJP, 35*(2), 62–72.

Stams, G. J., Dekovic, M., Buist, K., & de Vries, L. (2006). Effectiviteit van oplossingsgerichte korte therapie: Een meta-analyse [The efficacy of solution-focused brief therapy: A meta-analysis]. *Gedragstherapie, 39*(2), 81–94.

Stoffer, R. (2001). *Het vijf-gesprekkenmodel: Een handleiding* [The five-session model: A guide]. Delft, Netherlands: Eburon.

Susskind, L., & Cruikshank, J. L. (1987). *Breaking the impasse: Consensual approaches to resolving public disputes*. New York: Basic Books.

Tomori, C., & Bavelas, J. B. (2007). Using microanalysis of communication to compare solution-focused and client-centered therapies. *Journal of Family Psychotherapy, 18*(3), 25–43.

Tompkins, P., & Lawley, J. (2003). *Metaphors in mind*. London: Developing Company Press.

Van der Veen, D. C., & Appelo, M. T. (2002). Rationele rehabilitatie: Korte oplossingsgerichte therapie [Rational rehabilitation: Solution-focused brief therapy]. In C. A. L. Hoogduin & M. T. Appelo (Eds.), *Directieve therapie bij psychiatrische patiënten* (pp. 65–73). Nijmegen, Netherlands: Cure & Care.

Van Tongeren, P. (2004). *Deugdelijk leven: Een inleiding in de deugdethiek* [Living virtuously: An introduction to virtue ethics]. Amsterdam: Sun.

Verbiest, A. (2004). *Als ik jou toch niet had: De taal van complimenten* [If I didn't have you: The language of compliments]. Amsterdam: Contact.

Walter, J. L., & Peller, J. E. (1992). *Becoming solution-focused in brief therapy*. New York: Brunner/Mazel.

Walter, J. L., & Peller, J. E. (2000). *Recreating brief therapy: Preferences and possibilities*. New York: Norton.

Wampold, B. E., & Bhati, K. S. (2004). Attending to the omissions: A historical examination of evidence-based practice movements. *Professional Psychology: Research and Practice, 35*(6), 563–570.

Watzlawick, P., Weakland, J. H., & Fisch, R. (1974). *Change: Principles of problem formation and problem resolution*. New York: Norton.

Westra, J., & Bannink, F. P. (2006a). "Simpele" oplossingen! Oplossingsgericht werken bij mensen met een lichte verstandelijke beperking, deel 1 ["Simple" solutions! Solution-focused interviewing with people with mild intellectual disabilities, part 1]. *PsychoPraxis, 8*(4), 158–162.

Westra, J., & Bannink, F. P. (2006b). "Simpele" oplossingen! Oplossingsgericht werken bij mensen met een lichte verstandelijke beperking, deel 2 ["Simple" solutions! Solution-focused interviewing with people with mild intellectual disabilities, part 2]. *PsychoPraxis 8*(5), 213–218.

White, M., & Epston, D. (1990). *Narrative means to therapeutic ends*. New York: Norton.

Wittgenstein, L. (1968). *Philosophical investigations* (G. E. M. Anscombe, Trans., 3rd ed.). New York: Macmillan. (Originally published 1953)

Web sites
·················

www.authentichappiness.com
Site of Martin Seligman, the founder of positive psychology

www.brieftherapy.com
Site of Bill O'Hanlon, author of numerous books about solution-focused interviewing

www.brieftherapy.org.uk
Site of BRIEF, "Europe's largest provider of training in the solution focused approach"

www.brieftherapysydney.com.au
Site of the Brief Therapy Institute of Sydney, Australia

www.ebta.nu
Site of the European Brief Therapy Association, which hosts the annual European solution-focused brief therapy conference

www.edwdebono.com
Site of Edward de Bon

www.fredrikebannink.com
Site of Fredrike Bannink, the author

www.gingerich.net
Site of Walter Gingerich with outcome studies

www.korzybski.com
Site of the Korzybski Institute, a training and research center in solution-focused brief therapy

www.reteaming.com
Site of Reteaming Coaching at the Helsinki Brief Therapy Institute

www.solutionfocused.net
Site of the Institute for Solution-Focused Therapy

www.solutionsdoc.co.uk
Site of psychiatrist Alasdair Macdonald, with many outcome studies

www.solworld.org
Site for "sharing and building Solution Focused practice in organizations"

www.talkingcure.com
Site of the Institute for the Study for Therapeutic Change and Partners for Change, the authors and designers of the SRS

www.centerforclinicalexcellence.com
Site of the ICCE, a worldwide community of practitioners, healthcare managers, educators, and researchers dedicated to promoting excellence in behavioral healthcare services (Scott Miller).

Index

problem-focused medical model, goal in, 141–42

problem-focused meeting model, solution-focused meeting model vs., 134, 135*t*

problem-focused model, 1

problem-focused professionals, 129

problem-focused sessions, solution-focused sessions vs., 132–33

problem-focused therapy, phases of, 208

problem-focused way of talking, interventions for, 146–47

"problem-seeking" therapy, 1

problem-solving therapy, 217–18

Prochaska, J.O., 28

professional(s)
  problem-focused, 129
  working with other, 128–40. *see also specific types and* working with other professionals

projection into future, solution-focused skills for, 111–13

protocol(s)
  EARS, 230
  externalizing problem, 231
  finding exceptions, 226–27
  first session, 222–23
  for formulating feedback, 228
  goal formulation, 224–25
  subsequent sessions, 230

question(s)
  about competencies, 23–24, 157–62
  about exceptions, 21–22, 155–57
  about first session, 21
  about future, 214–15
  about goal, 21
  about goal formulation, 149–55
  about medication, 185–86
  about relapse, 186–87
  about situations when desired behavior or cognition has been observed, 214
  about situations when problem has been absent or less of a problem, 214
  about skills, 23–24
  for children, 177–80

for clients in cognitive therapy, 183–85

for clients in complainant relationship, 168–70

for clients in conflict, 190–93

for clients in crisis situation, 174–76

for clients in visitor relationship, 166–68

for clients who have experienced traumatic events, 170–73

for coaching managers, teams, and organizations, 187–90

for externalizing problem/conflict, 176–77

for general use, 149–66

for groups (couples, families), 180–83

for increasing hope, 173–74

miracle, 64

1001 solution-focused, 149–93

open questions, 68

opening, 76–85

for referrers, 170

scaling, 22–23, 110–11, 162–64

solution-focused, 13. *see also specific questions and* solution-focused questions

solution-focused interviewing–related, 20–24

in specific situations/with specific clients, 166–93

"What else?", 21

with which to conclude and evaluate session, 164–66

reality, as defined by observer, 11

reality of system, creating, 11

referrer(s)
  questions for, 170
  solution-focused questions for, 232
  working with, 129–30

reflecting on session, 194–203
  by client, 202–3
  solution-focused questions for professional, 194–97

reinforcement, extrinsic, 28

reinforcing, 230
  in subsequent sessions, 77

relapse

Fredrike Bannink is a clinical psychologist, health care psychologist, and child and youth psychologist (specialist-level) of the Netherlands Institute of Psychologists. She has worked in mental health care at various institutions and currently has a therapy, training, coaching, and mediation practice in Amsterdam. She is a trainer/supervisor with the Dutch Association for Behaviour and Cognitive Therapies and chair of the association's Solution-Focused Cognitive Behavioural Therapy Section. She is also a lecturer at various postgraduate institutes.

She teaches solution-focused therapy courses to psychologists and psychiatrists, and courses in solution-focused interviewing to medical professionals. She is a trainer of the Mental Health Team of Doctors Without Borders. In addition, she provides numerous in-company training courses in solution-focused therapy at mental health care institutions; for companies, she organizes solution-focused coaching trajectories for employees and managers.

Fredrike Bannink is also a Master of Dispute Resolution, a Netherlands Mediation Institute–certified mediator, and a mediator for the Amsterdam District Court. She is the author of many publications in the fields of solution-focused therapy, solution-focused interviewing, solution-focused mediation and positive psychology.

For more information go to www.fredrikebannink.com.